P9-DSX-480

THE BRASS RING

Mauldin farmhouse where I was born in 1921, at Mountain Park, New Mexico. Built by Uncle Billy, my grandfather, it is still occupied by my brother, Sidney, and his family.

Books by Bill Mauldin

THE BRASS RING

UP FRONT

I'VE DECIDED I WANT MY SEAT BACK

WHAT'S GOT YOUR BACK UP?

BILL MAULDIN IN KOREA

BILL MAULDIN'S ARMY

A SORT OF A SAGA

BACK HOME

STAR SPANGLED BANTER

UP FRONT (re-issue)

THIS DAMN TREE LEAKS

MUD, MULES AND MOUNTAINS

BILL MAULDIN

THE BRASS RING

W · W · NORTON & COMPANY · INC ·
NEW YORK

SBN 393 07463 3

Library of Congress Catalog Card No. 78–152671

Published simultaneously in Canada
by George J. McLeod Limited, Toronto

PRINTED IN THE UNITED STATES OF AMERICA

2 3 4 5 6 7 8 9 0

To all the nice people whose names got left out

THE BRASS RING

1

"Dear Sir," a preacher writes, "I understand your editorial cartoons are printed daily in almost three hundred newspapers. How I envy your pulpit and congregation. Think of the cumulative impact you have upon the public conscience—of your potential for doing good. Of course, you have probably never thought of yourself in a ministerial light. . . ."

The hell I haven't. Between the ages of six and twelve, it was one of several careers I considered, along with those of airplane pilot, deep-sea diver, and Sheriff of Otero County. Lest the preacher who wrote the letter think I'm trifling with him, let me point out that not only did I consider taking up his line of work, but I was no stranger to the pulpit. A hundred feet north of the upper end of the Mauldin apple farm, seven thousand feet above sea level and ten miles east of Alamogordo, New Mexico, stood (and still stands) a weathered, white clapboard, tin-roofed, one-room church which served the communities of Mountain Park and High Rolls. There, during Sunday-morning services I often crawled under the keyboard of the organ and worked the pedal bellows with my hands for my mother. She was the only person around who could play the thing and was too short to pump with her feet.

Later in the week I would sometimes climb back up the hill to the church, which was never locked, containing nothing of value but the leaky organ. I would compose myself behind the pulpit and speak at length to the empty benches and folding chairs about things which troubled my soul and what I thought might be done about them. Aside

Two bull calves in our back yard at Mountain Park. Earliest known photo of author.

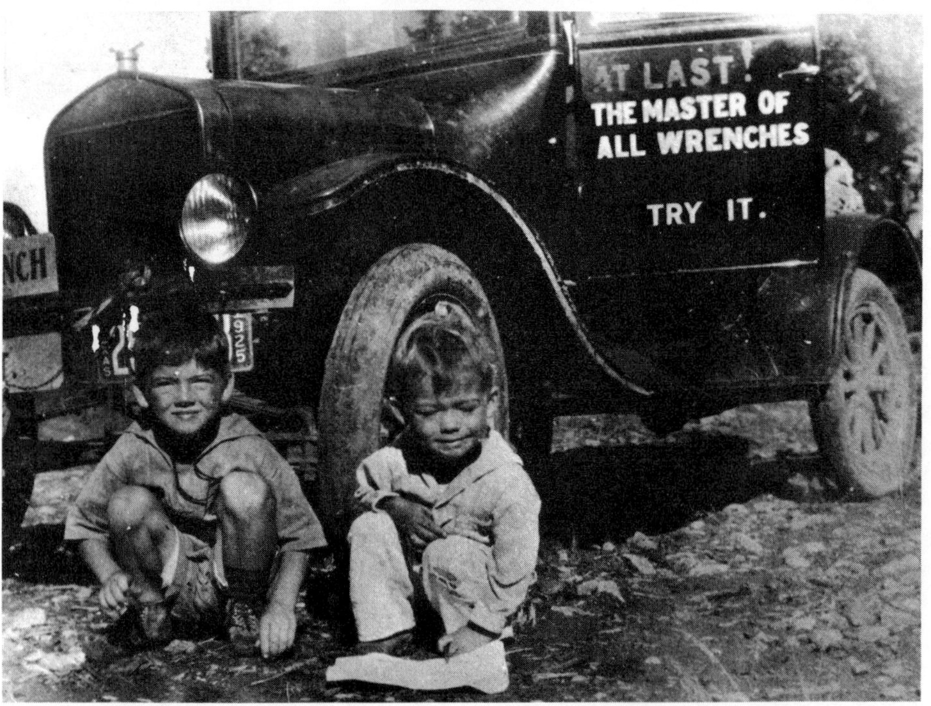

First known photo of author thinking up cartoon ideas. It was always a strain. Note date on Texas license plate behind Sid's head. This was our father's car during his brief career as wrench salesman.

from an occasional chipmunk or jackrabbit which might have paused quizzically in the doorway for a moment, I never had an audience reaction from which to judge my efforts, but I did feel that I had a knack for speaking meaningfully to and for the sinners of our time.

If this sounds a bit precocious, I should point out that we started everything young in the hills of southern New Mexico: smoking at ten, hunting at eleven, driving at twelve, drinking at fourteen, and if you were a virgin at sixteen you didn't admit it. As for me, I started inhaling at ten, but in other respects pretty well followed the norm, including being a virgin at sixteen and denying it. We even had pot. A coarse grade of it proliferated as a local weed, along with skunk cabbage, morning glories, and stinging nettle. Personally, I shied away from marijuana, having been convinced by the *Reader's Digest* and other medical authorities that the stuff was addictive and would lead straight to hard drugs such as heroin, which was not indigenous and would cost money—a rare item among farm and ranch kids in the early thirties. (Once I concocted a sort of reefer, using coffee grounds, dried horse manure, and brown Bull Durham paper. It was one of the first things I inhaled, and it gave interesting sensations: lightheadedness, nausea, and a touch of megalomania. But let me caution experimenters and would-be shitheads—there is no other possible word for it—that our horses ate mostly alfalfa hay and that their offerings lay baking for weeks under a dry Southwestern sun. Satisfaction is likely to be less than complete in other climates.)

Anyway, whereas most ecclesiastical careers begin with a "call," mine ended with one, on an afternoon in my thirteenth summer. The setting suited the event. A retreating sun put on its daily magic show of fluorescence, thirty miles out on the plains below, among the dunes of the great White Sands (one of Nature's showpieces, not then yet requisitioned and fenced in by the air force) and painted the San Andreas range, another thirty miles beyond, with gentle reds and purples (to be replaced in a decade by the shock light of the first nuclear bomb). The mountain breezes, having bustled uphill all day in the heat, were now cooling and sloughing downward through the piñons and ponderosa pines rimming our west bog. My grandfather liked to call it the lower pasture, but in the years since he had come up from Texas and carved our place out of the hills, the soft spot in the middle of the bog, where the cattails grew, had trapped and slowly swallowed an assortment of livestock, including a couple of stray horses, some goats and several cows.

I was milking one of the survivors at the time of my call. Actually, I had finished milking and was "stripping," a tedious business of flattening a teat at its top between thumb and forefinger and sliding the digits firmly and slowly downward to extract the last drop—repeating this with each teat in turn, around and around, until the udder was dry. Otherwise, I had been told, it would "cake." I had not been told how calves who didn't know about stripping kept their mothers from caking. I had learned that if I stripped too roughly this particular cow would put one hind hoof in the bucket of milk and try to get me with the other. The daily milking exercise gave me strong wrists and an abiding aversion to overstuffed udders.

I remember watching my fingers at work on that afternoon and considering a comment my grandmother made after I had told her that I was thinking of becoming a preacher. She said she thought I had the hands of a surgeon. My mother, who was present, agreed that I had fine hands, all right, but she in turn insisted that they were more those of a painter or a sculptor. My father, also on the scene, said a little more farm work would give them strength and character. Naturally, all this talk made me somewhat hand conscious. Mine were conversation pieces. Still studying them, bemused by their future, I butted my head into the cow's soft flank to move her an inch or two closer to the center of the bucket, and began a fantasy wherein I removed a tumor from President Franklin Roosevelt, as student nurses and cabinet members hung bug-eyed with admiration over the railing of the operating-room gallery. Now my fingers, so deft with hemostat and catgut, pinched a teat, whereupon the cow kicked me and stepped into the bucket in a swift double motion, hardly shifting the far hind foot.

Losing the milk wasn't so bad. Except for my grandmother, who liked cottage cheese, and for an occasional churning of butter for the rest of the family, I was the only real consumer of the stuff. The bucket, however, was badly bent. That was something else. The Great Depression was at its depth. Our apple crop, upon which we were almost entirely dependent, might have been worth as much as $500 that year if it hadn't been pounded off the trees by hail earlier in the summer. Oh, we weren't going to starve. Farm people can always manage to find or grow something for the table. We had a vegetable garden and the forests were full of fat deer, which would have been amazed to learn that they were legally immune from stealthy mountain kids with .30-30s and skinning knives. However, any piece of hardware which cost money was just about irreplaceable. I tried to hammer the bucket's bottom flat with a rock, mashed a finger, threw the rock at the cow and missed. But I hadn't cussed. If the Lord was testing me, I had passed, aside from throwing the rock.

At this point, I got my call.

"Hey, Big-Head!" It came from the other side of the cow. My brother, Sidney Junior, a year my senior, got some sort of peculiar satisfaction out of referring to the fact that an early case of rickets left me with an oversized skull on a scrawny, pot-bellied frame. Sid, on the other hand, at fourteen was almost six feet high, outweighed me by fifty pounds, and had the kind of face that later caused people to think he was related to Gregory Peck. He really could have afforded a more charitable attitude toward me. With a muttered comment that I couldn't hit a bull in the ass with a bass fiddle, my brother took the bucket, found another rock, and with a few deft knocks straightened the thing almost like new.

"What I came down here to tell you," he said, "is that the folks are breaking up and we're going to be on our own."

"You mean we're gonna have to *feed* ourselves?" Goddamn, things sure happened fast in our family. I hadn't left the house more than a half hour ago, and things had been peaceful then. But then, my parents were like France and Germany: peace for them was a pause between wars. He drank and roared; she sulked and clawed. He would threaten to blow his brains out and she would tell him it was a good idea. It was that sort of marriage. But in the past, no matter how stormy things had got, Sid and I enjoyed a surprising amount of security. Even when our father became restless and took us on journeys to new careers he found for himself, such as mining in Mexico or homesteading in Arizona, we always had some sort of roof over our heads and there was always food on the table. No matter how hard and constantly he and my mother fought and bickered, he always managed to bring something home and she always managed to cook it. But, aside from this rather loose teamwork, our family had no assets or resources at all. Even the New Mexico apple farm, to which we always returned from our far-flung adventures, belonged to our grandfather. If our parents were really splitting, what would happen to Sid and me? Suddenly I felt young enough to be helpless and old enough to be scared.

My brother and I walked back up the hill together. I suppose parental battles were about the only things that made us feel close. The two-bedroom frame house, which my grandfather had built, and in which I had been born, was empty. It turned out that our father had gone muttering off into the hills with a pistol and a bottle of gin, and our mother had started walking down the road toward Alamogordo. She wasn't going to see anybody in Alamogordo; it was simply the only handy road. Sometimes in the past she had walked the other way, toward Cloudcroft. Sid and I got the kerosene lamps lit and played cards until they both came home.

But Sid had been right. The atmosphere was changing. When people fight that much something vital begins to tear. Something else begins to calcify. This time, for the first time, we really knew that our family

Photo courtesy of Mrs. C. F. Moore

First Cavalry Division troopers on maneuvers in mid-twenties.

Pancho Villa holding my cousin Marjorie Schumacher during the baby-kissing phase of his career, just before his assassination. My Uncle George Bemis at left. Picture taken in Parral, Mexico, where my father worked in mines.

Sid cranking our first jointly owned Model T. Author offstage to left getting ready to switch to kerosene tank after warm-up.

Early (age ten) portrait of author during law-enforcement phase. Witness in box at right is being urged to confess crimes.

ship was sinking. Daydreams about the future began to go glimmering. In our situation you didn't consider a "calling"; you thought about a job.

A few days later Sid and I sat on a fence and watched the 1st Cavalry Division go by on its way to summer maneuvers in the hills behind us. This was one of the grandest sights a boy could ask for. The famous old division was based at Fort Bliss, near El Paso, on the Mexican border, ninety miles south of us. In those days cavalry still meant men on horses. It took hours for them to pass: thousands upon thousands of dusty-faced troopers clip-clopping up our narrow, rocky mountain road on great, barrel-chested mounts (nothing like our jug-headed, broom-tailed local ponies), with leather creaking, campaign hats turned up in front, carbines in scabbards, officers with pistols on lanyards (maybe I'm being carried away by the memory, but I could swear some of them had sabers, too), and lance corporals with guidons fluttering. Some of the wagons and fieldpieces with caissons were pulled and hauled by trucks, but you could tell that the cavalry still distrusted machinery and preferred horse or mule power for every possible job.

Here, it seemed to me, might be a sensible and not unpleasant solution to the problem of what to do with myself when the crunch came. After all, I wouldn't be the first hayseed to begin a distinguished military career from hunger. The fact that my grandfather, for whom I was named, once worked for the cavalry as a civilian scout during the Geronimo wars, and that my father, an artilleryman in France during World War I, used to regale us with stories of his adventures overseas had done nothing to alienate me from the martial life. In Mexico we had lived in Parral, a mining town garrisoned by government troops drilling for great battles with rebels who never showed up. At the age of three I had learned how to roll cigarettes from mustachioed stalwarts in glittering uniforms with bandoliers full of great brass cartridges. At the same time I became a sort of mascot in the Mexican army's favorite Parral whorehouse until apprehended by my parents, who understood that I only went there because the nice ladies made salty tortillas for me.

When drawing pictures of myself in various careers during my childhood, I sometimes fooled around with soldier scenes when I wasn't depicting my favorite hero as a scientist or an inventor or a pilot, sheriff, or preacher. I suppose one of the reasons I had such an active fantasy life was that I could draw before I could talk. It came so naturally to me that when a schoolteacher would berate me for drawing in class I would reply that I had only been thinking. It was the truth, since that was how I often put my thoughts together. Anyway, I was older now, facing rather more reality than I had bargained for, and the soldierly me, which had played a comparatively minor role among the other pen, pencil, and watercolor images of myself, now seemed to stand up as a real possibility.

"Sid, I think I'll go to West Point," I said, above the muted thunder and flinty clicks of the endless parade of hooves, with their accompaniment of snorts, farts, and exhortations to close up that goddamn file or keep that frigging interval. "That is," I added, "if the family stays together long enough for me to get through high school."

"Haw," he said. "The family's not your problem."

I reminded him that there was nothing wrong with my scholastic record. I had been valedictorian of our eighth-grade class of six. I shouldn't have brought it up, since my brother had been near the other end of that stick.

"Oh, we all know you're a smart-ass, Big-Head," he said. "Your trouble is that you have to get appointed to those schools." He reminded me that, even if our parents had ever so much as laid eyes on such an exalted personage as a U.S. congressman or senator, they certainly didn't know one, nor was one likely to want to know us. Although the apple farm had been our home base, we had treated it more as a refuge and had branded ourselves as gypsies, not as reliable members of anybody's constituency. Also, my brother pointed out, when we were home we ran up unpaid bills. Why, he asked, would a New Mexico politician be interested in doing our parents an important favor, such as appointing their snot-nosed, chicken-breasted, bat-eared, string-muscled, gourd-gutted, fumble-footed, squeaky-voiced brat to West Point?

"Besides," Sid asked, "what makes you think you could pass the physical?"

"Well, I'll lie about my age, join up, and rise through the ranks," I said. "I'll bet I could pass the tests for an enlisted man."

"You couldn't pass a test for a barracks rat," he said.

At this point in our conversation one of the few mechanized portions of the 1st Cavalry was going by. One of the troopers' despised trucks, carrying a field kitchen, broke down before our eyes. The crew got the hood up and began fussing and peering futilely at the innards. Sid jumped off the fence, approached the men, and craned over their shoulders. I mentioned earlier that Sid was a tall, well-knit specimen for his age. He was also a good mechanic at the age of fourteen. He had been trained by an expert. Our father might have had problems with wanderlust and thirst, but not with talent. He was a designer and builder of spraying machines and other farm equipment from odds and ends of scrap metal, as well as an accomplished, practicing carpenter, mason, plumber, distiller, hunter, motorcyclist, and prospector. He could dismantle and rebuild automobiles and trucks blindfolded—a good thing, since the average Mauldin vehicle had passed through the hands of at least a half-dozen owners and needed all the help it could get.

"Beat it, buster," one of the troopers growled at my brother from under

Author, two friends, family Maxwell, Sid, and milk-goat on Arizona homestead west of Phoenix.

Recent photo of remains of father's hand-built spraying machine, sans wagon wheels.

Uncle Billy (right, with vest) and friend i Mountain Park, about 1910.

Uncle Billy and his first wife touring the mountains shortly after he learned to drive.

[M]y father taught him. Here he's teaching my mother.

Sid in one of his later bombs.

the truck's hood.

"Your coil wire vibrated loose from your distributor cap," Sid observed respectfully, backing away.

"Well, son of a bitch if it didn't," another man said. They shoved the wire back in and clanked away in a cloud of blue smoke.

"They could use a ring job, too." Sid grinned at me, turned his back on the military spectacle, and sauntered away. His future, at least, seemed cut out for him.

Sid and I started high school that fall in Alamogordo, riding a bus over a dirt road which wound eighteen miles through canyons to make good ten straight miles. The altitude differential was about three thousand feet. Alamo, as we called it, was the county seat and a sawmill town of some thirty-five hundred people, cutting pine logs which were felled in the heights above our farm and hauled down what was known among train buffs as the steepest standard-gauge railroad in the world.

There was still a touch of the frontier about that country then. The state had still been a territory only nine years before I had been born. My Grandfather Mauldin was one of the early mountain settlers, and had among his acquaintances several heroes and rascals of his time, including Pat Garrett, the sheriff who shot Billy the Kid in Lincoln County, just north of us, and Oliver Lee, a cow baron with several thousand head in terrain where one head required seventy acres for grazing. The sun set daily on Lee's holdings, but it had to work at it. The rancher was a tough guy who kept his image up.

This was the country of a judge named Roy Bean, who has spawned as many legends as any man of the West. My favorite Bean story concerns a Mexican lady who came into his courtroom with a quart bottle of milk, while he was on the bench in El Paso. She was a customer of Bean's dairy. It was one of his many commercial enterprises. The customer went straight up to the bench, plunked the bottle in front of Bean, showed that the cap was still sealed, pointed at a live minnow swimming inside, and accused him of watering the milk.

"Damn," he said, "I told that stupid herd boy not to let those cows drink in the Rio Grande."

I was never able to find out if my grandfather killed anybody. I knew him well while I was growing up (he lived to be a hundred, stayed mentally sharp, read most of the larger type in his newspaper without glasses, and chewed his last meal with some of his original teeth) and must have asked him a hundred times if there was any blood on his hands. Naturally, I hoped there was. One of the problems even today of growing up in the West is that with all the rustlers dead and the Indians on the reservations you still get guns all mixed up with masculinity, and whether you realize it or not you tend to measure a man by how much violence you figure is bottled up in him. Uncle Billy, as my grandfather was called, never gave me any satisfaction in this matter, and I was too stupid to realize that he didn't have to prove a damned thing. Everybody who knew him in the old days told stories about Uncle Billy's talent with a gun. When he and his young bride settled their first place in Wills Canyon, above Cloudcroft, he bagged deer and wild turkey with a pistol. Any turkey hunter will know what this means. Uncle Billy did not do it to be a showoff, but because he couldn't afford a rifle.

We mountain kids were often called hillbillies by our classmates in Alamogordo. There were about two dozen of us riding the school bus. Most of us wore Levi's or overalls, with long-handled union suits underneath in winter. I remember being stuck for a few weeks with a pair of corduroy *knickers,* for God's sake—hand-me-downs from some cousin—which I wore because they were the only pants I had until I managed, after several unsuccessful tries, to ruin them on a barbed-wire fence, forcing my mother to scrounge something else for me. The Alamo youngsters knew that we all used "coal-oil" lamps in the hills, dressed around the kitchen stove in winter, shot deer out of season for meat, and relied heavily upon wallpaper and magazine cutouts to block drafts through the cracks in our walls. Today I suppose we would be called poverty cases. We just thought we were broke.

As a result of all this, town girls didn't exactly fall over most of us mountain boys. Even my brother, with his good looks, hand-waved hair, and extra-long sideburns, had a hard time getting dates at first. Another problem was that, although we all drove, we had no car. When a farm family went to the movies on Saturday night it took its pickup truck, with the elders up front and the kids in back. My folks didn't even have a pickup. Except for a brief period when my father worked as a foreman on a WPA outdoor-toilet-building program and drove an almost-new Pontiac, our vehicle was an ancient Maxwell with the back hacked off by an axe and a truck bed bolted and wired on. This alone would have been enough to keep the belles from standing in line to ride with the Mauldin boys.

I did meet one Alamo girl who seemed to take a shine to me. She was a lovely little blonde with a double first name. I think it was Teddy-Lee. I mooned over her with all the intensity of a pubescent boy's first love. Possibly my main attraction for her was my drawing ability. I did numerous portraits of her, and she was always asking me to draw horses, which I did well. One noon I was in the drugstore with her, at the soda fountain, blowing the proceeds of a long Saturday's work at fifteen cents an hour on a neighbor's farm. The druggist asked me, right in front of my girl, when my father was going to pay his bill. Teddy-Lee took it in her stride—in those days it would have been a reasonable assumption that

Author, Sid's girl, and Sid on Arizona desert.

Sid, my girl, and author in New Mexico mountains. Photo accidentally became crumpled after girl switched to Sid.

her old man could have been having bill trouble, too—but I was unable to pursue my courtship seriously after that. She became a part of my humiliation. I dumped all the change I had left on the druggist's counter and have hated him to this day.

I mention all this to show that there were burrs under my saddle even aside from the pressure of an impending family split and the knowledge that Sid and I might be on our own at any time. I've never been able to figure out exactly where this overload of touchiness and ambition came from. Some of it was probably natural aggressiveness. I had gained a certain notoriety in grammar school for starting more fights than anybody else and winning none of them. (Sid would loyally bail me out of these situations whenever he could, then beat the tar out of me himself when he got me home.)

Whatever the psychology, for a variety of reasons I found myself ending my thirteenth year in late October, 1935, in a normal state of fright, anger, resentment, humiliation, and insecurity. Thumbing through a tattered copy of *Popular Mechanics* while sitting in a wrecked Marmon touring car my father dragged home in order to salvage the brass fittings, I came across a group of ads for cartoonists' correspondence schools. One ad was topped by the notation that some practitioners of this art made as much as a hundred thousand dollars a year. This was it. Not only was I going to save myself, but the family honor would also be salvaged. The answer to everything had been in my hands all along.

"You're not without an artistic background, Billy," my Grandmother Bemis said that night at our supper table, after I had announced my final decision on my life's work. "That is to say, there has been a history of art appreciation, among your Boston and Chattanooga ancestors especially, but very few actual artists."

She sounded dubious. She believed heritage was everything. She belonged to the D.A.R., and she swore you could tell a person's breeding by the skin on the back of his hand. The thinner and more venous the better. Besides, she wanted a surgeon in the family.

"What about artists from the Texas side?" my father asked.

"There are no artists in Texas and there is no art in Texas," my grandmother replied.

Later I followed her up the hill to her house. The correspondence course in cartooning I had selected, after sending for brochures from all those listed in *Popular Mechanics,* was the Landon School in Cleveland. The price was twenty dollars, payable in advance. I would have preferred to keep my grandmother out of the deal, and would have approached my parents if I had thought there was a chance either of them had that kind of money. My father was always sympathetic to the idea of learning any new craft. He collected careers as an Eagle Scout accu-

Uncle George Bemis, his wife Naomi, Uncle Guy Loomis, Aunt Louise Schumacher, my father, Nana, Waldron Schumacher, my mother, Pauline Loomis.

Mother and brother, in Mountain Park at about time this book begins.

mulates merit badges. My mother had always been an enthusiastic and uncritical supporter of anything I did that looked like self-improvement. When I had taken up reading at the age of four, she had buried me in borrowed and scrounged books of all kinds, from *Tom Swift* to Agatha Christie. She always dreamed of being a writer herself. During one of our leanest periods, she managed to buy on installments the Miller Bookhouse series of six heavy volumes which took the young reader from Mother Goose up through serious biography. Now, however, twenty dollars was clearly beyond my parents' resources, even for the sake of my career. To have asked them for it would have made them feel bad, and they were having enough troubles between themselves already.

There was little doubt in my mind that my grandmother had that much somewhere among the crockery on her kitchen shelf, or that she would part with it. The trouble with her money was that she knew how to attach strings. She was concerned with my purity. Once she set me up in the fruit-vending business, watched with equanimity while I almost lost my shirt, then became distressed when I turned the corner, made a small profit, took it to Shorty Miller's pool hall in Alamogordo, and doubled the money in a domino game at the back of the room. (Miller had a sign, MINORS DISCOURAGED, but admitted he didn't have much respect for easily-discouraged minors.) My grandmother never forgave my father for teaching me stud poker at the age of ten, nor could she ever understand his motive or method. He owed me seventy-five cents for five hours of setting out cabbage plants; not having the money handy, he spent several patient evenings getting back his IOU from me and teaching me the fine points of the game, whereas he could easily have taken me in a few minutes if he had merely wanted to win. It was his way of being fatherly, but she couldn't see it that way. She said that when she looked deeply into my big brown eyes she saw something fine there and aimed to keep it there.*

I found my prospective angel in her backyard trying to split kindling with a butcher knife by lamplight. I located her missing hatchet on top of her privy (where I had left it after using it as a hammer to nail a loose section of corrugated roofing at her request a week or so earlier), finished the kindling job for her, and was invited in for late tea. This was a good sign. She knew I wanted something, but negotiating with my grandmother was like dealing with a trade union or an Indian chief: much ritual and smoke signaling. In her well-ordered world, tea was

* Footnote: One little anecdote about my grandmother really has no place in this narrative but deserves telling as a sidelight to her character. In her youth, while departing from Chattanooga on a train and waving to some friends, she dropped one glove of a treasured new pair out her window onto the platform. There wasn't a chance of retrieving it. Without a second's hesitation, she threw the remaining glove after its mate.

something you began at sixteen, coffee at eighteen, tobacco—if you must—at twenty-one, and so on. Even though in the outside world I was a practiced sinner who consumed upward of a sack of Bull Durham a day when I could afford it, had sampled whiskey, debated with myself the pros and cons of trying the local breed of hashish, watched girls swim raw under the waterfall at the head of Box Canyon, and had given aid to a nanny goat in a trying breech birth, I was flattered to be offered evening tea in my grandmother's house, in full knowledge that she would drown it in milk so it wouldn't keep me awake.

"I need twenty bucks," I said, after the tea ceremony had been performed and the chitchat was out of the way.

"I suppose an artist needs paints and things," she said.

"Nana, you don't understand. It's drawing. Cartooning."

"Cartooning? Oh, those things in *Esquire*." (My uncle, Waldron Schumacher, a mining executive in El Paso, sent her a pile of magazines from time to time, including *Esquire,* which she called a belly-button book.) "Well," she said, "I suppose someone has to draw them."

"Nana, I'm going to make a bucket of dough."

For a while she just stared at me with disbelief, and maybe a touch of delicate horror. I had to keep thinking of my humiliation in the drugstore to hold my spine stiff.

"People make money out of flowers, and pets, too," she said. "But there are two kinds of seller. One loves plants or animals. The other just loves money. They both peddle their wares, but one of them is committing a sort of blasphemy, because life in any form is a miracle and if you don't respect it you've got no business handling it. A talent is a sort of special gift, too. You didn't earn it. You don't own it. You're merely its keeper. There's nothing wrong with earning a living with it, but that should be incidental. Do you think Rembrandt just wanted to make a bucket of dough?"

"Can anybody prove he didn't want to?"

"I think so."

"Rembrandt was no cartoonist." The tea had sharpened me. I felt I was giving as good as I got.

"Well," she said at last, "I suppose cartooning is a legitimate way to use artistic talent. I probably don't appreciate what I see in *Esquire* or the newspapers because something is lacking in me. If you make people laugh, you've created some happiness. That makes the world a nicer place. I can't stand people who go through life without wanting to tinker with it and change it a little. You go ahead and make funny pictures."

I thought this was fine reasoning on her part, and said so, reflecting to myself that laughter also made money, which made even more happiness. I showed her the Landon School brochure.

"Oh, my," she said. "It takes training to draw cartoons?"

"This is a business proposition," I said, bearing in mind that our part of the West was the traditional land of the grubstake. "Lend me the twenty and I'll pay you back double. Triple. Quadruple."

She looked at me for another long spell, then got up and went to her bedroom without a word. I felt I had not only failed; I had probably driven her to tears. I went to comfort her and found her standing on a chair in her closet with a fistful of ones and fives. All the time I had thought she kept it in the kitchen.

"I told you I had no spare cash," she said. "These are savings I'm giving you."

Overcome, I swore on all that was holy that it would be the soundest investment of her life. I would not only pay her back a dozen times over but would see that she was never in want for the rest of her life.

"Listen," she said, "I'm going to lend you the money at no interest and with only one condition. Promise me that you aren't *really* going into a profession for what you can get out of it. And if you should ever decide it was the wrong career—that you'd contribute more and get more happiness doing something else—you'll drop the whole thing, and forget about paying me back."

"Sure," I said. "I promise." My tongue was only halfway in my cheek. I was reasonably certain that cartooning would turn out to have its esthetic satisfactions, too. Like Carnegie, I would make my pile first and then devote myself to the uplifting of souls. If a poor cartoonist could bring joy to mankind, think what a rich one could do.

"Good God, boy," my father said next day. "Why didn't you tell me you needed lessons? Fellow I got to know up in Ruidoso is a cartoonist. Professional. We built a government outhouse for him. Name is Larry Smith. Signs himself Hillbilly Larry. Nicest kind of a guy. I'll take you to him. He'll teach you the ropes and save you twenty bucks. Let's go."

From the way his eye lit up when he said twenty bucks, I decided not to mention that an hour earlier I had sent the money to Cleveland from the combination post office and general store across the valley and had watched the conductor of the logging train scoop up the mail sack on the way to Alamogordo. Imagine a real cartoonist within reach! I hadn't thought one existed in the whole state. Ruidoso was a mountain resort some forty miles north—then a sort of honkeytonk town among the tall pines, with a saloon in just about every other building, a thriving trade from El Paso and the Panhandle country, and a crying need for sanitation. A lot of my father's WPA toilet-construction time had been spent there.

"Whatever people might say about your old man," he said as we got into his car (the green Pontiac he had acquired toward the end of his

A two-page album of Pop.

Here he's eleven, on his horse, Cricket.

On his first motorcycle.

As an artillery corporal overseas in World War I.

With a bevy of post-war admirers.

Father, Sid, and author in front of family tent-house on desert homestead. Out-of-focus effect probably due to 120° July heat waves.

Above. Pop and his second wife, Emily, shortly after their marriage.

Right. A recent photo in front of his trailer.

brief job), "I do have a way of getting around and knowing the right people. By the way, I might need a little of that twenty for gas."

I gave him a dollar out of a side fund I had accumulated for drawing supplies.

"Junior! Junior!" he hollered after tramping on the starter for a moment. "Where's the damn battery?"

My brother came out of the tool shed, looking defensive. "You told me you had to take the car back to Ruidoso because you couldn't finish paying the dealer, so I took a few things out of it, like the spare tire and jack and lighter, stuff like that. I was going to swap the battery for one of our old ones, but I forgot to put ours in."

"No matter how rich you get drawing pictures," Pop said, as we sailed up through the tall woods, "remember to always stay on the right side of your brother."

I felt all the excitement of a boy fiddler on his way to meet Heifetz. In my case maybe it would be more accurate to say an ambitious young speculator on his way to meet Jay Gould. I wasn't even worried about how we were going to get back from Ruidoso. As we pulled onto the town's long, narrow main street, half blacktop and half mud, we stopped at the first tavern, a rustic affair made of edge slabs, with bark attached, which a sawmill cuts off a pine log before making planks from it. They were cheap, and practically every building in Ruidoso was made of them.

"Pop, I already mailed the twenty dollars," I said hastily. "You ought to know before you go in there."

"Oh," he said. "Well, we'll take a look anyhow. This is one of Larry's favorite hangouts and he just might be here."

"Listen," I said, "I do have one more dollar extra." I began to feel like a rat.

"Nope," he said. "This is professional business we're on."

Smith wasn't there, but his work was all over the place. The bar mirror was framed by cartoons, and the opposite wall was a solid mass of drawings, some overlapping. I strolled over to this collection, trying to look like a connoisseur rather than an excited kid, but after I got there I could contain myself no longer.

"Pop!" I yelled. "They're *originals*. They're real, not just prints."

"That's how Hillbilly pays for his booze," the bartender said, grinning.

"The sprout here is taking up cartooning himself," Pop told the barman.

"Well, if he drinks like you and draws like Larry, we'll have to build a new room for him."

I only half heard the rest of the conversation. I was engrossed in the gallery. The artist had a free-swinging style—plenty of action. His humor was earthy and abundant. The predominant theme was lady tourists in hilarious predicaments. Most of all, I think I admired the economy and precision of line. Zip, stroke, zap, squiggle, dot, dot, and there was a buck-toothed cowboy. No hesitation of execution; very little sign of agonized pencil underdrawing and erasing. They were cheerful, happy drawings by a man who knew his stuff.

Pop pulled me away and said we ought to look for Larry in person before we found ourselves spending that dollar.

We worked our way through the business section. Practically every bar, restaurant, dry-goods store, drugstore, grocery, and dancehall was decorated by the cartoons.

"That Larry," said the owner of the little movie house—whose entryway had such a display of Smith creations that you could hardly tell what was playing—"he sure does like movies."

"You just missed him. He was headed up the hill," said the man in the souvenir shop, peering from behind a display board full of Hillbilly's postcards. So Smith's stuff was published, too!

"Larry's trying to bring the barter system back into style," my father told me. "Most people do their work, get paid for it, and spend it on what they need. He cuts out the middle stuff."

We came to a row of one-room cabins in a grove of pines. All were built of the inevitable pine slabs, with tarpaper roofs. One had a brand-new WPA outhouse behind it, and it was here that we found our man.

"Hey, Sid!" he yelled, unwinding a long, gangling, incredibly skinny frame from a rickety chair in front of a plank table, on which rested a huge, ink-encrusted breadboard and a half-finished cartoon. The floor around Larry's feet was ringed with cigar butts, and the whole room had the cheerful disorder of a happy bachelor and artist. Everywhere were bits of paper, clothing, and bottles of colored ink. "Hi!" he yelled at me. "You must belong to old Sid. Those ears!" He made great swoops with his pen, drawing ears in the air. He had a huge pair himself. He also had the biggest, friendliest, most infectious grin I ever saw, and he positively twitched with nervous energy. He turned out to be the only man I ever met who could outtalk my father.

"Well! So you want to learn to draw!" he cried delightedly before Pop had half finished explaining our mission. "Okay, let's get started right. See what you can do." He plonked me down at his board—the highest honor I could have imagined. He tossed his own cartoon into a corner, pulled a fresh sheet from a stack of heavy drawing paper, hacked off a chunk, and set it before me. "Two-ply bristol," he said. "Never stint yourself on materials." I reached timidly for a pencil and he snatched it out of my hand. "First thing to realize, you gotta *produce!*" he said. "Some people will tell you to mess around with a pencil first. To heck with that. If you know what you're doing you got a picture in mind and you get it down on paper fast before the next picture comes. Watch!"

He grabbed the breadboard with my still-blank paper, sank a pen into a quart of Higgins ink, and as Pop and I watched, transfixed, he slammed out a drawing of the south end of a fat tourist lady riding north into the pine woods on a tiny horse. Even if I had had a stop watch I wouldn't have been able to look away from the drawing, but I'll swear the entire performance, from the first curved stroke of the lady's rear to the last branch of the tree, took less than a minute. His hand was a blur of motion over the board, stabbing out at five-second intervals for a fresh dunk in the ink bottle. He dropped the pen, seized a brush, and with more rapierlike passes at various other bottles he had colored the picture in even less time than he had taken to draw it. I've never since seen a man who could approach Hillbilly Larry Smith for speed.

"Wow!" I breathed.

"Well, Billy, I sure brought you to the kingfish himself, didn't I?" Pop asked, proudly.

"Wait a minute," Larry snapped. "We got a drawing; we need a gag."

"Oh, don't you think of that first?" I asked.

"Why? It's already funny. Fat dame, little horse. Everybody laughs at a big butt like hers. Make a funny drawing, the words write themselves. Let's see—usually I think it up while I'm drawing, but I'm dragging now. Wrong time of day to be working, I guess. But, man, in this business you gotta produce—wait a minute. . . . I got it! We'll stick long ears on the horse," he suited action to words in about ten seconds, "and now she's riding a burro. Now it doesn't need any words." He prodded at me with a long, ink-stained finger. "Remember that. The best kind of cartoon has got no words."

"I don't get it, Larry," my father said apologetically, peering over the artist's shoulder.

"Aw, for Chrissake, do I have to spell ass for you? Okay, how about this: we stick a couple of sympathetic-looking cowboys in the corner"—it was no sooner said than done—"and one of 'em says—see, we put it in a balloon; that's what you call the line around a cartoon character's words—he says, 'Look at that sweet little ass.' And then we have the dame saying: 'Thanks.' "

"Well, that's better, I guess," Pop said. "I get it now."

"*Better!*" Larry roared good-naturedly. "Sid, if you saw that in a bar you'd be rolling on the floor."

"I think it's pretty funny," I declared, embarrassed for my father.

"It's not great, but it'll do in a pinch," Larry said. "Pinch, pinch. There's an idea. . . ." He became a man possessed. He grabbed another sheet. "Pinch. Now wait a minute. . . ." The muse was not on his shoulder; it was astride his ear, beating at his head. "All right, now here's a man helping a girl into the saddle. Nothing about pinching here, but it shows you how one idea leads to another. . . ." As the girl took shape under the cartoonist's hand I thought how near to God you can be at a drawing board, creating any kind of people you want when you know how. "All right, now watch how I draw this horse," Larry said. "I don't claim to be Charles M. Russell when it comes to animals, but I got confidence with cartoon horses and your work shows when you're not afraid. Wait a minute. . . . I got the gag now! He says: 'You ought to wear pants when you go riding, miss.' And she says: 'Awww, you been peekin'!' "

This one got a satisfactory chuckle out of Pop.

"See what I mean, kid?" Larry said to me as he flashed his brush among the bottles and flooded the drawing with color. "Don't fool around. The way to be a cartoonist is to draw. Keep busy and knock the stuff out. I'm hungry. Let's take these two drawings out and eat 'em."

I don't think we'd been in his place ten minutes. We went out and traded the cartoons for all the hamburgers we could put away. I began to see some sense in the barter system. If I could spend twenty minutes a day on grocery drawings, plus thirty minutes, say, on rent drawings, and another half hour or so on cartoons for clothing, laundry, and sundries—why, I would have the rest of the day to draw for sheer profit.

Back at Larry's place, he showed me his collection of originals from other cartoonists. Reverently, I held in my hands comic strips from nearly every master in the field: McManus, De Beck, Crane, Branner, Goldberg, Caniff, Gray, Leonard, Smith, Raymond, Capp, and a dozen more. As I laid each one out on the board and studied pencil blurs and corrective razor scratches, I took heart at the realization that each great cartoonist had to struggle every day with each little strip. Also, I think it would have pleased my grandmother to know that as I handled each drawing I was not just thinking of how much money these guys made. I was handling the work *they* had handled. The originals. Larry must have felt that way, too. I noted that of all the things in his place these were the best cared-for.

"Okay, let's get on with the lesson," Larry said at last, putting the treasures away. "Let's see how fast you can make me a drawing."

"Just think," Pop mourned, "he sent money away for lessons and you were here all the time, Larry."

"You should have told him sooner." Hillbilly was leaning over my shoulder nervously as I tried to draw without planning in pencil and once again found legs and arms getting away from me and figures running right off the sheet. When I dropped a blob of ink from the pen and took out my knife to scrape it off, Larry could stand it no longer.

"You've got to step it up," he cried. "Quit scratching. Get confidence. Never take out a blob. You know what a blob is at the bottom of a

EDDIE THE 2ND. LOOEY

EDDIE, FRESH OUT OF WEST POINT, IS DRILLING A COMPANY OF OLD TIMERS TO SHIP OVERSEAS, AND THEY RESENT HAVING A MERE BOY BOSS THEM—

BY- BILL MAULDIN

An early (pre-Landon School) comic strip, heavily influenced by father's army jokes.

An editorial cartoon of approximately the same vintage.

The Landon School takes effect. I become conscious of expression and caricature.

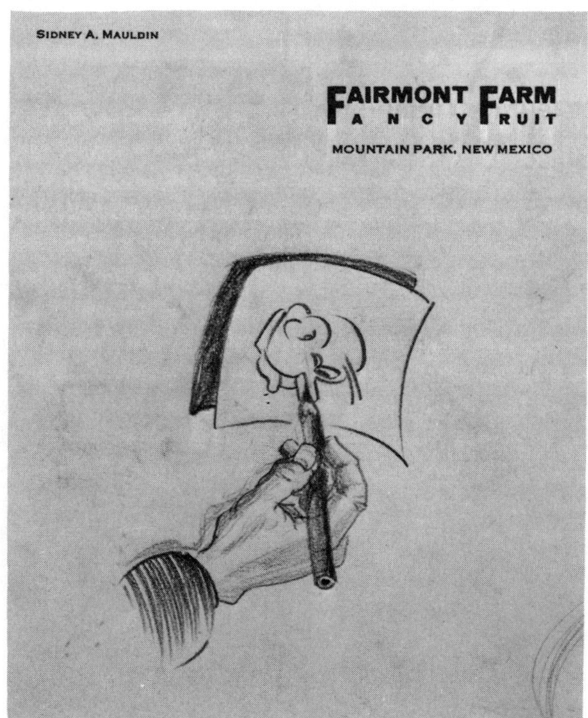

I depended heavily upon my father's letterhead supply for drawing paper.

drawing? The middle of a daisy. Draw petals around it. You know what it is up high in a drawing? A polka dot. Draw a dress around it and put a dame in the dress!"

"Think he'll get there, Larry?" Pop asked, looking on with real concern.

"*Sure* he'll get there!" My mentor slapped me on the back encouragingly, creating enough polka dots on the drawing for a fashion show. "It'll take a few years of practice, but as long as he starts out with the right system he'll make it. Took me years, too, and he's starting out as good as I did. Produce, that's the thing. Don't mess around. Get it out."

"Tell me, Larry," I said when it was time to go. "How did you get all those original strips? Do you know those guys?"

"Met a few. Got 'em mostly by writing and asking for 'em. Haven't been turned down yet. You'll find that cartoonists are the nicest class of people in the world. They'll always take time out for other cartoonists—especially young ones like you or fellas like me who haven't hit the top yet."

"Larry," I said, feelingly, "for my dough you're already up there."

"My advice to you is to see if you can get a refund from that school," Pop grunted.

"Naw, he ought to keep on with it," Larry said. "Don't worry, I'll see him around from time to time and if he gets any wrong ideas I'll straighten him out. But you can learn a lot from schools."

We gave the Pontiac back to the dealer and caught a ride home with a truck driver. I still had my dollar and the first pro I'd met thought I would make the grade.

The Landon course was not bad, considering that this was an interim period when the Mutt and Jeff type of crude drawing was still popular and the more sophisticated Milton Caniff style was just developing. The Landon people couldn't teach you to draw like Caniff or Al Capp, but they could put you a jump ahead of Happy Hooligan or Andy Gump. For example, the old-fashioned, rough-and-ready comic artist would draw head, hands, and feet where he wanted them, then figure out a way to connect them with limbs. The new school thought in terms of true anatomy, bone structure, and could tell the difference between a heel tendon and a triceps. The Landon school taught a basic, pragmatic approach to the subject, in which you thought of the torso as a sort of flexible bean, from which extended two-part cylindrical limbs, rather like broken cigarettes. I remember three little hints from Landon which were always useful afterward. One was to remember that the main part of the hand is as long as the fingers. Beginners always make the fingers too long. Another was to think of the foot as a triangle. The mark of the tyro here is to forget that some heel protrudes backward. Possibly the most valuable tip was to think of the human pelvis (which you added to the bottom of the bean) as a trapezoid, with the large end up in the male and down in the female. This means that if you draw a line of alternating men and women their pelvises will neatly fit next to each other. A practical application of this is when you try to put three women and three men in a small car. If you put a woman between two men in front and a man between two women in the back seat they will be more comfortable.

As we'll see a little later, there are some drawbacks to this streamlined, trick-of-the-trade method of learning. Today any aspiring cartoonist who thinks he should bypass a serious, academic study of anatomy (no matter how wildly and crudely he means to draw later) through correspondence schools would be better advised to send off for a mail-order course in plumbing. But for a New Mexico mountain boy in a hurry Landon was the ticket. At the end of each lesson you were assigned drawing projects to mail to the school. Back they would come, with onion-skin overlay sketches by skilled teachers, showing what you did wrong and suggesting ways to improve yourself. These sketches were superbly drawn. It didn't occur to me for a long time to wonder why these fellows were working for a correspondence school instead of making that advertised hundred thousand per year. All in all, it was well worth the twenty dollars, even in those days, and it gave me enough confidence to try spreading my wings a bit.

My first published work was in the Alamogordo high-school paper, a two-page mimeographed affair which the English department published as an experiment. I applied for the job of cartoonist, and filled one of the pages with comic faces, some of which were intended to look like the teaching staff. Normally, poking fun at the establishment is an effective circulation gimmick, but the teachers didn't recognize themselves, nor did the students seem to catch on, and the paper lasted for only one edition.

I took a crack at advertising. We had bought some Sargent's worm medicine for a dog. Shortly after taking it, he was run over. With this as inspiration, I drew two grieving children at a dog's grave, stating underneath that a dose of Sargent's, given in time, might have saved him. I mailed this, with return postage (Hillbilly Larry had warned me always to send return postage if I wanted my free lance drawings back), to the company. Back came a letter, with a dollar bill pinned to it, explaining that my idea was negative advertising, which Sargent's did not use, but that the company was pleased with the cartoon and would like to buy it to hang on the wall, even though they couldn't print it. It was a sort of sale.

A week or so later, I got a genuine freelance job. Halfway between Mountain Park and Alamogordo was the La Luz Pottery Company, which made the local red clay into roof tiles, flower pots, and decorative urns.

A postcard effort, drawn under the influence of Hillbilly Larry. I was unable to market this one.

Poster for an Alamogordo jewelry store.

The proprietors were a friendly couple from somewhere in the East who had originally gone to New Mexico for reasons of health. My father had told them I was studying cartooning, and next time I saw them they asked me to design an advertising postcard.

"We know you're turning professional now," they said, "and pros get at least fifty dollars for this sort of thing, but ten is all we can afford. Will you accept it?" They knew my family and me, and our circumstances, very well. I kept my voice under control, but I'm sure my eyes must have given me away. I allowed that the price was acceptable since it was a new account. Half the Landon money back in one crack! I spent a week sketching and rejecting ideas until I came up with something I considered worthy. The customers liked it. They paid me with ten brand-new one-dollar bills. Those people had class. They knew I would want to take the loot home and spread it out on my cot, which was what I was doing when my father came in.

"Billy," he said, "I'm in a jam. I got a ticket for driving the truck through Alamogordo without a muffler. That damn whelp of a cop was dead wrong: I did have a muffler, but since there was nothing connecting it to the exhaust manifold I didn't feel like arguing the case. It's going to cost me five dollars. I'll pay you back in no time."

Remembering that he hadn't drunk up my dollar in Ruidoso, and considering that in a sense he had been the agent responsible for the pottery job, I felt the least I could do was to give him half my pile. The pain of parting with five of those sleek new bills was offset by the feeling that if I was really going to be the guy who redeemed the family honor, the traffic court would be as good a place as any to start. Was that judge going to be surprised to see my old man come in with cash in hand!

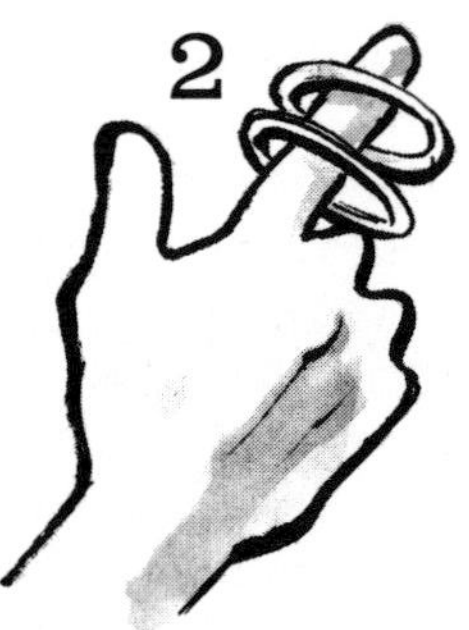

We had a lot of snow in the mountains that winter. There were two sources of heat in our house: the kitchen stove and a small fireplace. This meant we spent a lot of time together as a family, but it didn't bring my parents any closer to each other. By spring my brother and I knew that it was all over with them. There was no question about young Sid's ability to look after himself. His renown as a mechanic had spread and his services were in demand. As for me, I knew I couldn't expect commissions on the scale of the La Luz pottery job every day, but I felt reasonably sure I was onto something that would keep me afloat.

I bought a roll of white oilcloth, some poster paint and lettering brushes, and trudged up the hill to Cloudcroft, where I lucked into a price war between the two gas stations. I charged ten cents per square foot. A ten-by-three-foot banner, with whatever words and figures the customer wanted, plus appropriate cartoon illustrations thrown in free, cost three dollars. The colors ran in the frequent mountain thundershowers, but there were few complaints because prices kept changing and new signs were needed every few days anyway. A couple of stores in town gave me some window-sign business. Doing these on the inside of the windows so they wouldn't get rained on necessitated lettering backward. I learned that for some strange reason I could read, spell, and work backward as fast as forward. Maybe being left-handed had something to do with this. The only establishment in Cloudcroft I could never get business from was the Lodge, a resort hotel which boasted the world's highest golf course but out of contrariness wouldn't commission me to paint a sign advertising its remarkable claim.

About this time my Grandmother Bemis and Grandfather Mauldin, both of whom had been widowed several years, decided that loneliness was for the birds, and even as their children were breaking apart they got married. It turned out to be a sensible union. She moved to his La Luz house, which had a milder climate and indoor plumbing. As a sort of wedding present, my Uncle Waldron, the mining executive, gave the couple his 1932-model Lincoln touring sedan, a seven-passenger behemoth with a curb weight of about three tons. This was a lot of car for Uncle Billy, who stood about five-three in his boots. I wasn't much bigger, but I was younger, so I enjoyed driving the big machine, especially on long trips to the Texas boondocks to visit various Mauldin relatives. They all thought we were rich as Croesus with that automobile. Their illusion might have been bolstered by the fact that before each trip I spent eight or ten hours simonizing all that thick, black paint. What they didn't know was that the tires were thin as paper and that I didn't dare go over forty miles an hour. Uncle Billy had saved a little for his old age, but there was no room in the budget for Lincoln tires. There really wasn't enough for Lincoln gas, either, but the car gave a great ride.

Best of all, it freed for my occasional use my grandfather's little Chevrolet, enabling me to expand. The Chevy's tires were pretty thin, too. I remember patching and pumping four flats on one trip to deliver posters to Ruidoso. Even so, the car meant a lot to my business. You would think I would have had the courtesy to stay out of Hillbilly Larry's bailiwick, but I was operating on a mixture of ambition and desperation. It made sense to work territory which had been softened by a competitor. Larry himself appeared delighted to see me, was generous in his praise of my progress, and actually threw some work my way which he said he was too busy to handle.

My steadiest Ruidoso account became Weldon's riding stable. My brother had recently sold Weldon a worthless bay gelding named Jack. Humane people don't usually sell horses to Western livery stables, because too many customers think the way to get their money's worth is to run the poor animals to death. In Jack's case it was all right. Nothing could make Jack run: not the sharpest spurs nor the heaviest quirt. Jack wouldn't even walk if he didn't feel frisky. More than once he had simply lain down while Sid was aboard. He was named Jack because although he looked exactly like a horse he had the cussedness of a prospector's burro.

My brother was probably the only person who ever got the best of Weldon. Although I hadn't been with Sid when he sold the horse, the stable owner knew I was associated with the deal, or at least related to it. Jack didn't help matters by giving me an effusive greeting (we had been good friends) every time I passed the corral, where he spent most of his time. No customer rode him twice. Sid never told me how much he was paid for the horse, but Weldon tried to get as much as he could back from me. He would order five or six posters at $1.50 apiece, then when I delivered them his first ploy was to claim he was broke, and wouldn't I take it out in rides? Ruidoso was full of little El Paso and Amarillo girls who would do anything for a long canter in the piny woods on horseback. A few of them were always sitting around on the fences. I refused because I knew Weldon would stick me with Jack. It usually ended with a settlement for seventy-five cents or a dollar per poster, which was really all right because I had a sliding scale and that was all I charged a lot of customers, anyway.

During the summer my parents split permanently. If Sid or I had chosen to remain with either, undoubtedly we would have been taken care of somehow. We simply felt our own interests would be better served if we struck out for ourselves. We were not tearful waifs adrift in a storm. Our hearts ached a little, probably because we loved our parents almost as much as they loved us, but we felt we knew how to survive on our own and had long ago plotted our course.

We headed for Arizona. Back in 1929, when Sid and I were nine and eight, respectively, our family tried homesteading on 320 acres of desert about fifty miles west of Phoenix. The farming part was not a success, but two little boys had the time of their lives, scampering barefoot among greasewood, cacti, gila monsters, rattlers, scorpions, lizards, horned toads, rabbits, kangaroo rats, and roadrunners, seldom taking baths because water cost fifty cents a barrel and we didn't have the money. We lived under canvas most of the time, the whole adventure had a sort of *Swiss Family Robinson* flavor, and we swore we would go back there someday. The desert is forbidding only to people who haven't lived in it. Snakes, you say? Rattlers don't bite people who give them time to wriggle away, and two boys that age send out plenty of vibrations ahead of themselves. As for scorpions, it would have taken a sharp stinger to penetrate the skin of feet that had become used to running on rocks hot enough to fry eggs. We still owned the property, which was then valued at about a dollar an acre. I believe the taxes were six dollars a year. We hoped that eventually Sid would open a garage out there and I would start a desert studio. First, however, we had high school to finish. Among our homesteading neighbors on the desert had been a family named Beauchamp, with whom we were good friends. Sid and I knew that Mr. Beauchamp's mother owned a boardinghouse in Phoenix. We wrote to her; she remembered us and offered to put us on cots on her back porch and feed us breakfast and supper for twenty-five dollars per month apiece.

The trip was four hundred miles. Sid and I jointly owned a stripped-down Model T Ford: a bare frame with two seats and a tool box, all attached with baling wire, and a pretty good engine which Sid had rebuilt. It was understood that we would split expenses except for gas and oil, which I would pay for because Sid had done the engine work. It didn't occur to me until we were on our way that the only real expense would be gas and oil, since we had some canned goods in the tool box and blankets on the seats. The trip was easy, with only three or four flats. We kept my fuel costs down by starting the engine on a priming charge of pure gasoline, then cruising on a mixture of cheap gas and kerosene in the main tank. I believe today's jets run on this formula and call it JP-4; we were ahead of our time. Our oil consumption was heavy, as always in Mauldin cars. The answer to this was to carry a bucket and straining cloth, and buy used oil that service stations had drained from other people's crankcases. This cost only a few cents a gallon. The cloth removed heavy sludge and random chunks of metal. An engine which used as much oil as ours obviously had plenty of clearance between bearing surfaces to pass any smaller particles which got through the strainer. We used almost as much oil as fuel, which was all right, since the oil cost less.

Three days later we arrived in Phoenix in the middle of an August afternoon. I remember we had wrapped a thick layer of friction tape around a rupture which went through the cords of one of our front tires, to keep the tube from ballooning out like bubble gum, and were fascinated by the fact that the street asphalt was so soft in the 120-degree heat that our tires cut sharp tracks and the tape left a perfect imprint of itself with every turn of the wheel. That tire looked like something out of a comic strip (*Mutt and Jeff* style, not Caniff school). Arizona summers were old stuff to us, but we had been cooling in the New Mexico mountains for a few years, so our blood must have thinned. When we pulled into Mrs. Beauchamp's backyard at 816 North Central—we weren't going to embarrass her by parking that thing on the street in front—steam was coming from our ears as well as from our radiator.

The back porch was comparatively cool, the cots were comfortable, our landlady seemed genuinely pleased to see us again, and we already knew she was a good cook. Our only worry now was making money. As Mrs. Beauchamp showed us through the house she pointed out the telephone in the front hall and said all boarders had reasonable calling privileges, long distance excepted, of course. It was the first dial phone I had ever seen. When our tour was finished, I opened the classified pages of the Phoenix directory and began hunting for poster customers. I was motivated partly by commercial instincts and partly by fascination with that phone. You stuck your finger in holes, twisted, electronic switches shuffled and clicked in some huge control box in the bowels of the city, and you were in touch with a human being you had chosen miles away. There had been a phone in Mountain Park, in the store, but it was one of those oaken-box affairs with a crank on the side, and people had to scream so loudly into it that you wondered if they really needed connective wires to the other end.

Unfortunately, it was a Sunday, so not many establishments answered my calls. I did get a number of gas stations, which would have been all right in Cloudcroft or Ruidoso, where they were a mainstay of my poster business, but in Phoenix none seemed interested in having me come around with samples. After I had been on the phone about an hour, Mrs. Beauchamp explained to me that she was automatically billed for every call that was answered. It hadn't occurred to me that the same genius who had invented the dial system would have fiendishly figured out a way to charge for it. I offered to pay for the damage already done; she wouldn't let me, but she asked that I confine future business calls to the pay phone down the street.

Phoenix Union High was the city's only public secondary school in 1937, except for a tiny, segregated one in the Negro section. I was told that PUHS had seven thousand students and was the biggest high school west of the Mississippi. Coming from an Alamogordo class of a few dozen, and having graduated from grammar school in a class of six, I was ready to believe anything about this behemoth of an institution in which I enrolled. It looked more like a university than a high school, with broad lawns, acres of buildings, and stately rows of palms. There were so many of us that we were issued serial numbers. I remember mine was 6,644. In spite of this impersonal touch, it was a fine school, and the fact that I turned out to be a poor student was my doing, not the institution's. What interested me most about the school was the fact that it had a large journalism class which produced a weekly paper. The *Coyote Journal* often ran to eight or twelve pages, with drawings and photos. It was a good newspaper by any standard, published under the amiable direction of a man named Scott Nelson. Also, PUHS had a first-rate art department. My teacher was a young woman named Frances Kapanke. Knowing that I would never get within hollering distance of a college, and would be lucky to manage to finish high school, I deliberately concentrated on art and journalism and let the rest of the curriculum go to hell. In those days this was not a rare outlook. Many kids concentrated on vocation rather than education. Phoenix High School had an extensive manual-training department, with elaborate shops. Here my brother swam happily at first like a goldfish in a horse trough, until he realized that he knew more than most of his teachers about putting engines together; then he became bored. This was not the case with me. Stumbling into that high school was one of the luckiest things that ever happened to me. It was not, however, necessarily the best thing that ever happened to the school. While I was a model of industrious application in journalism and art, I was a pain in the neck to teachers of subjects I had chosen to ignore—or barely pass, if these were required for graduation.

I did intend to graduate, but an imp seemed to possess me. Whenever I was bored, or felt unnoticed, even in classrooms where logically I should have welcomed anonymity, I felt compelled to irritate whoever was in charge. One mandatory course was laboratory science. In biology I happened to sit near the skeleton of a small lady whom we called Gertrude. She looked uncomfortable one day hanging there by a wire through the top of her head. I thought she might like to have a smoke. When the teacher seemed busy elsewhere, I lit a cigarette and stuck it between Gertie's spring-loaded jaws. She seemed to smile in gratitude. As the smoke curled up through her eye sockets the entire class grinned with her. The cigarette went out after a minute or two. I removed it, stuck it into my own face, relit it, took a couple of deep drags to make it go better, and gave it back.

"All right, Mauldin," said the teacher, a serious young man, "I tried to overlook the cigarette at first, but when you smoked it yourself I officially saw you."

He threw me out of the class. I never did make up the quarter credit that semester's biology would have given me, and eventually missed graduating by just that much.

Scott Nelson encouraged me to write as well as draw. Once he even printed a satirical piece I wrote to accompany a feisty cartoon about what I considered an unconstitutional edict that PUHS students couldn't smoke within two blocks of the school. The campus, I felt, belonged to the establishment but the streets were ours. Besides, it made me late to classes, where I was already in trouble because of my grades. (This was probably my real beginning as an editorial cartoonist. I was still thinking ahead in terms of doing comic strips or something else highly remunerative, but basically I was a pop-off, not a storyteller. I believe Nelson realized this and nudged me in that direction.) While nurturing the verbal side of my journalistic career, Nelson inadvertently introduced me to another important aspect of the game—expense-account swindling. One Friday afternoon he offered me the assignment of covering the next day's football game our team was playing against a high school in San Diego. I was well into my fifteenth year by then, and Nelson would probably have had no qualms about my going alone, but he wanted pictures, too. My companion for the trip was the *Coyote Journal* photographer,

Jack Foley, about a year my senior. He owned a Rolleiflex. We were each given twenty dollars for expenses and told to be back on Monday with copy in one hand and a detailed expense account in the other.

"Twenty measly bucks!" said Foley. "Let's head for the freight yards." It turned out he was a year ahead of me in experience, too. How can you have fun in San Diego if the Greyhound Corporation has your money? We entered the yards just at dark. A bum obligingly directed us to a westbound freight. There were many hobos around, of all sizes and sexes. This one decided, on second thought, to escort us to our train.

"Look at the size of the bastard," Jack muttered to me. "He can't take his eyes off my Rollei."

On tiptoe, we peered into an empty boxcar, then swung aboard.

"Thanks a lot, fella," Jack hollered at the bum, whose head was two feet away. "Be seeing you."

Our hobo said nothing but got one leg over the sill. I began pulling on the opposite door to make sure we had an exit. The train started with a jerk. To our relief, the man slipped off. Then he ran alongside, cursing, grabbed a fresh hold, and we knew for sure he was up to no good. As he came swinging up this time, Foley got a grip on the very end of the long leather strap of the camera case and clouted the fellow's jaw with the heavy instrument. The blow was at least doubled by the fact that the target was coming up fast to meet it. It made the guy miss our train.

Scrounging through the debris in the car, we found enough cardboard and wrapping paper to make beds and composed ourselves for the long night ahead. Just as we were dropping off the train stopped on a siding, then moved again. There is no sound like that made by a long freight starting, when you are two-thirds of the way toward the caboose, with your ear to the floor. As each coupling and each drawbar on each car is jerked taut, there is a chattering, clanking roar that draws nearer and louder until it reaches a crescendo. Then it hits you, and if you have made the mistake of bedding down at the front of the car, as we had, you find yourself displaced in a hurry. We slid the length of the car. The Rolleiflex, which had survived being used as a weapon, finally ended up with a dent.

Each time the train stopped, we went back to sleep, then were awakened by that long-drawn-out clickety-clickety-cliCKETY-CLANKETY-WHAM! as we started again. No more head-over-heels stuff, though. We had moved to the back of the car. While the train bucketed along, we dangled our legs out the open door and watched the moonlit cacti go by. When we began to get a little cold and hungry, we thought of all the hell we were going to raise in San Diego. At about midnight we became tired enough to fall into a deep sleep.

We were awakened at 4 A.M. by flashlights in our faces, and were jerked to our feet by a pair of men in leather jackets. For a terrible moment we thought the Phoenix character had recruited a friend and caught up with us, but to our relief these newcomers turned out to be Yuma cops. The sense of relief didn't last long. They didn't say a word to us as they handcuffed us and hustled us into their car. Their faces were grim. It seemed to Jack and me that they were handling us pretty roughly, considering that we were nothing more than a couple of junior-grade hobos. The Great Depression was still on, and free riders on freight trains weren't that rare.

"This might strike you as funny," said Jack, trying to break the ominous silence, "but we're really working for a high-school newspaper. See the camera?" He held up the Rolleiflex.

"Yeah, we saw it," the cop behind the wheel said. "We're going to talk about that camera, and the other stuff, too." In the police station, we learned that the evening before, west of Phoenix, two teenage boys, respectably dressed, had hitched a ride with an elderly, lone motorist. They had knocked the man in the head, taken his wallet, watch, and baggage, including a camera, and left the car and its presumably-dead owner near a siding where our train had stopped. The police pointed out that our cooperation would be of benefit mainly to ourselves, not to them, since the victim would be able to identify us as soon as he got out of the hospital.

"When do you think that might be?" asked Jack.

"Oh, two or three days," they said. "You kids didn't hit him as hard as you thought."

"That would be too late for us," Jack said, as the cops and I stared at him in puzzlement. "I guess we've got to wake the Chief up," he said to me. (There was a sort of tradition around the *Coyote Journal* that the staff called Nelson the Chief. Maybe it embarrassed him, but it made us feel professional.) I'm sure Jack would have preferred to remain under suspicion of attempted murder and highway robbery for a few more hours rather than to have Nelson learn that we had hooked a freight for the obvious purpose of messing around in San Diego with school funds. But if we had to wait for the victim to clear us we would miss the game, stay in jail, and the fat would be in the fire anyway.

"Who's this Chief?" asked the cops. What had they stumbled onto—a teenage Mafia? They finally let us call Nelson's home, collect, at 6:30 A.M. After a short, pungent conversation with us and a long, detailed one with the law, Nelson got us freed. We went straight to the bus station, and while checking schedules to San Diego, found ourselves taken into custody again and hustled back into the police car.

"The sheriff's daughter works on the high-school paper," the now-friendly cops said. "He thinks she'd like to meet you guys."

We had a sumptuous breakfast at the sheriff's house, were driven to our bus, covered the third quarter of the football game, and got back to Yuma in time to join the sheriff's daughter and her girl friend at a Saturday-night square dance, with a moonlight picnic in the desert afterward. Foley had had the right idea all along. You can get straight news by following orders, but you risk missing the sidebar feature stuff.

Many male students on tight budgets in Phoenix Union High School solved their clothing problem by joining the ROTC battalion, which required members to wear uniforms four days per week. These were standard army serge jackets, trousers, and caps, and khaki shirts with blue lapels on the jackets. They were issued free by the government, along with brass buttons and a 1903 Springfield rifle with the firing pin removed.

If you didn't take ROTC you had to go out for sports or physical education. Being a prototype of the ninety-seven-pound weakling, I had long ago given up trying to do anything to improve my physique by doing handstands or knocking around with a ball of some sort and getting grass stains on my pants, and had decided to wait for age and success to fill me out. The free ROTC uniform appealed to me too. Cadets were even allowed to wear them at night, which meant you could get along socially without buying a suit. Still another advantage of ROTC was its rifle club, which provided a target range and free ammunition. All in all, the military offered a great many little fringe benefits to kids who had no other way of obtaining them.

Aside from the material advantages, I took to ROTC like a duck to water. I guess sitting on that fence in the mountains and watching the horse cavalry go by had really got to me. Every night I polished my brass, borrowed Mrs. Beauchamp's electric iron, pressed my trousers under a damp towel, and shined my shoes, giving them a top gloss with saliva and a flat shoestring. I don't know what there is about rubbing with a shoestring, but there is no substitute. I not only won inspections, with my shiny shoes, but I practiced the manual of arms every day instead of racking up my rifle under the stadium after drill period, and got myself on the exhibition drill team. Nowadays you hand your rifle up from "order arms" to port position. We little high-school squirts had to flip those standard, nine-pound army pieces—literally throw them up with one hand and catch them with the other—without twitching a shoulder. On the fancy team, we had to twirl as well as flip them, so that they spun one complete revolution around their longitudinal axis as they came up. And they had to arrive together: forty or fifty slings in the platoon cracking as one.

We did the Queen Anne salute, too: from a position of "right shoulder arms," without ever moving the left hand, you jerked back on the rifle's

A young dude on his way up in Phoenix.

High school ROTC uniforms solved a clothing problem.

butt, bringing the weapon erect and balanced on your hand, then you hurled it into the air and caught it with right hand reversed on the small of the stock, then swung the piece in a great arc as you came down on one knee, so that you ended up genuflecting with your rifle butt on the ground and the foreend straight up and behind your arm. Getting back up was the tricky part: you really threw the rifle this time, so that it did a somersault as you rose. If all went well it ended up on your right shoulder as you arrived back in position. We usually practiced this over a wrestling mat until we had it perfectly: the army's ROTC fund did not provide for bent sights or broken stocks. I have gone into this in some detail because my proficiency on the parade ground, especially with the Queen Anne salute, comes up again later in this story.

Aside from journalistic adventures and military spit-and-polish, I found myself doing all right in the nitty-gritty department almost from the start in Phoenix. It turned out that Weldon, the Ruidoso riding-stable man, ran a thriving winter business in Papago Park, east of Phoenix. He needed posters, which I provided in abundance. These were hung in places like gas stations and store windows, which led to a fair trickle of other commissions. There were plenty of show-card lettering experts in town, but what made my posters competitive was that I illustrated them for free.

One day Weldon and I stumbled onto a new art form. He mentioned that he was thinking of getting a new paint job on his pickup truck but hated to spend the money. I suggested dressing it up by putting white sidewalls on the tires. Many people had tried it, but most efforts looked sloppy because painting rubber was tricky. Under my hand Weldon's tires came out looking as if they had arrived from the store that way. We settled on a price of twenty-five cents per wheel, plus materials. When Weldon's friends saw his truck, I began getting as much sidewall business as I could handle. Not only truck owners but hot-rodders came around.

Another sideline developed when my brother Sid and a bunch of his hot-rod friends came around to the boardinghouse one evening in a shiny Model A roadster with squirrel tails on the windshield posts, chrome headers poking through holes in the hood louvers, and a white canvas cover on the spare tire behind the rumble seat. They wanted a naked girl painted on the canvas. Price was no object, they said, if the nude lived up to my brother's claims about my ability. Touched by Sid's loyalty, I made a price of four dollars, half payable in advance, and told them to leave the tire cover for a couple of days. I hadn't had much experience with nudes, so most of that first two-dollar advance went for flesh-colored oil paints, turpentine, and a copy of *Esquire*. The girl who emerged under my brush was my own creation, but I never could have done her without George Petty and two or three other *Esquire* regulars, upon whom I depended heavily for anatomical data. From then on it was clear profit. For weeks after my first girl's debut on the streets nudes on spare-tire covers enjoyed a small vogue, with attendant profits for me, until my hot-rodder customers discovered that suddenly the cops had begun harassing them even more than usual. My nudes were not explicit —usually one leg was drawn up coyly over their pubic regions and their nipples were a quiet pink, not a flaming red—but even in those days Phoenix was a conservative town.

My white-sidewall-and-spare-tire-cover clientele led me back into more social contact with my brother Sid. Almost from our arrival in Phoenix we had gone our own ways. We sometimes walked to school together, and on Saturday night often joined the penny-ante poker game which began in Mrs. Beauchamp's house after she had retired. We depended upon the game, to a certain extent, to augment our income, having learned from our father to throw away nine hands out of ten in a seven-hand game, to drive our opponents rather than try to suck them in, and to be satisfied with small pots. We became known as a pair of mean, hard-nosed players, and the only reason we weren't thrown out of what had once been a social game was that everybody hoped to get even with us. We seldom won more than seventy-five cents or so apiece, but since a school-day lunch usually consisted of a five-cent doughnut and a five-cent carton of milk, any income went a long way.

Aside from this, however, we had quickly drifted into our own orbits and associations. Mine were nearly all connected with my aspirations, social and professional. Sid would never have gone along with one of my favorite weekend diversions, which was to put on my one good pair of civilian trousers and a white duck sport jacket which I had bought from a bank teller in the boardinghouse for two dollars, and take the elevator to the eleventh floor of the Westward Ho, an elegant hotel only a couple of blocks south of Mrs. Beauchamp's place on Central. Strolling past bellhops and waiters with a cigarette hanging out of my mouth, hands in pockets, head down as if trying to remember where I had mislaid my last million, I would go out on the sun deck, try out such exotic equipment as reducing vibrators (I was still about thirty pounds underweight), lounge about on the deck chairs for a while, then slither away as the terrace waiters began to zero in on me. This excursion always gave me strength for the coming week. It reminded me what lay ahead if I kept my nose to the grindstone and my eye on the ball.

I hate to think what Sid would have said if he'd caught me at my little farce. I remember how he used to hoot at me for spending long hours simonizing our grandparents' old Lincoln. Appearances meant nothing to that boy. He was concerned about how well a car ran. He was a pragmatist about material objects, whereas, I'm afraid, I tended to be that way about people. Sid's pals included some of the scruffiest characters I ever saw. Usually, their worst crimes were drinking beer, getting into their girls' pants (even though their girls seldom wore pants) siphoning gas, and being noisy late at night. From time to time Sid would try to get me to go out with them. I was touched and flattered, since this meant I was no longer an involuntary outcast from his personal wolf pack. They were a gang of sorts, including a few mean-eyed types with weapons stashed about them, but they treated me with a certain solicitude. They would open a beer bottle by hanging the edge of the cap on a bumper and whacking it with the heel of a hand. Sometimes I would start to follow suit—it really isn't much of a trick—but some goon in a leather jerkin with mutton chops thirty years ahead of his time would remind me that mine were the hands that could draw naked broads and would actually open my bottle for me. They were all determined to get me laid for the sake of my complexion, which tended toward chin pimples, and several times arranged for me what could euphemistically be called set-ups. In almost every case I chickened out, necked with the girl, and pretended I didn't know she had another end. Looking back on it, those were pretty raunchy girls and I'm only slightly sorry that I let most of them go by. Sulfa drugs hadn't even been invented yet, let alone antibiotics. Anyway, the boys were tolerant of me. Partly this was because of Sid's being a member in good standing and a first-class hot-rod doctor, but I suppose some of it was the same wary gentleness that savage tribes traditionally show toward zanies and eccentrics.

Frances Kapanke spent a lot of time trying to knock the Landon School out of my system. The problem, as she explained it, was that I had the ability to go beyond mere tricks-of-the-trade and could only live up to my potential by learning to draw seriously. Since she put it so beautifully I could only agree. I tried to stop thinking of the human body as a flexible bean and began to see such things as girls' behinds as more plastic than trapezoids. At Miss Kapanke's urging, I carried a pad and pencil and began "blind sketching." The idea was to make full-figure drawings of people as I saw them walking, sitting, playing, lounging, eating, busy, idle, or whatever, keeping my eyes on the subject, allowing myself only ten seconds or less, and not permitting myself to lift pencil from paper or look down at the sketch until it was finished. Of course, what I saw at first looked like a skimpy serving of spaghetti. But when I looked again I realized that, although I had made the feet come out of the chest and had put hair on the shoulder, I had caught the essence of the subject's movement with an accuracy and a fluidity that would have been impossible by any other method. After a little practice, this sort of sketch can become linear poetry. By the way, anybody can do it, whether he thinks he's an artist or not, thereby proving that drawing is really a universal gift. As with music, some people can sing on the stage and some sound better in the shower, but everybody can warble.

The upstairs bathroom at Mrs. Beauchamp's had a mirror on the door and one on the medicine cabinet, hinged so that I could arrange a sort of double-reverse image. Sketching with my left hand, I could use my right one as a model and make it appear to be on either side. The same with arms, legs, and feet. This system was good for learning wrinkles in clothing, too. Milton Caniff's wrinkles in *Terry and the Pirates* were by now the envy of the profession and it was clear that Miss Kapanke was right: you'd better know how to draw a thing correctly before you begin exaggerating. I spent so much time in the bathroom that the other boarders complained. Mrs. Beauchamp, after learning what I was up to, removed the three-sided vanity mirror from the top of her dresser and let me stow it under my cot when I wasn't using it.

Frances Kapanke felt, along with Scott Nelson, that I should take up political cartooning. As they both put it at various times, I was a born troublemaker and might as well earn a living at it. My stuff in the *Coyote Journal,* although usually drawn in the form of gag strips and panels, continued to carry enough editorial sting to raise some eyebrows in the school administration. Not only did Nelson intercede for me on occasion, but I suspect somebody might have had to speak up for him once or twice, since I worked under his aegis and had his approval. Somewhat ahead of my time, I thought students should have a lot to say about school policies. Actually, Phoenix Union High was not backward in this respect, having all sorts of freely elected student leadership groups. I suppose it was as modern in its outlook as any public high school of its time. But you could still find things to criticize if you were so inclined. I was. I wish I could say I concerned myself with matters of import. Most of the time my beefs were frivolous. The school said girls could wear boys' shirts if they tucked them in. I thought girls looked cute with their shirttails popping in the breeze, so that's how I drew them. When I decided a rule was chickenshit I found a way to defy it in print. As an editorial cartoonist I showed early form without much content.

Besides, I still intended to get rich. Whoever heard of a solvent editorial cartoonist? Thomas Nast almost made it late in the nineteenth century when Boss Tweed of Tammany Hall offered the artist a bundle (different versions of the legend put the amount from a hundred thousand to half a million dollars) to get off his back. Nast refused the bribe and continued attacking Tweed until eventually the poor old tyrant's power was broken and he died in prison. Scott Nelson first told me that story. It gave me a lot of respect for Nast, but I couldn't help reflecting that as a comic artist he could have made as much as Tweed's proffered bribe or more in a single working year. You can see that I was torn in this matter. My printed barbs had earned me some notoriety among my classmates. God knows, if I wanted anything even more than money it was recognition. I could see that becoming a strong editorial voice would pay off handsomely in prestige. But what about my standard of living? Did any political cartoonist ever stay at the Westward Ho? Bud Fisher, the creator of *Mutt and Jeff,* once stopped there, and the bellhops were still talking about the suitcase full of Scotch they helped him unpack.

Phoenix had an editorial cartoonist, named Reg Manning, who had established a national reputation. I began visiting Reg shortly after my arrival in Phoenix. He was kind and encouraging. His own eminence in the city gave me a clue that some of the fringe rewards of this profession might be as much fun as money. Aside from his daily editorial efforts about national and world affairs, Reg drew a Sunday page called *The Big Parade*: a cheery, folksy hodgepodge of cartoons about local affairs. The page had considerable power. Once Reg decided that Phoenix street lights should be mounted on fake saguaro cacti. He had long ago adopted the familiar organ-pipe shape of the plant as his own trademark and he felt it belonged to the capital city of Arizona as well. *The Big Parade* promoted the idea until the city built a prototype concrete saguaro street light and planted it in a test location downtown. There it stood, arms akimbo, in green-painted glory, until even its proponents recoiled at the idea of a city full of the things.

My parents had been getting back onto their respective feet since their divorce. My father had given up his bottle and was headed for California, where he eventually got a job in the kitchen of Brown's Military Academy and married Emily, the school nurse. My mother ended up in Phoenix with a job as housekeeper for an elderly gentleman named George Curtis, who was a topographical draftsman for the government. In the days before aerial photos, precise artists like him converted surveyors' data into exquisitely-drawn charts which even showed shadows on the sides of the hills. Eventually, because she admired talented people, my mother married her employer.

Midway through my seventeenth year, while I was still trying to decide on a branch of a profession in which I was already making something of a living, my class graduated without me at Phoenix Union High School. In spite of myself I had made friends, formed associations, and developed a sense of belonging with my classmates. Why else would I have parted with several dollars to get my picture printed with the other seniors in the yearbook? It was called the *Phoenician.* I designed its cover that year as a project in Miss Kapanke's class. I realized the diploma would have meant a lot to me; I knew it was all my own fault, and I felt bad.

"You've really burned your bridges, haven't you?" said Frances Kapanke. "From now on you can't afford not to improve your work." She suggested that I find a way to attend the Chicago Academy of Fine Arts, which had a good cartooning course and didn't care whether I was a high-school graduate.

I headed back to New Mexico to see if my grandmother was still in a grubstaking mood. Of course, she was married to Uncle Billy now and I would have to get around him, too. How would a man who had matched wits with Geronimo's skulkers and hunted wild turkeys with a six-shooter hold with this art stuff? As it turned out, I needn't have worried about Uncle Billy. My grandfather said he was relieved to see me get back safely from Phoenix.

"Not everybody can stay out of jail in Arizona," he said. I was never able to get him to explain that remark. He was also pleased that I had found a trade. He shared my father's dim view of my prospects as a farmer. Best of all, he thought cartoons were entertaining, especially the ones in magazines about hillbillies. Hallmarks of the true frontiersmen were tolerance and humor. After consultation with my grandmother, Uncle Billy gravely offered to advance me the price of one year's tuition at the Chicago Academy of Fine Arts. This came to five hundred dollars, a staggering investment for an aging couple with perhaps eight times that amount as their total combined assets. Of course, I would have to find a way to feed myself in Chicago, but that seemed a minor problem. Miss Kapanke had already assured me that plenty of art students found ways to support themselves in the city.

"You understand the rules of grubstaking," Uncle Billy said, his mouth a thin line under his white mustache and his blue eyes fierce.

"Of course Billy knows," my grandmother said. "Besides it's not a grubstake. It's a tuition stake."

"Quiet, Callie," he said. "Whatever happened to that twenty dollars you advanced him?"

"He's had expenses," she said. "Besides, I never intended to let him pay it back. I kept hoping he would decide to be a surgeon someday."

"Well, I intend to let him pay this back," he snapped. "Billy, do you know what will happen if you don't share booty with us?"

"You'll come after me," I said.

"He understands, Callie. Give him the money."

3

One of the nice things about Chicago is its tolerance for rubes. For a century or so they've been flooding into the metropolis on cattle trains, barges, wagons, and trucks. For me as for most of them (I arrived by bus) a really big city was a new experience. On my very first day, en route to the Lawson YMCA where I had booked a room, I managed to embarrass myself on the Michigan Boulevard drawbridge over the Chicago River. To me it was just a big bridge. Who could imagine a thing that size breaking in half and hoisting itself into the air? There I stood on the middle of it, admiring the tall buildings all around and marveling at the fact that an ocean-sized ship was coming up the river and was going to pass under my feet. I had studied some perspective under Miss Kapanke and in the Landon correspondence courses, and was reasonably certain that the ship's masts and funnels all were higher than the bridge. The longer I looked at them and the nearer the ship approached, the more positive I became. Breaking out of my trance, I looked around for someone with whom to share this revelation, and discovered that I was alone, except for a cop who was running toward me. He was yelling something which I couldn't hear over the ringing bells, the honking of horns, and the hooting of the ship's whistle. It finally dawned on me that since the ship couldn't duck the bridge would have to do something to get out of the way. I beat the cop to land by a nose, feeling the structure tremble into action at my last step or two. The ship, which had gone into reverse and was churning up gobs of muddy river bottom in an attempt to stop,

Michigan Boulevard Bridge (closed position) shortly before author's arrival on the scene.

passed through unscathed; the cop chewed me out, and everybody else thought it was funny. I still wonder what they would really do if somebody stayed on the bridge.

The Chicago Academy of Fine Arts taught many subjects: everything from industrial design to fashion illustration. The cartooning class was quite large, which dismayed me; one of the attractions of the profession, I had thought, was lack of competition. All courses took two years. On my first day at the academy, reporting to the director, a large lady named Ruth van Sickle Ford, I explained that I had only enough money for one year.

"All right, we'll make you concentrate on life drawing and composition," she said, after some thought. "You won't be able to cartoon as much as the rest of the class."

"But that's what I'm here for," I protested, thinking of the grubstake. "I've got to make a living at this."

"That's the idea," she said. "The day is gone when you could draw crude characters and get away with it. Readers and editors are more demanding now. Exaggeration is all right—when you know what you're exaggerating. Everybody thinks he can paint like Picasso if he puts both eyes on one side of the nose. But look at Picasso's early work and you'll see that he learned his academic ABC's before he started fooling around."

I listened as patiently as I could to this lecture, considering that I had already heard it from Miss Kapanke. When it was over, I explained that I already knew how to draw "academically"—why, I even knew how to blind sketch. I showed Mrs. Ford some samples. She riffled through them, smiled at me, and led me into a large room full of benches, with a model's platform at one end. A blonde chick in a robe lounged in the curtained entrance to a dressing room at the side of the stand, talking to a dapper little old man with a snow-white Van dyke and a string tie. Mrs. Ford told me he was Wellington J. Reynolds, who taught anatomy and painting. She added that two of his students in the academy had won the Prix de Rome. As we approached him she warned me in a whisper to never, never let him know I wanted to be a cartoonist, because he hated the breed.

"Mr. Reynolds, here is a boy with some talent but absolutely no training," Mrs. Ford said. "Please look after him. His ignorance is complicated by cockiness."

The model grinned and the old painter looked me over.

"Do you think you know anything about the human figure?" he asked.

"A little, sir," I said, cautiously. "I've studied a few books." This was a lie. I had once looked through Gray's *Anatomy* in a doctor's office.

"How many heads high is this girl?" he asked.

"Well, I never thought of it that way," I said.

"All right, how far down the length of the average head is the center of the ear?"

"About a third," I said.

"My God," he said to Mrs. Ford, "what's he doing here—understudying to draw Popeye?"

I learned later that one of Reynolds' former students had been a gifted fellow named Segar. The teacher had high hopes for the young man, possibly seeing him as another Prix de Rome candidate, but Segar couldn't care less about that stuff. He wanted to do a comic strip. Reynolds, disappointed, began needling him in class. Segar bided his time. Later, he created Popeye, the one-eyed, spinach-eating sailor. Popeye became a huge success, both as a syndicated strip and as a series of animated movie shorts. The cartoonist went out of his way to mess up his hero's anatomy. Popeye's upper arm was pencil-thin, whereas the lower part was huge, as if that was where the biceps lived. It is hard to imagine the effect this had on Reynolds, who was known to make a student repeat a drawing of a kneecap a dozen times or so until he had it right. Worse, Popeye's best friend was named J. Wellington Wimpy, a sloppy, lazy, paunchy, greedy bum who was the very antithesis of Wellington J. Reynolds, the natty, diligent, wiry, ascetic scholar, artist, and teacher.

During my first encounter with Reynolds, the classroom filled up and the model stepped onto the stage and shucked her kimono. I knew this sort of thing went on in art school, but had expected a chance to brace myself. I had seen naked dames before, cavorting around the waterfall in Box Canyon, but from behind some boulders. Here was one looking back at me—a magnificent specimen, blonde all over. I found a bench, settled down with charcoal, pad, sandpaper, and fixative, and dared to look again. There was nothing to it. Cool as anything, I started drawing her as if she were a vase or a leg of mutton.

Finally, a rest period came. Students leaned back, gossiped, or wandered about looking at each other's work. The model stretched, yawned, and rubbed a cramped leg muscle, with nobody paying any attention to her. Another long posing session, with everybody drawing furiously, then class was over. The model stepped into her curtained booth and began putting on her clothes. She had pulled the drapes tight, but one had slipped an inch or so. Every male eye in the room was glued to her as she stepped into her pants, and by the time she had hooked up her bra and slid her dress over her head every boy's brow was faintly beaded with sweat. When she saw us gawking there long after the bell had rung and realized what had happened, she blushed in genuine embarrassment and hurried out. Reynolds gave us hell and said we'd be lucky if she ever came back. She did return and posed nude many more times, but she never gave us another peek.

I understand that Reynolds eventually learned the truth about my being a cartoonist, but not from me, and not until long after I had left the academy. Meanwhile, my efforts in his class were well spent. Not only did he teach the structure of the human body from the bones outward, but he also taught its movements. He was a classicist. Reynolds was not dotty, in spite of his great age; he knew that people he taught not only sometimes became cartoonists but even abstract painters, which was worse in his mind. He simply didn't want to hear about it. As far as he was concerned every student of his wanted to be Michelangelo. In one year I learned enough to realize how little I knew, which was not bad going for me. Since Reynolds, I have never missed a chance to draw from models and have never failed to profit from it.

Don Ulsh, a contributor to the old *Life*, *Uncle Billy's Whizbang* (no relation to my grandfather), and other publications, taught gag cartooning at the Academy. He showed us how to prepare pencil sketches, called roughs, to submit to editors. Ulsh warned us not to show teachers anything good in the way of ideas. He told about a recent student in another school who showed his instructor a rough about a man trying to mail a container full of helium. In the cartoon the postmaster informed the man that according to his scales the government owed him a dollar and a half. Ulsh said the teacher drew it over his own name and sold it to the *Saturday Evening Post*. When the student saw the cartoon in the magazine and complained, his mentor told him that learning to guard against plagiarism was one of the most important parts of the course. Don told us the way to start a cartoon was to lay out a rectangle, sign your name, and add a picture if any room was left. In many ways he was my kind of teacher. I remember spending a lot of time practicing eye-catching signatures after that.

Political cartooning was taught by Vaughn Shoemaker, a two-time Pulitzer Prize winner who was then at the peak of his career with the Chicago *Daily News*. Informal and friendly with students, he encouraged us to call him Shoes. He never stinted on telling us everything about his work he had learned the hard way, in hopes he might make things a little easier for us. I suppose I must have picked up practically everything I know about editorial cartooning in Shoes' class. Although he taught only a half day every week, I considered him one of my most valuable teachers. Years later, he admitted to me that I was not his favorite student.

"I was a little scared of you," he said.

"Come off it," I said. "I remember you took physical culture almost as seriously as religion, and must have weighed about a hundred and eighty to my hundred and ten."

"Oh, I probably could have handled you," he said. "But you sat there

A first-week life class effort. I had not yet learned proportion, but was careful to sign my name.

"Boy! I've always had an urge to do that!"

Highly detailed locomotives were one of my favorite subjects.

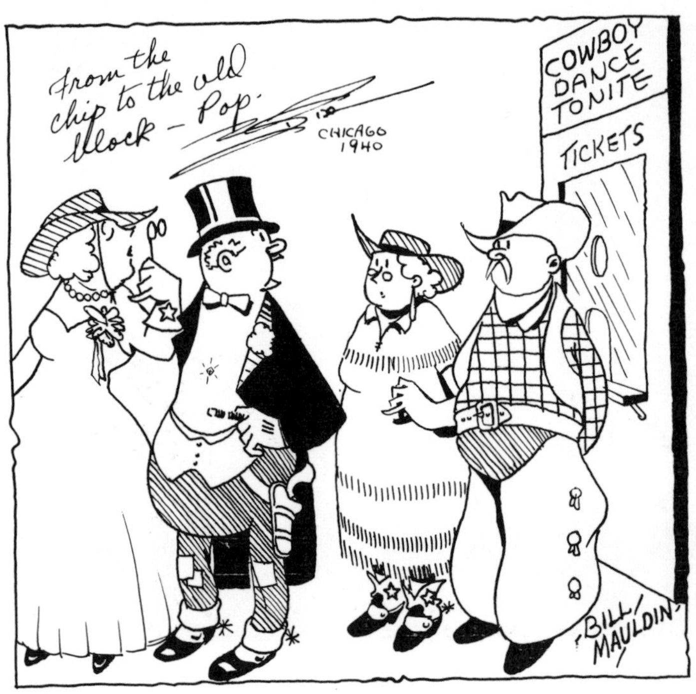

"We weren't sure whether it was formal or informal!"

Arizona Highways bought th one. My father asked for the original, hence the inscriptio upper left.

"Hey, Maw, I missed the turkey, but I bagged me a Hatfield."

Next to locomotives, I liked drawing hillbillies best.

"The main trouble seems to be in the distributor!"

More *Arizona Highways* cartoons. Indians and cars were viable topics.

The effects of life class began to show slightly after a while.

with those eyes burning out from under those sullen brows and I was convinced that if I criticized your work too strongly you'd attack me right there in class. Who wants to get bitten by a chihuahua?"

Chicago had a lot of cartoonists. I tried to get to know them all. Joe Parrish, one of the top hands on the Chicago *Tribune*, showed me his studio in the *Tribune* tower. His working quarters could only be described as stately, with Gothic arches in the ceiling and a magnificent view of the city. A contrast was the office of Paul Battenfield, editorial cartoonist for the old Chicago *Times*. His room couldn't have been more than six feet square. He shared it with George Lichty, the gag artist, who still draws *Grin and Bear It*. The two men's boards were jammed up against each other like spinet pianos for a duet. In order to make room for the cartoonists to sit, the boards had such a high tilt that I doubt if their owners ever saw each other except when they got up to go home. Because Lichty's seat was nearest the door, he was the one I got to know best. One day Battenfield told me that Lichty, whose real name was Lichtenstein, was headed for a distinguished painting career as a student at the Chicago Art Institute until one night he sneaked around pasting typed gag lines on the bottoms of the frames of about thirty million dollars' worth of old masters in the museum part of the institute. Nobody knew it had happened until the next day when visitors in the galleries started breaking up with laughter. The captions were traced to the school typewriter; eventually the trail led to Lichty, and he was expelled.

Next to Hillbilly Larry, and Walt Kelly, the Pogo man, whom I knew in later years, Lichty had the fastest drawing hand I ever saw. George used a Winsor Newton Number Three, Albatta Series Seven watercolor brush. I know because I picked up one he had discarded, have used the same brand and number myself ever since, and still treasure the one I swiped out of that wastebasket. Lichty would spend about two or three minutes roughing in a panel, about four minutes inking it on the reverse side of a sheet of Coquille board, and perhaps a minute shading it with the flat of a black pastel stick. If he didn't like it, he threw it on the floor and started over. I picked up a number of his rejects, and took them home for study.

Like most art students, I was very style conscious. We assumed that in a competitive profession our work had to have distinction and we sought quick ways to get it. We tried everything. I remember once even dividing the hairs on a brush so that vertical strokes came out double and horizontal ones single, The resulting drawing had a jangling effect, like trying to focus with a hangover. It was distinctive, though. One day Vaughn Shoemaker chewed a bunch of us out about this. He said the real trick was to master enough ways of drawing so that you could match the picture to the subject.

"The game is communication," he said. "You want to get an idea across. Don't make readers have to fight their way through some phony 'style' to see what you're trying to tell them. Most of them won't bother."

Then came the valuable part of the lecture.

"Style takes care of itself," Shoes said. "When you've learned how to draw and have been at it a while, your work takes on a special and recognizable quality without any effort on your part. You can't force it."

Another fallacy I shared with most students was that good drawing requires top-quality materials. On the same day I got a job washing dishes for two hours daily for my supper at a place called the Piccadilly Tea Room I laid in a large supply of twenty-five-cent drawing pencils. Only a Gillotte's Number 70 pen point would do for me, and my paper carried such sterling names as Strathmore Kid Finish or Whatmans' Cold-pressed Water-Colour Block. It was some time before I got smart enough to spend my money on hamburgers, steal my pen points from the post office, and scrounge my pencils from the nearest secretary. The ultimate in this sort of practicality was reached by Daniel Fitzpatrick, the veteran cartoonist of the St. Louis *Post-Dispatch,* who once told me that after he became successful he sometimes used a chewed matchstick as a brush. I'll bet as an art student he starved to buy one made of red sable.

My year at the academy had included summer courses. By the time the fall term started my life was pretty well organized. With classes all day, dishwashing late in the afternoon, and academic homework, I found I still had some hours left. My eighteenth birthday was coming up late in October; as I got older I seemed to be developing an even more acute awareness of time sliding by. Also, I never forgot that I had bought exactly one year. If I didn't make it by then I was sunk. There were no scholarships available to me, and no chance of borrowing another five hundred dollars.

With the help of Don Ulsh and an article he showed me in the *Writer's Digest* about freelance gag writing and drawing, I compiled a list of magazines which used cartoons, rating them by their pay scale. I remember *The New Yorker* was first, at a hundred dollars and up, *Collier's* second at fifty up, *Saturday Evening Post* third, and so on. The *Digest* piece contained helpful tips, such as the fact that *Saturday Evening Post* was easier for unknowns to break into than *Collier's* and paid as much, but that Gurney Williams, gag editor for the latter magazine, was touchy about getting first crack at ideas. If a rough sketch had too many thumb smudges from other editors he wouldn't even look at it. So Williams came first with me—after *The New Yorker.* There were about twenty-five magazines on my list.

Daily on my way home to the YMCA, I stopped at a little store on

Chicago Avenue and bought a quart of milk and a package of tailor-made cigarettes if I was flush—Bull Durham or Duke's Mixture if I wasn't. Either way, the milk was necessary to the regime I had set for myself. Every night, Monday through Friday, I forced myself to think up ten cartoon ideas and develop them into roughs suitable for mailing to editors before I would let myself go to sleep. The reason for the milk was to settle my stomach from all the cigarettes I smoked. Nowadays, as an ex-smoker, I have dutifully warned all of my sons about the agonies of tobacco withdrawal and told them they would be better off not to start. But I don't belabor the subject. I don't think I could have gotten through that year in Chicago without my nicotine crutch. Who am I to decide that a kid in late high school or college, loaded with studies, doesn't need a crutch, too? Anyway, at two or three or four in the morning, I would finish the tenth rough, rubber-stamp my name and address on each sketch's back, stick the bundle into a manila envelope addressed to *The New Yorker,* fold and insert an identical envelope, stamped and self-addressed (otherwise, I had been assured, the roughs were almost certain to end up in a wastebasket), and be asleep before I hit the pillow, more often than not fully dressed, or with one shoe off and a sock still clutched in my hand next morning.

The point of all this was not just to make money. It seemed to me that the biggest problem of being a professional cartoonist would be getting ideas day after day. I knew that many of them bought some or all of their ideas—in fact, there has always been a thriving freelance trade in this, with contributors making up lists of cartoonists according to their pay scale just as the artists indexed editors. I decided early that I wanted none of that: that if I couldn't think as well as draw I would do something else for a living. So it seemed to me that while I was young and could do without sleep I should rigorously train myself in the idea department. Surely there must be one good idea in ten. Ten became my number. As a discipline, it worked. I must have boiled out almost twenty-five hundred roughs that year. Although now I'm slowing with age I still find myself thinking up a half-dozen or so every night. It's as much a habit as eating dinner. I usually find in the critical light of morning that none of them are usable. However, the fact that I go to sleep thinking about cartoons means I wake up thinking about them, so that somehow I've always managed to come up with something before deadline time.

Useful as it turned out to be for working habits, the commercial side of my Chicago project didn't work out so well. Possibly my midnight inspirations just never have been viable. Every morning the mail cage at the YMCA presented me with a pile of manila envelopes addressed to me with my own rubber stamp. I would quickly take them up to my room, open them, and shake the rejection slips into the wastebasket.

Occasionally there wouldn't be a slip. I would wildly fan out the ten roughs, looking for the magical O.K. with the editor's initials which meant go ahead and send us a finished drawing. Invariably somebody had just forgotten to put in the slip. I would put sketches *The New Yorker* had returned into a fresh envelope for *Collier's,* the *Collier's* stuff to *Saturday Evening Post,* and so on down the line. By the time a dozen or so editiors and their assistants had pawed over the roughs, the paper, not a very fancy grade to begin with, had gotten a little scruffy. At this point I would become selective, resketching the worst ones, and send out hunting and fishing gags to outdoor magazines, soldier jokes to the *American Legion Magazine* and so on. When I happened to meet Gurney Williams a few years later he told me that he felt he knew me well after seeing ten of my sketches every working day for a year. He never bought any, though. Nor did any of the other important national magazines. The only time I came close to scoring was when *Esquire* kept two of my roughs out of one batch, returned the others, enclosed a check, and appended a note saying they were buying only the ideas for five dollars apiece and would turn the final drawing of the cartoons over to a professional. I wish I had had the guts to demand my roughs back, but I needed the money.

The man who saved me that year was Raymond Carlson, editor of *Arizona Highways,* one of the most handsomely illustrated magazines in the country. Carlson had never bought anything from me while I was in Phoenix but had always been friendly and encouraging. Now, even though he knew he was just about the last editor on the totem pole of my mailing system because his price was two dollars, he always O.K.'d two or three, and sometimes even four, of my roughs every month. He was mainly interested in Western or travel gags, of course, but I did plenty of those. If it hadn't been for *Arizona Highways,* my system would have broken down simply because I couldn't have afforded all those envelopes and stamps. One day the *New York Times* reprinted one of my cartoons from *Arizona Highways.* When I got to school a couple of fellow cartoon students hoisted me onto their shoulders like a football star. Not only did Carlson buy my stuff, but he printed everything he bought. His effect on my morale would be hard to calculate.

My winter wardrobe in Chicago consisted of a pair of heavy trousers, numerous sweaters (my grandmother knitted to kill time while she organized quilting bees), a brown wool suit which had turned sort of purple, and a heavy blue overcoat. The last two items were gifts from Charles Curtis, my new stepbrother. Charlie, an Arizona mining engineer, had gone all the way through Harvard on scholarships in that overcoat, selling brier pipes to make expenses, and had graduated third from the top of his class in 1930, so you could say the garment already had a pretty elegant academic tradition. In fact, Charlie later admitted, it had been

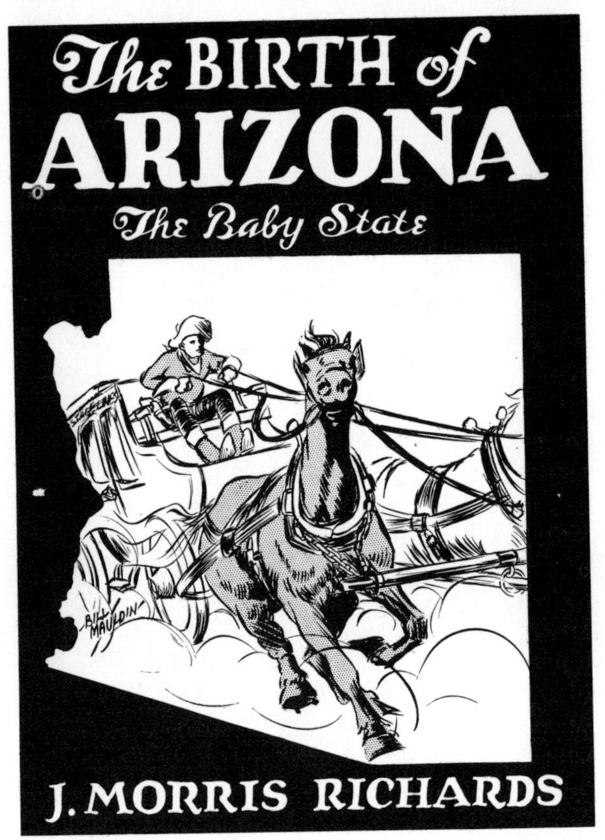

A genuine commission for a book jacket!

"Don't worry, Zeb! It won't last!"

This cartoon for *Arizona Highways* was reprinted in the *New York Times* travel section. My cup ran over.

passed on to him by an earlier graduate. The only thing wrong with the coat after all those years was a torn lining in one sleeve. The warm Arizona sun was responsible for the peculiar color of the brown suit. Charlie had hung it out to air one morning and had forgotten about it until the next afternoon. Fortunately, the clothesline was oriented north and south, so that the front of the suit got the morning sun and the back got the stronger dose of ultraviolet, and when you wore it you looked more purple going than coming. If the line had run the other way, you can see that the result head-on would have been a sort of hopeless domino effect.

Chicago couldn't have cared less about how an art student just beginning his eighteenth year was turned out. I always gave myself weekends off and quickly learned that most of the best things in the city were free and informal. On warm Saturdays you could go to Grant Park and listen to music; when the weather was bad you could prowl around the near north side, go in a saloon's back door because you were underage, and spend all the time you wanted nuzzling a ten-cent beer. If you wanted to fight you could immediately find somebody who knew how to fight better. In any weather there was the view, which could awe you if you were careful to observe only the lake, the parks, or the skyline. For a nickel you could see the rest of it, riding the El past unbelievable miles of jammed-up, tumble-down, gray, wooden, multifamily firetraps full of immigrants, sons of immigrants, and descendents of slaves, all of whom in Chicago seem to have always had more fun snarling at each other than at their circumstances. Eventually you came to Brookfield Zoo, where the inmates were separated from you only by camouflaged trenches. You could wander down a wooded path and suddenly meet a lion or a zebra eyeball-to-eyeball. I don't think I had a dull weekend that year, not even when it got so cold that I had to start wearing the overcoat.

Along with the Brookfield Zoo, one of my favorite places for weekend sketching expeditions was Riverview Amusement Park. I usually went alone, not only because I liked to set my own pace when I worked at something, but because I had a secret craving for merry-go-rounds. Possibly it started on the playground of our grammar school in the New Mexico mountains, where my father built a wild carousel from a bunch of two-by-fours and a universal joint from a truck's drive shaft. The Riverview machine was surely one of the world's largest and fanciest, with a calliope that would tear your heart out. I seldom had to buy more than one ticket to ride as long as I liked it, because I had an uncanny knack for snagging those little brass rings that hung out on a wooden arm as I went bobbing by on my green-spotted chartreuse horse. Each ring was good for a free ride. I was so good at this that I couldn't resist showing off a bit by snagging rings with one finger at a time, beginning

A couple of editorial efforts for Shoemaker's class, showing some early brushwork.

"Full Speed ahead. . . ."

Note British spelling of *defenses,* a rare lapse for author, who used to win spelling bees in school.

with the forefinger, until each digit was loaded to its end with brass. By the time my hands were full the attendant would come around complaining that they were running out of rings; I would grandly dump the lot into his hat without bothering to count. He would look at me askance, clearly wondering what a big boy like me was doing on that little horse, and would let me ride as long as I wanted, which was usually at least an hour. You can see why I chose to keep this obsession private. One time I arrived at Riverview with only return carfare in my pocket and blew it on the merry-go-round. Anybody who knows Chicago and remembers Riverview will realize that meant a hell of a long walk home.

The amusement park had one of those infamous monkey cages full of black teenagers sitting on planks suspended by triggers over a tank of water. If you bought three balls and could hit a target under the boy of your choice it would trip his plank and he would tumble into the drink. What bothered me wasn't seeing the kids get wet—on really hot days they might even have considered it a fringe benefit—but the method used to attract business. Obviously acting on instructions, and equally obviously putting their hearts and souls into their performance, the black boys screeched obscenities, lewd suggestions, and pointed insults at every passing white couple. If they saw a swain's neck grow red as his girl covered her ears in horror, they really poured it on. Lacking a gun, the gallant had only one means available to satisfy honor: three balls for a dime, mister, ten for a quarter. See if you can soak that little jig in the corner. He's the one making the most racket. Even sounds like an ape, don't he?

4

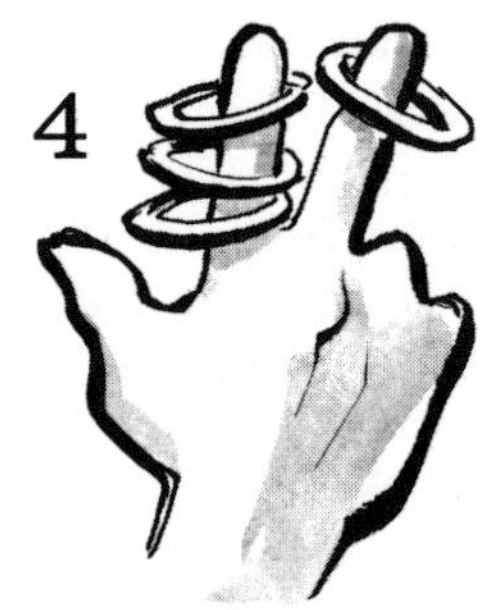

As much as I admired and liked the editorial cartoonists I had met so far in my life, by the time my academic year was two-thirds over I still hadn't committed myself to any special branch of my profession. For me, this was unheard-of vacillation. At eighteen I considered my life almost half finished. I was convinced that creative people accomplished everything worthwhile before forty and if they hadn't died by then they should do society a favor and commit suicide. I remember putting on my purple suit one night and going with one of our rich students to a party in one of the grander Lake Shore Drive apartments. The canopy in front was blue, the doorman had epaulets, the lobby paneling was mahogany, the elevator was brass and velvet, and the apartment contained a genuine Rembrandt. No editorial cartoonist made enough to buy a Rembrandt.

Spiritually, however, I liked the world of opinion more and more. Having already decided that I was on the Allied side of the war, I was outraged at the anglophobic *Tribune*'s editorial posture. It seemed to me that if McCormick wasn't outright seditious, he was the next thing to it.

"If we have to fight the Germans, I hope they hang the *Trib*," I said to Bruce Goff, an architect who taught composition at the academy.

"Someday," Goff told me, "you're going to oppose a war the *Tribune* supports, and when they talk about hanging you for treason it'll be your turn to holler about freedom of the press."

More weeks went by. The academy had delivered my money's worth:

it had knocked a great deal of nonsense out of my drawing and had put my work onto a sort of foundation. I was ready to go. But where? It began to dawn on me that the form of my livelihood within the profession was no longer a matter of my choice. The Depression was still on; the wartime economy had not yet begun. There were no jobs. Some students talked of going to New York. I wanted no more big cities for a while. I was homesick and knew it, yet I couldn't face Uncle Billy under these circumstances. Maybe he wouldn't have cared, but I would have. There was a rumor for a while that Walt Disney, an academy alumnus himself, was hiring new animators at twenty-five dollars a week. According to people who had worked for him, the pay didn't get much better and your eyes gave out after a while, but if his talent scouts had tapped me at that point I'd have jumped into their pockets.

One night I was reading a note from Ray Carlson, complimenting me on the improvement in my drawing, and I talked myself into going back to Phoenix. Surely a town that size could support a commercial artist. Before going to Chicago I had been merely a crude cartoonist and an untrained sign painter. Now it would be different. A travel-agency ad in the *Tribune* asked for drivers to take new cars to California. The agency told me a new Willys was about to leave with two other westbound fellows; if I would pay fifteen dollars I could help them drive as far as Phoenix. I packed my Harvard overcoat and some of my better nude figure studies and headed back west. My new stepfather said he would put me up until I found a job.

The Willys was a brand-new coupé. I don't know how much the owner saved by having it delivered in this fashion, but whatever the amount it wasn't worth it. This was in the days when you were supposed to break in a new car under thirty-five miles per hour. For the first five hundred miles, while I was merely a passenger, we never drove under seventy. Two or three times I tried to hint to the driver that this was not only a hell of a way to treat machinery, but that the car might not get us all the way if we ruined it. I got a dirty look for my pains. He was a big bruiser, an unemployed butcher, who smelled as if he hadn't bathed for ten years. It was the hot end of July, the coupé had a narrow seat, and during one of our gas stops, the other man aboard, a college student, said he felt sorry for the car but was grateful for the speed because it kept the air moving through the windows. By the time I got the wheel, somewhere east of Kansas City, the engine had stopped smelling like a burnt-out furnace. I figured it was broken in, one way or another, and kept up the 70-mph pace.

We never stopped except for gas and oil—for some reason the engine kept demanding more and more oil as we went along—and we bought candy bars at the filling stations. Less than a day and a half after leaving

One of the jobs Reg Manning passed on to me.

Sid, mother, and George Curtis about time I joined army.

Chicago, we were zipping through northern New Mexico, which I had never seen before. I remember passing a red neon sign in Albuquerque: MAULDIN'S JUNKYARD.

"Well, Bill," said the student, "you said you went east to get famous, and they've already got your name in lights in New Mexico."

In Phoenix my mother and stepfather put me up on their porch. During the next few days I quickly learned what I should have known: as far as freelance art in Arizona was concerned, it was a buyers' market. I went to see my old friend Reg Manning, the *Arizona Republic* cartoonist, who had encouraged me to go to Chicago. He was surprised to see me back so soon. When I explained the circumstances, he was sympathetic. Better, he was helpful. He phoned me at my stepfather's house one morning and dropped a bonanza into my lap. Reg explained that early in his career he had built up an election-year clientele among various local politicians around the state, drawing cartoons which were made into campaign posters and newspaper ads. Sometimes the clients wanted a comic-strip-style series of panels depicting their rise from rags to statesmanship; sometimes they merely wanted single panels, showing their opponents as the rapacious scoundrels they surely were. Reg went on to explain to me that as soon as he became a respected and prominent part of the editorial page of the biggest paper in Arizona he had to cut out all that moonlighting.

However, his work had been so effective that his old customers had never quit coming around. Now it was 1940, an election year, and an important Presidential one at that. Manning had already had four calls from upstate candidates for sheriff, county treasurer, and so on. This time, instead of refusing them, he had said he might be able to provide them with a talented substitute. The suggested retail price, he told me, was twenty-five dollars per drawing.

Reg's call bailed me out of trouble with my stepfather. George Curtis was not an inhospitable man, but, like my grandmother, he worried about my character. He couldn't understand why I had gone east for professional training, and then had come back to Phoenix, when I could have worked my way up in a respectable Chicago advertising agency. He had watched me hit the street every morning with samples under my arm, and had seen me come home, with growing discouragement, from my rounds of stores, printing shops, trade papers, and what not. The sidewalks of Phoenix get hot in summer, and nobody had seemed to need cartoons, illustrations, or drawings of any kind. My stepfather suspected, correctly, that I was about to swallow pride and go back to my old high-school business of painting white sidewalls on tires and making posters for such establishments as Weldon's riding stable in Papago Park. In fact, the old gentleman was even beginning to suggest this course, with an urgency that bordered on insistence. His salary as a government map maker was a living in those days, but didn't allow for leeches.

Now reprieved for the moment, I put all the skill I could summon for the next week into four pictures to help elect four obscure but sterling public servants in Coconino County and points east and west. None of the candidates wanted a hatchet job on the opposition; they merely wanted their own lives depicted in heroic adventure strips. Photos were provided, along with biographical material. Thanks to some quiet coaching from Reg here and there, my efforts were accepted, paid for, and, as far as I know, printed.

Chin high again, I landed some more political-cartooning jobs on my own. Arizona was about as solidly Democratic in those days as it is Republican now. Battles for important state jobs were to be fought in the approaching summer primaries. A Phoenix businessman was making a strong bid for the governorship, which was held by a professional politician. I called the aspirant's campaign manager, told him I was a political cartoonist in town to observe the local scene, and asked for an appointment with "the next governor."

The challenger and his manager were disconcerted by my youth when I showed up, but by the time I finished telling them what Thomas Nast did to Boss Tweed, they were listening with as much respect as any eighteen-year-old could reasonably hope to command. They decided they could use two cartoons, both attacking the incumbent governor. I said that a bulk order deserved a special price, and that they could have both drawings for only fifty dollars. They agreed, with payment to be upon acceptance. I was too green to hit them for half as a retainer.

The trouble with clobbering the governor pictorially was that I couldn't find much wrong with him. When I asked Reg for help, he told me the only thing he had against the fellow was that he was a Democrat. I think my mentor was appalled by what I had taken on. In the end, I fell back on the political cartoonists' device of trying to make a man look ridiculous when you can't make him evil. Fortunately, the governor was not physically beautiful. I believe one of my drawings showed him as a rodeo clown, and the other portrayed him as a buzzard circling over some unidentified bones on the desert. My customer was delighted, and said he would think of something to write on the skeleton. Again, I was naïve. I should have protested that my integrity demanded that my work not be altered.

Fifty dollars richer, and with probity still part of my future, I made tracks to the statehouse. Arizona was not a very populous or busy state then, so that even youngsters were admitted to important people, and in no time I was in the presence of one of the governor's campaign advisers. I said I was a cartoonist from Chicago, in town to draw pictures of the campaign. I felt that this was bending the truth without breaking it. I said that mine was a very close-knit little profession with few practitioners especially in Arizona, and that we all knew what the other fellows were up to. Thus, I was able to state for a fact that the governor's enemies had hired a political cartoonist to attack him. Would he care to fight fire with fire? Another adviser came into the room during this conversation. The two men huddled for a moment. The consensus was that the governor would not stoop so low. I described the offensive cartoons. The men looked at each other, then agreed to see my samples. In the end, they ordered one drawing. They were not interested in counterattacking. They wanted their man's accomplishments dramatized in a few modest subpanels within the cartoon.

When this job was finished and paid for, I offered to reimbuse my stepfather for my back room-and-board. He reminded me that there are dry spells between elections, and suggested that I use my loot to buy a one-way ticket back to Chicago. Reg Manning thought it might be a good idea for me to leave town, too. He was thinking of all those gubernatorial cartoons appearing at once. He asked if I had signed them. Of course, I told him—any cartoonist ashamed to sign his own work, I felt, should be kicked out of the profession.

Chances are I never would have had enough sense to get out of Phoenix if I hadn't run into Jack Heinz, my old high-school ROTC buddy. Heinz had owned a Model A coupé with a rumble seat; together we had courted a pair of North Phoenix sisters and become good friends. Now Jack was a corporal in D Company of the 120th Quartermaster Regiment of the Arizona National Guard, which was a part of the 45th Infantry Division. The 45th was drawn from three other states as well: Oklahoma, New Mexico, and Colorado, and was about to become the very first Guard division to be "federalized," or made a part of the regular army, which at that time numbered fewer than a quarter-million men.

Heinz and I talked about the war in Europe, which was quiescent at the moment. This period was being called the "phony war" by some American observers and editors. Considering ourselves men of some military experience, at least as far as close-order drill went, we agreed that whatever sort of war it was, the United States would be drawn into it sooner or later.

"Why don't you join Company D?" Jack asked. "When we get into the mess there'll be a draft and they'll catch you anyway. In the National Guard you'll be among friends, you'll stay out of the infantry, and you'll solve your civilian unemployment problem. We just got a bunch of new Dodge trucks and maybe I can get you assigned to one."

I remember his words because they kept coming back to me later on. I understand the army still gets some volunteers out of this sort of conversation among friends. Possibly one reason I was so easy to persuade was that I had never really gotten over my old enchantment with the army. Whatever my potential as a soldier might have been, I should have guessed that I wouldn't realize it in a quartermaster regiment, which concerns itself with transportation, storage, and distribution of blankets, underwear, footgear, mops, garbage cans, contraceptive kits, sides of beef, unpeeled potatoes, window screens, tent ropes, toilet tissue, coffee beans, soda pop, cotton webbing, helmet liners, chopping blocks, and stove lids.

Also, I should have been warned by the physical examination, which I took on the same day with several other volunteers, that Company D was not destined to be one of the army's elite units. They didn't really test our eyes; they sort of counted them. I never saw so much as a stethoscope that day. The doctor turned out to be an old acquaintance who had treated me for the flu and a couple of minor injuries during my high-school days. When I arrived before him he seemed to be having more trouble filling out forms than looking over naked recruits. He knew that I pushed a pencil with some dexterity, so he pulled me out of the line, made me his clerk, and gave me a grandstand view, so to speak, of the proceedings.

He seemed interested in nothing but hemorrhoids. In retrospect, it makes sense. These men were going to be lifting and hauling a lot of crates in and out of trucks and warehouses. I'm sure now that the doctor was acting upon instructions. At the time, however, I was horrified by what appeared to be his preoccupation with all those scruffy butts. As soon as each man bellied up to his desk, the doctor spun him around and barked, "Bend over and spread those cheeks." He kept each subject in this posture for what seemed a long study. I had no idea what hemorrhoids, or "piles," as they were generally called, looked like. Later, when I was able to get my hands on some medical books, I made a point of finding out, and I can tell you that several of those men had them, all right. Apparently, the military concern with the affliction was quantitative, not qualitative, because everybody passed that day. I remember one of the fellows had a testicle that seemed to have strained its moorings and had left its colleague hanging some four or five inches higher.

"Mark that man with a left varicocele," the doctor instructed me. Heretofore, I had been following orders to mark everything "normal" in the long and complicated forms, which covered everything from scalp eczema to athlete's foot.

"Isn't that some kind of rupture?" I asked. The testicle's owner brightened. Anything sounded better than varicocele.

"We're not running a premedical school," the doctor grunted. Then he relented. I had been a good clerk. "Everybody tends to develop a varicocele on the side he hangs his pecker," he said. "Perfectly harmless. Got to make room for the thing somehow."

When it was over, I reminded the old man that I hadn't had my own physical. I dreaded going around the desk and assuming that posture, which seemed the most humiliating thing a human could do. The doctor's fatigue saved me. He asked if I was in good health. I said I thought so, except that I probably had a very slight left varicocele, myself.

"Put it down, then," he said, "and mark everything else normal. I'll sign it." Thus, I completed my own pre-induction physical.

Since I was eighteen, the matter of parental permission came up, but that was disposed of with the enthusiastic help of George Curtis. Together, we convinced my mother that the army was going to be a sort of advanced Boy Scout encampment. We explained that in Company D her boy would be among friends like Jack Heinz, whom she already knew and liked, and we even took her to meet the company officers. They said that they would personally keep an eye on my welfare.

"My, the army has certainly changed since I dated a lieutenant from Fort Bliss," my mother told them. "That man treated his soldiers like peons."

"Mrs. Curtis, we are technicians in this outfit," the captain said. "We're not just dumb cannon fodder. You don't treat specialists like dirt."

In the spirit of specialization, I listed my primary civilian occupation as truck driver. This was partly on the advice of Heinz, and partly because I really was capable of handling trucks—off the highway, anyhow. Back in Mountain Park, we sold nearly all of our apples in bulk to haulers who came to our orchard in every kind of rig from ton-and-a-half Chevies to Whites and Macks pulling huge semi-trailers. I often got the job of backing and maneuvering these things among the trees. Anybody who can back a semi through a hilly orchard without breaking too many limbs is qualified to call himself at least a truck maneuverer, if not a driver.

A day or so after I was sworn into the Guard, we became "federalized," as expected, when President Roosevelt declared a "limited national emergency." We were now part of the standing army. It was fifteen months before Pearl Harbor. I reported at the armory where Company D was organizing itself for the convoy trip to Fort Sill, Oklahoma, the 45th Division's home base, and waited to be given my truck. Several days later I was still waiting. All the new Dodges were assigned, then the old GMCs. I didn't even get onto the assistant driver roster. It was clear that I was doomed to ride a thousand miles in the back of an army truck.

"It's practically a violation of contract," I complained to my friend Heinz.

"Are you asking for special treatment?" he asked, busily checking off some cargo against a sheaf of papers on his clipboard.

"You could put it that way, Jack, old buddy, if that's the way you want to put it."

"This is the army now, Bill, not the old Guard, where guys could take care of each other that way. I really did put in a word for you as an assistant driver, but there are a lot of men waiting who joined before you did. By the way, while we're on the subject, you can keep on calling me Jack in private, but it's Corporal Heinz when anybody's around."

My second lesson in soldiering came a few nights later, when we bivouacked, en route, on the outfield of a baseball park in Midland, Texas. I was assigned to sentry duty, with a flashlight and an unloaded Springfield rifle. The corporal of the guard was Heinz, who was now solicitous toward me. I had been assigned to the back of his new Dodge, and I think his conscience had begun bothering him from watching me through his mirror as I bounced over mile after mile of two-lane Texas blacktop full of dips, humps, and chuckholes.

"You can sack out on the front seat of our truck," Jack whispered to me. The way he said "our" truck almost made me hope again. "I'll cover for you," he added. "They've got too many guys on guard anyway. Who's going to attack a ballpark?"

"Like you told me, Jack, it's the army now, not the Guard," I said, not fully trusting him, "I've heard they can give you the firing squad for sleeping on sentry duty."

"We're not at war," he said. "The worst they can give you for anything is jail. But suit yourself."

At the beginning of my second watch, shortly after midnight, I saw two figures approach through the park gate. I recognized one of our lieutenants and our first sergeant, a tall young man with spectacles. He and the officer had gone to town much earlier in the evening.

"Who goes there?" I challenged. I had read the General Orders for sentries. Also, I had heard, as part of my accumulation of military lore, that it was a favorite trick of sharp, discipline-oriented officers to bull their way past sentries who clearly recognized them, then nail the poor devils for dereliction of duty.

"Who goes there?" I cried again, blocking their path with my empty rifle at high port. My flashlight, unlit, was tucked under my arm.

"If you don't know us by now you never will," the sergeant said. "Who are *you,* anyway?" He beamed his own flashlight full into my face. "Aw, it's *him.*"

"Who goes there?" I said, holding my ground. I remembered that after the third challenge you were authorized to shoot, or, presumably, throw your weapon if unloaded. I couldn't remember whether the General Orders specified that you *could* or *should* take such action.

"Maybe he just wants a little old password," the lieutenant said, laughing. His breath was soaked with bad whiskey.

"Is there a password?" the sergeant asked.

"Beats me," chortled the officer. "Let's ask him. Soldier, what's the password?"

"Sir," I said, "I don't know. I don't think there is one."

"Then what the hell do you want from us?" the sergeant hollered. "Get your silly ass out of the way and get back on your job."

He stopped briefly at the guard tent on his way to bed. Shortly after, Heinz came to see me at my post.

"You're hopeless," he said. "I told you to sleep in the truck. You had to stand out here and make a jerk of yourself. That topkick doesn't look like much but he's got a short temper and a long memory. If you got on his shit list tonight I never heard of you, old buddy. Better get back on your job now."

"You can all go to hell," I said. "Everybody tells me to get back on the job and I never left it."

"No need to get snotty about it," my friend said.

Riding in the back of Jack's truck the rest of the way to Fort Sill, it began to dawn on me that I was probably a failure. I was making twenty-one dollars a month in a truck company where I couldn't get behind a wheel. When I let Heinz talk me into this, I had a crazy notion in the back of my head that maybe there would be some way in which I could combine my artistic and soldierly talents. Hell, at the rate I was going, I would be lucky to get a job painting latrine signs.

The 45th was what the army called a "square" division, with two infantry brigades of two regiments each, an artillery brigade, and quartermaster, medical, and engineering regiments. All this was spread out in tents over the muddy prairie when we arrived at Fort Sill. I became aware for the first time of a phenomenon of meteorology which has puzzled soldiers for centuries: it is nearly always muddy where infantry is, no matter how normally dry the climate might be. Not all of Fort Sill was wet. There were paved streets and brick barracks for the permanent garrison of regulars, including the army's artillery school. We were definitely second-class citizens as far as they were concerned; we couldn't even use their post exchange.

Reserves and National Guard are anathema to regulars under the best conditions, and we were a sorry lot. Many of us, including myself, had been issued uniforms that had been in mothballs since World War I. My tunic, or "blouse," was a choke-collar affair made of a blotterlike fabric called "Melton." I even had breeches and wrap leggings. The latter came in rolls like bandages. They had to be coiled around your calves like anacondas: if you still had circulation in your feet you knew your leggings

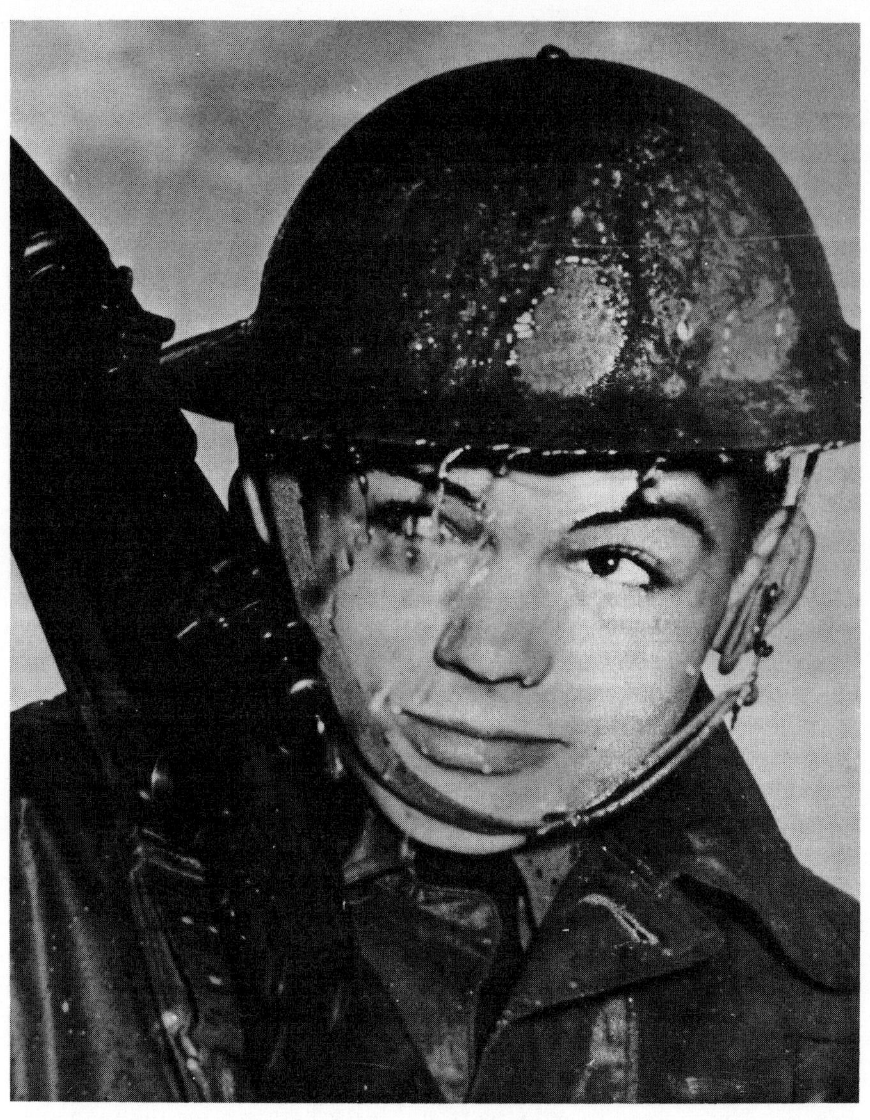

Note World War I helmet and Springfield rifle. Explanation of this photo, taken by A. Y. Owen, appears later in text.

were too loose and would work their way down to your ankles like a schoolgirl's stockings. My shoes had hobnails and cracks that went clean through the dry leather. I was not their first owner, nor even their second. My headgear was a floppy-brimmed, peaked "campaign hat" left over from the Pershing expedition into Mexico. My high-school ROTC uniform had been far better than this. Who could blame the regulars for not wanting us clowns cluttering up their canteens?

There were a few comforts. The 45th Division had used the encampment before during summer training periods, so there were wooden messhalls and latrines, as well as floors for many of the pyramidal tents. The 120th Quartermaster Regiment was blessed with these. Indeed, it would have been strange otherwise, since quartermasters are in charge of the procurement and disbursement of lumber. Our latrine even had flushing toilets and showers.

However, it was a long walk through the mud to this facility, with no lights on the way. Few of my comrades-in-arms bothered to go there after dark, preferring to piss in their tracks or on the sides of their tents. After a few days our mud was noticeably deeper, although not a drop of rain had fallen. Our first sergeant, who had a delicate side, became offended by the pollution of the good earth and commanded his men to use the latrine. Even in ROTC I had learned the stupidity of giving an order which couldn't be enforced. Clearly, the sergeant hadn't had the benefit of my training. After a few more days, he did what he should have done in the first place: he caused a twenty-gallon GI can to be placed each evening in the middle of the company street. Then he had an inspiration which even his detractors among us had to admit seemed intelligent and fair: each morning the can, full and foaming, weighing approximately 155 pounds gross, was carried to the latrine by the last two men to answer reveille.

Up till now, reveille had been like every other military exercise in Company D: ragged, sluggish, and sloppy. If my description seems carping, let me make it clear that I was no shining example as an early riser. Despite my previous love for the army, Company D was fast making a cynic of me. I managed to catch the honey-bucket detail twice during the first week after it was instituted. Being the very last man out both times, in each case I was assigned the downwind handle of the frothy can. The wind always blows on the Oklahoma prairie, even in the predawn darkness when elsewhere it is calm. After getting befoamed twice in this manner, I became almost an insomniac, jerking upright in my cot and grabbing for my socks at any whistling or bugling sound in the night.

Then, one morning I overreacted to the top sergeant's shrill, pre-reveille toot, found myself the very first man out of the tents, and learned that in the army it does not pay any more to be eager than to be tardy. The sergeant gazed at me as I stood at attention, fully uniformed, with even my wrap leggings done up tightly, and then he gazed at the honey bucket, which had a head of foam at least a foot high. He poked at it and stirred it slightly with his swagger stick. I think he got the idea of the stick from a Marine movie.

"Soldier," he said, "this thing is too full. Let's get it out of here before somebody knocks it over." You couldn't have upset that load of second-hand Oklahoma bootleg beer if you had hit it with a Mack truck.

The next man out was one of my tent mates, a former middleweight boxer of Mexican ancestry: a slightly punchy, good-natured lummox with whom I had been on friendly terms until now. The first sergeant assigned him to the can's other handle—at least I managed to get the upwind side this time—and as we staggered through the darkness with our load, the ex-fighter kept wiping at his cheek with his free hand and muttering about getting a transfer.

"Transfer out of the quartermaster?" I asked him. "Where will you go? Infantry? Artillery?"

"I mean transfer out of your tent," he said. "You are bad news, kid."

I was beginning to learn that the art of achieving anonymity in the military is like that of avoiding highway cops: bury yourself in a bunch of other cars and drive at their tempo, regardless of what the signs say. Once I got through a whole week in D Company without drawing attention or extra duty. This was made somewhat easier by the fact that although we were supposed to be undergoing basic training most of our time was spent in large groups doing chores, such as cutting and stacking firewood for the tent stoves, hauling crates to and from warehouses and railroad sidings, shoveling coal for messhalls, and washing trucks. It was like being in a union. If you carried exactly your weight at the common pace you got along. I was careful to do no less than my share of goldbricking and no more than my share of working.

Then I blew it again. One morning the first sergeant announced that division policy was for all units, even such noncombatant outfits as ours, to become proficient in close order drill. He confessed that few of our noncoms were trained in the stuff, that even he knew practically nothing about it, and asked which of us had had parade-ground experience. Like an idiot, I raised my hand. Heinz later admitted that he would have fingered me anyway, since I had been in his ROTC company, but that doesn't excuse me from the folly of having volunteered. They gave me a squad. After two hours of getting everybody's feet sorted out, I had the troops marching in step and executing right and left flanking movements. I was really pretty good at this. By the end of the day we were doing fancy stuff. On command, the rear rank would reverse direction while the front kept going. After a few paces, I would holler, "To the rear, HARCH," both groups would now head for each other, and just before the crash I would reverse the front rank. Now they were marching in their original positions and direction. The trick was for everybody to avoid flinching at the last second, which calls for confidence in the drill master, who must be on the ball at all times. Absorbed in what I was doing and having a fine time, I wasn't aware of the first sergeant's presence behind me.

"Well, well, well," he said. "How are you at the manual of arms? I'll bet you're great at that, too."

I suppose I still could have partially saved myself, but suddenly I didn't care. There was now no doubt that I was destined to be a yardbird in this company and I might as well face it with a flourish. Telling the sergeant to wait a moment, I went to my tent and got somebody's Springfield rifle. I adjusted the sling, moved the brass frogs so they wouldn't hurt my hand, tightened the leather until it cracked nicely in my palm, and took my sweet time about it, with the sergeant and the squad standing there watching me. I have already described the Queen Anne salute. Never was it done so well. Then, with my knee dripping mud, I ran through the manual forward and backward, spinning the rifle on its way each time. For a climax I did "inspection arms" as follows: with the piece at order by my right foot, I kicked sideward smartly against the stock so that it swung out, pendulumlike, then, as it made the return stroke to the left, I lifted and spun it so that my left hand could flip the bolt up. When the swing back to the right ended, momentum made the bolt snap open with a sharp click. I then brought the weapon up to the standard inspection position, proffering it to the sergeant. It was gratifying to observe that he didn't even know how to receive it.

"Keep it up, Bill, and you might get to be a corporal like me," Heinz said later, having heard about the one-man parade.

"That shows how much *you* know about the goddamn army," I snarled. I spent twenty-four days on KP during my next six weeks in D Company. Most of the remaining days were spent on guard and latrine duty. Somehow, though, it makes you feel better when you know you've asked for it.

Company D had a little Mafia of sorts, consisting of the mess sergeant and supply sergeant. In some ways those guys just about ran the outfit. Both were veterans of the regular army. They lent money on a simple basis of one hundred percent per month. That is, if you defaulted on a five-dollar loan, at the end of three months you owed forty dollars. Theoretically, that is. Defaulting was vigorously discouraged. The two sergeants ran the only poker and crap games in the company, taking a percentage from each pot. They were also the only bootleggers—no small thing in a state as dry as Oklahoma used to be. They had every racket tied up. I heard they even bought an interest in a whorehouse in Lawton, the only nearby town. The Gold Dust Twins, as we called them, had a fool-proof method of collecting from debtors. They simply sat by the company commander on payday, with their ledgers in front of them. When a soldier's name was called, he stepped up, signed the payroll, and then the captain handed his money—minus legitimate deductions for insurance, dependency allotments, and so forth—to the mess sergeant, who inspected his personal books, took what was coming to him, and passed the remainder to the supply sergeant, who did the same. If there wasn't enough left for the supply sergeant, he simply doubled the amount still owing and moved it forward to the next month, when it was his turn to sit next to the captain and get first crack at the roll.

The sergeants operated so brazenly that it was assumed they assuaged the thirst of key officers throughout the regiment as well as the company. They must have slipped up somewhere at last. The colonel himself stormed into the company area one morning, ripped the stripes off the Gold Dust Twins with his own hands, and personally placed them under arrest. They were sentenced to thirty days at hard labor. Since the division had no stockade, they were under guard in their tents by night and put to work by day chipping and shoveling mud from the gutters of the paved street which ran the length of the regiment. One day when I caught sentry duty it fell to my lot to stand over the evil pair with a rifle while they hacked at the mud. The weapon was empty—merely symbolic.* After an hour's half-hearted labor, the miscreants laid down their tools and told me they were going to have a cup of coffee down at the warehouse. They invited me to join them.

"I have orders to keep you working until I'm relieved," I said. "Maybe the next guy likes coffee more than I do."

"Don't be a dumb shitbird all your life, Mauldin," the ex-supply sergeant snarled. "We want coffee now."

"No," I quavered, as firmly as I could.

"Kid, let me tell you something," the ex–mess sergeant said. "We're not gonna be in hock much longer. When we come back, some of the officers are gonna be pretty thirsty. Do you follow me? We're gonna be sergeants again, and you waving that weapon around and doing your chickenshit duty isn't gonna put any stripes on *your* arm, so you're gonna have to deal with us again. How about that coffee?"

"Nope," I said. I felt there was truth in his words, though.

"Kid, I hope you got a file on you," the ex–supply sergeant said.

"Why?" I have always been one of those people who can be depended upon to ask why.

* In fact, the first time I ever heard of the National Guard carrying live ammunition was when the massacre at Kent State University occurred thirty years later.

"When we shove that gun up your butt it'll feel better if you rub the front sight off first."

"You bastards take one step toward me and I'll call the corporal of the guard."

"Go ahead. Hell, we'll do it for you. *Corporal of the guard! Hey! Corporal of the Guard!*"

That worthy came trotting right up.

"Corporal, we been busting our backs all morning and this little horse's ass won't give us a coffee break."

"For Chrissake, what's the matter with you? Give 'em their break." The corporal looked disgustedly at me and walked away.

"No hard feelings, kid," the ex-mess sergeant said, grinning at me over his cup in the warehouse.

"No hard feelings," I said, only about half-insincerely. I was beginning to get philosophical and to blame the environment, not the sharks who swam around in it.

Out of my twenty-one dollars per month, I paid premiums on my military life-insurance policy and put my grandparents on a dependency allotment, on which I paid a portion and the army paid the rest. I learned that I could legally do this because during the year before I enlisted the old couple stood *in loco parentis,* having paid my art-school tuition. My grandfather later told me he approved of the phrase, since he had felt loco ever since putting up the money. As for me, I felt it was a poor way to start paying back the grubstake, but at least it was a beginning. After deductions, I had about five dollars left each month for tobacco and candy. I would have preferred beer, but didn't want to get into the clutches of the bootleggers. For the same reason, I stayed out of the crooked poker games.

One day we got new uniforms, including denim fatigues, and were able to shed the stuff which had made us look like something out of an Irving Berlin musical. Orders were to print our names in block letters, using waterporoof ink, above the left breast pocket of the fatigues. Producing a bottle of Higgins and a Speedball pen from my foot locker, I quickly did the job on my jacket, adding a small caricature of myself below my name, and made sure a number of people saw it. Soon there was a line outside my tent. I charged twenty-five cents apiece. A week later I had done about two hundred names and caricatures, including a number from other companies, and had the only profitable racket in the area not controlled by the Gold Dust Twins. I was pleased but not proud. My nineteenth birthday had gone by. It had been almost six years since I had decided to be a success, and here I was on a muddy prairie drawing caricatures for a quarter each. I had done better than that at the age of fourteen in Cloudcroft.

Most of the 45th Division's troops, as well as its brass, were Oklahoma National Guardsmen. The assistant chief of staff for intelligence at divisional headquarters was a lieutenant colonel named Walter M. Harrison, who in civilian life was editor of the *Daily Oklahoman* and Oklahoma City *Times*, the state's two largest papers. Harrison had a national as well as local reputation as a distinguished journalist and was a member of the Pulitzer Prize committee. Late in 1940 he established the *45th Division News*, a four-page weekly.

There was no precedent for an army newspaper on a divisional level. Harrison didn't need precedents. He had clout. The *News* was set up in the colonel's G-2 office and under his aegis. Printing costs were paid partly out of morale and entertainment funds, and largely, I suspect, out of Harrison's own pocket. He owned considerable stock in the immensely successful Oklahoma City papers. The *News* staff members were put on special assignment to G-2. Their various company commanders probably assumed the men were being taken for cloak and dagger work. Then, as now, intelligence outfits had a lot of latitude in these matters, and sometimes, as in this case, it works out for the common good.

Of course, I knew nothing of these details at the time. I did see the *45th Division News* when distribution of the first issue reached D Company of the 120th Quartermaster. I noted that the paper had no cartoonist. Shortly thereafter, a letter from one of my tentmates went to the *News*, telling about the talented soldier-cartoonist and entrepreneur of portraits on fatigues in the muddy backwaters of the encampment. In no time at all a *News* reporter named Johnny Riddle came to our tent to get further information about me from the man who had sent the letter.

"Ask him direct," my friend said, pointing to me. "He wrote the damn letter. I only signed it."

The same day I shined my shoes and reported to Colonel Harrison at headquarters. A wiry, peppery little man with a ramrod back, trim mustache, and steely eyes that reminded me of Uncle Billy's, he barked like a martinet and didn't fool me for a moment. He was no more a professional soldier than I was. He was just playing at it. There was no question about his abilities as an editor, however. He riffled through my samples—I had managed to do a lot of soldier sketches in spare moments—and told me exactly what was wrong with each of them. He offered me the job of staff cartoonist.

I tried not to show what I felt. My luck had turned. My hand was on the ladder to fame. Joining the army had turned out to be the smartest gamble I had ever made. Farewell to Company D, to KP, latrine duty, guard duty; goodbye, Gold Dust Twins. Watch my smoke, you bastards. Then Harrison dropped the other shoe. Pointing out that it shouldn't take a cartoonist at my stage of development more than three or four hours to do a weekly drawing (his time estimate was distressingly accurate) he said he was not going to give me a full-time job at division headquarters, but would arrange with my company for me to be excused every Friday afternoon.

"Don't look so disappointed," he said. "After all, how can you find material for cartoons if you're not soldiering most of the time?"

"Sir, in D Company we're not exactly sol—"

"We'll give you a corner of your own here to set up your drawing board," Harrison added, "and of course you're free to come up and work any time you're off duty, day or night. Try to keep your pockets buttoned when you come up here, though. The rest of the staff already thinks I've taken on a bunch of Communists."

From then on, no matter how many pots I scrubbed or toilets I scoured, or how much coal I shoveled, at the end of every day that drawing board was waiting for me. Every night, except when I pulled guard duty, I walked the half mile or so to division and put in four or five hours. It was almost like Chicago again, in a way. I even resumed sending roughs out to magazines, although not so many as before. *Arizona Highways* started buying again. One day Harrison told me the *Daily Oklahoman* wanted to reprint my weekly *45th Division News* effort and would pay five dollars apiece. This came within one dollar of doubling my net monthly income. I opened an account in an Oklahoma City bank. Life in D Company became almost bearable. It didn't matter now that I wasn't making it in the army. I was back in my professional bag.

The "general aptitude test" had recently been adopted by the army. I have always been able to get good scores in this sort of thing. In high school I depended upon exams to help me pass courses I hadn't studied. This new test was my favorite kind, with pyramids of blocks to count, word associations, and arithmetic. I made the second-highest score in the entire division, leaving the first sergeant, who fancied himself as something of a brain, way behind in my intellectual dust. Next day, not at all to my surprise. I found myself on permanent KP assignment. If I had been still hoping to get ahead in D Company, I would have been smart enough to play dumb with the test, but now I thought I had an ace up my sleeve.

"Colonel Harrison," I pleaded on the following Friday afternoon, having been excused from the kitchen sink for my half day at the paper, "I could draw KP cartoons from now till doomsday without going near another messhall. It looks like I won't be able to get any other kind of material in the quartermasters from now on."

"What's wrong with doing more KP cartoons?" he said, grinning. "Everybody enjoys them."

"Colonel, I'll lay it on the line," I said. "I've got to get out of that outfit.

First *45th Division News* cartoon. Joe is hook-nosed Indian and Willie plays straight man.

At first Joe spoke comic-strip English, although Indians were most literate men in division.

If I don't my drawing might just go to pot. I mean, even cartoonists have got morale problems."

"Speaking of morale," Harrison said, "this paper is an experiment they're letting me try, but we're on thin ice. There's a certain amount of resentment because there hasn't been a puff story about a commanding officer or even a picture of one since we started. Not only are we running the paper for the enlisted men, but your cartoons have an irreverent quality about them which has not escaped notice.

"Now don't get me wrong—this happens to be exactly the kind of paper I had hoped for," the colonel went on. "In the end I think its morale value will speak for itself. Soldiers need outlets for their gripes, and if they can pick up a paper and see somebody griping for them they go back to work feeling better. But my theory still needs proving, and meanwhile I'm cluttering up division headquarters with a bunch of wild men who don't even have a place on the tables of organization. One more of you—especially a jug-eared kid who can't really justify full-time duty up here—and we might all get wiped out by some literal-minded personnel juggler over in the G-1 section."

"Sir," I said, "playing my last card, "if I can't transfer up here full time, I'd rather be anywhere else in the division. Even the infantry."

"Even the infantry?" he stared at me. "Nobody—absolutely nobody in the entire military history of the world—ever voluntarily transferred out of the quartermasters into the infantry. Do you know what you're saying, or has all that kitchen work really fried your brain?"

"Even the infantry," I repeated.

"As soon as you finish your cartoon this afternoon, report to your orderly room," he said.

Back in D Company I found everybody staring at me.

"Holy cow, Mauldin," an orderly-room clerk said, "we knew you were a fuckup, but what have you done to somebody up at division?"

My captain told me I had been transferred, effective immediately, to K Company, of the 180th Infantry, where I would hold the title of rifleman.

"And may God have mercy on your soul," he said. "I never heard of anything like this happening to anybody before, so quick! I feel bad for you, kid. I'm going to have somebody drive you over there with all your gear. Save your feet. You'll need them."

5

Although I'd have snorted if anyone had suggested that Harrison had done me a favor, in my heart I knew it was true. My old truck company happened to be one of those outfits at which the regular army likes to point when it talks about the National Guard. Besides, at best the quartermaster was a hewer of wood and hauler of water, a counter of buttons and sorter of socks. He could take pride in his work, but could hardly think of himself as a warrior. What does a quartermaster say when his grandchildren ask him about his role in the great war? Almost from the moment I arrived in the 180th Infantry, a certain pride of soldiering began to return to me. It started at first call in the morning, as I awakened to the music of the regimental band instead of the cursing of some lost drunk entangled in tent ropes. When K Company fell out for reveille we found our officers dressed, shaven, and waiting for us, instead of a red-eyed first sergeant wearing bedroom slippers and tucking in his shirttail beside a can of foaming quartermaster piss. In the infantry we formed straight lines, with clickings and rustlings of weapons and webbing. Squad leaders sang out to platoon sergeants, lieutenants barked their reports to the captain; all down the line you could hear other companies doing the same . . . and the band played on. It was still winter, with some mornings near zero on the Oklahoma prairie; I remember wondering how the players of the big brass instruments got their lips unfrozen from their mouthpieces in time for breakfast.

Most of the men in my new company were from McAlester, Oklahoma,

First staff of the *45th Division News*. Top picture: John Waddell, Sam St. John, John Riddle, A. Y. Owen, John Pepper. Bottom: Joe Stocker, author, Bob Duncan.

and environs. They were a rugged bunch of small-town and rural boys, at home with weapons and outdoor living. We had a lot of Indians. By and large, these were our best-educated soldiers. In fact, I learned that the only two men in the outfit who lacked high-school diplomas were the first sergeant and me, both white. A number of our Indians had been to college. One of my tentmates, a big private first class known as "the Medicine Man" because, it was rumored, that was his father's tribal rank, had the eyes of a turkey buzzard, a broken beak, a slit mouth, a lantern jaw, a deadpan sense of humor, a degree from the University of Oklahoma, a talent for memorizing and reciting epic poems, and a conviction that there would never be peace with the white man until it was legal for Indians to buy whiskey.

The Medicine Man was kind to me during my early days in K Company, teaching me the proper way to roll a pack and other little tricks of the trade to make life easier. I was grateful. Nobody gave me a bad time, but it was clear that breaking into this new society would take a while. Aside from the natural clubbiness of a group whose members have grown up around the same town, there was the fact that everybody knew I had come to the infantry from the quartermasters. Was I a foul ball or a nut? Only time would tell. At first I tried explaining the reasons for my transfer, but only the Medicine Man seemed convinced. He told me he had a special tolerance for cartoonists because he had once done a term paper on pictorial satire from Hogarth through Daumier. He remembered most of the material and taught me the history of my chosen profession.

The first weapon issued to me in K Company was a Browning automatic rifle, a massive hunk of steel which seemed to weigh almost as much as I did. At first I assumed this was part of my initiation—a sort of minor ordeal to test my endurance—but later learned that it was customary in the infantry to hang BARs on the smallest or scrawniest soldiers, perhaps in the hope of developing them. Actually, I was proud of the thing. Shortly after I got it, we had our first public parade, with the division marching through Lawton, a nearby town which made its living selling campaign ribbons and cherry pie á la mode to the regular Fort Sill troops. The residents couldn't have cared less about a National Guard division trooping through. A dozen or so people turned out, chewing gum. To me, an audience was an audience. I had just sewed on my new shoulder patch (the 45th Division's insignia had always been an Indian good-luck swastika, but thanks to the Nazis this had become unfashionable and we had been ordered to replace it with a golden thunderbird in a red diamond), pinned on my new regimental lapel pins (three arrows on a blue shield surmounted by a silver Indian head), and shined the stock of my BAR with linseed oil. When we snapped our heads to the right as we passed the reviewing stand, you could have heard my eyeballs click.

"Hey, Mauldin," muttered the Medicine Man, marching alongside, "did you ever take ROTC?"

"Me?" I said. "I went out for basketball."

Marching was K Company's thing. A typical week would start with a fifteen-mile hike on Monday, twenty miles on Tuesday, and so on up to thirty-five on Friday. This was done while carrying full field packs, including two-blanket rolls, and all equipment, including weapons. Sometimes the routes included surfaced roads, which we stared at wistfully while walking on the muddy shoulders, keeping five-yard intervals between men, as if walking into battle. Usually we kept to the back country, where the mud was really deep and there were no pretty strips of asphalt to distract us. Our equipment included heavy, old-fashioned, buckled galoshes. We used to speculate on whether dry feet were worth the monumental effort of wearing the things, but the choice was not ours.

We were allowed ten minutes' rest out of every hour on the marches. The most useful thing I learned in the army was the K Company trick of falling asleep instantly and waking exactly ten minutes later. I would blank out hitting the ditch when the whistle blew for rest, and wake up struggling to get my BAR slung over my shoulder. I can still switch myself off and on—in a chair, at a table, or even on my feet if there is something to lean against. For an infantry outfit, the hikes made sense and we knew it. In the history of K Company none of its men had ever dropped out of a march. If a soldier developed blisters his buddies would lend him their Band-aids, or if he seemed to be ailing they would carry his equipment, but he was supposed to finish on his own feet. This might not sound like much of a tradition, but it was an important thing in the company and a thread in whatever mysterious fabric makes esprit.

My chance to make it, socially speaking, in my new outfit came about during one of the marathon marches. On a rainy Thursday morning, with a thirty-miler ahead, I woke up feeling terrible. I thought it was a cold and knew I should report for sick call, but there seemed to be no fever and without a temperature an infantryman who reports sick is considered a malingerer unless he can come up with a broken bone. Besides, I knew I wouldn't have to make the next day's thirty-five-miler because my Friday-afternoon cartooning privileges had continued after my transfer to the infantry. I wouldn't have given up my weekly session at the drawing board for anything, but it had not been an unmixed blessing. Company K's captain had already told me that I could never seriously hope to become a noncom as long as I was merely a part-time dogface. Also, my afternoons off had let me in for a certain amount of ragging from the other foot soldiers. There was no malice in it; I think they sort of enjoyed having the cartoonist for the division newspaper around as a conversation piece. Still, you can see why I decided a slight headache and malaise shouldn't keep me from doing my best on that Thursday.

My best wasn't good enough. By noon, at about the eighteen-mile point, with freezing rain coming down in sheets, I remember the Medicine Man, who was marching alongside across the road, coming over and taking my pack. I would have preferred giving him that damned BAR, but in the infantry the last thing you give up is your weapon. The rest is hazy; I remember concentrating on planting one galosh in front of the other. During a rest stop one of our medics poured a couple of ounces of what he claimed was grain alcohol down my gullet. Back at camp I didn't stop but kept plodding through the mud like a little wind-up tin soldier, until I had crossed the parade ground to the hospital, where I was told I had measles.

When I emerged I found in a dozen subtle ways that I had become part of K Company. The first sign was that they gave my BAR to a bigger man and issued me a brand-new M-1 rifle. We had only recently graduated from bolt-action 1903 Springfields. Some infantrymen contended that this was not progress—that the M-1 couldn't touch the '03 for accuracy and that semi-automatic rifles would merely cause men to waste ammunition. The Medicine Man was one of our Springfield diehards. On the range one day, after throwing shots all over the target with his own new M-1, from a prone position, he borrowed one of the few '03s still around, slipped a canteen cover over the stock to make a recoil pad out of the thick bottom, and, disdaining the steadying sling, shot a perfect score at two hundred yards, standing up. He said that proved which rifle was best. The platoon sergeant said it proved that the Medicine Man's feet were flatter than his belly.

For a long time after the arrival of the M-1 you could tell an old soldier from a new one by watching the thumb of his trigger hand. If he draped it carelessly over the stock, in the most natural position, you knew he came in after the Springfield was phased out. A thumb in that position was often driven into the shooter's eye by the lusty recoil of the older weapon; an '03 man learned to tuck the member out of the way on the outboard side of the stock. Compared to the '03 the M-1 had the kick of an angel's shrug and you could stick your thumb up and hang a flag on it if you wished. Those of us who wanted to be identified as old soldiers hung our thumbs outside our M-1s while firing and hoped people would notice.

Lieutenant General Walter Krueger, the Third Army's commander, whose military domain covered most of the U.S. Southwest, was a tough old bird who liked to sneak up on his troops. Twice in the same month I encountered him while my company was doing field exercises. It is an awesome experience when a man with three stars on each shoulder steps

"The Army just fascinates me! I could stay here all afternoon asking questions."

Strictly an inside gag. The convoy has stopped for a "bladder break."

ning midnight oil in the corner of the 2 office. The shelf holds anatomy and ıce books, and two filing cases containing y pictorial "morgue": clippings from gazines of everything from azaleas to zebras.

When the draft started, the division greeted its new men with a cheery little booklet which I illustrated. Later, when asked why I never used my talent for constructive purposes, I always showed the booklet.

out of the bushes and demands to see your bare feet. As we sat on the ground and peeled off footgear, Krueger picked up our socks, inspected them for holes, and ran his hands inside our shoes to check for nails. Then he had us spread our toes as he peered between them, his august nose not six inches away. On one visit he had us unbutton our shirts so he could see if we had the proper long-handled underwear and were wearing our dogtags. When Krueger caught a soldier without dogtags there was hell to pay—for the culprit's regimental commander. The colonel naturally took it out on the responsible company commander, who clobbered the lieutenant, the sergeant, and the corporal. When Krueger found an infantryman with untreated blisters, athlete's foot, or leaky socks, the soldier's noncoms lost their stripes and his officers got official reprimands. We in the lower echelons sort of loved the crusty old boy, were delighted to learn that he had enlisted as a private and risen through the ranks, and were not surprised when later he turned out to be one of the most distinguished generals in the Pacific Theater of Operations.

One Friday afternoon at division headquarters I learned that a master sergeant from Krueger's office had arrived during the week and created a sensation by reporting directly to General William Key, the division commander. The grizzled sergeant, who had the build of a wine cask, hashmarks up and down his arm, and ribbons all over his chest, had brushed past Key's secretary and aides, handed the general his orders, and announced that he had come to teach the infantrymen of the 45th Division how to use their bayonets. It turned out that our visitor had always been something of a cutlery specialist. When stationed in the Far East shortly after the Russo-Japanese War, he had put on a demonstration with trench knife and bayonet for the edification and amusement of a young Japanese battalion commander named Tojo. The officer, fascinated, admitted that he had considered pointed weapons relics of the pre-gunpowder age, and asked the American to give him personal instruction. When Tojo became head man of the Japanese forces the bayonet was given strong emphasis in the training of his infantry. Some of the goriest news pictures of the thirties had showed Japanese troops using live Chinese prisoners as targets for this training. The idea was to cure squeamishness. If you can stick a poor bastard whose hands are tied behind him, you shouldn't have any trouble bayoneting some guy who's trying to do the same to you.

The Tojo story made good telling (Third Army headquarters swore it was true) and we all agreed that the least the sergeant could do was prepare us to defend ourselves against what he had wrought. My company had gone through bayonet drill, but it was nothing compared to what we learned when the old boy got around to us. He worked with my regiment a week, got us fairly proficient, then told us his real secret of successful combat with bayonets and knives.

"It's all in your form and your attitude," he said. "If you stick out your blade like you know what you're doing, look the enemy straight in the eye, and move in on him, he'll chicken out most of the time. It's common sense for *somebody* to quit. The thing is to make the other guy believe he's the only one with enough brains to do it."

Early in 1941 the division moved to new quarters at Camp Barkeley, near Abilene, Texas. I continued struggling with the sword by day and the pen by night. One day Walter Harrison stopped by my drawing board outside his office and observed that my new life as an infantryman was being reflected strongly in my drawings. He said he was pleased. I said I was certainly finding plenty of material in the 180th. Then I sought to amuse the colonel by pointing out that with all the marching I'd been doing since being transferred to a combat unit my feet had grown a full size from 8-C to 9-D.

"Very interesting," he said. "Your head seems about two sizes smaller, too, so that balances things."

Although at Camp Barkeley we still lived in tents and walked in mud, life was an improvement over Fort Sill because of the nearby town. Abilene had never depended upon the army for a living—indeed, it had never seen the army before—and so the people didn't resent us, at least in the beginning. Abilene had several colleges crowded with female students. We soldiers were mostly still adolescents, to whom schoolgirls and soda fountains were more familiar than whores and bootleg booze. In no time at all at least half of the men in the 45th had been adopted by one Abilene family or another. When the division pulled out some fifteen months later, there was hardly an unattached female left in town or on campus.

Herschel Schooley, the public-relations man for Hardin-Simmons University, was my local host. The Schooleys had a niece from Mexico, Missouri, who went out with me from time to time. One day Mrs. Schooley asked me why I didn't wear civilian clothes in town like most other soldiers. With Pearl Harbor still to come, the U.S. was technically not yet at war and we could dress as we pleased off duty. She said I was welcome to hang my suit in their hall closet. Was this a hint that the niece would like me better in mufti? I didn't have a suit—Charlie Curtis's brown one had finally turned completely purple and had been left in Phoenix—so I caught a bus to Dallas and bought a gray sharkskin at Neiman-Marcus. It cost over forty dollars, but why not? My bank account in Oklahoma City was able to absorb the blow. It turned out that the niece preferred me in my uniform. We continued dating casually and the suit gathered dust in the hall closet.

On Saturday afternoons and Sundays I hung around the Abilene *Reporter-News,* which printed the *45th Division News* for a modest fee. I made a particular point of getting to know the photoengravers, having learned that these guys are to a newspaper artist what accompanists are to a singer. They can make a bad one seem passable or a good one seem terrible, depending upon their ability or their mood. The *Reporter-News* engraving crew showed me everything and taught me to do some of the work. The news staff of the Abilene paper were astonished at the latitude given our little division weekly. At the time I didn't have enough experience to appreciate the fact that we had more editorial freedom than many civilian journalists. This was partly due to Walter Harrison, of course; when we outraged some officer or other and the propriety of the very existence of the *45th Division News* was questioned, our little colonel would snarl back at the critics and circle about us protectively, throwing up smoke screens like a destroyer escort. Didn't our detractors believe in freedom of the press? Didn't they consider soldiers human beings entitled to opinions of their own? Were the officers just sore because their pictures hadn't been printed? Most of the division's highest-ranking officers were in business or politics in Oklahoma and knew they would have to reckon with the waspish Harrison when he went back to being a journalist himself. Even after we lost Harrison later that year to the Command and General Staff School in Fort Leavenworth, his spirit prevailed. The *News* came under the hands of a series of officers: Major Tom Johnson, Captain Fred Stoft, Major William Ruggles, Major Lee Gilstrap, Lieutenant Richard Hagood, plus a few others—and all went along with our raunchy spirit. Some even contributed to it. Of course, what really made the *News* viable was the fact that it was equally lucky in the succession of division commanders over the next four years. Like William Key, our first general, they seemed to feel that we were more useful than painful. We continued our policy of ignoring the doings of brass hats and printing mostly news about soldiers. A couple of times I even lampooned Key himself, to the consternation of our friends at the *Reporter-News,* who assumed I was bucking for a month or so in the stockade. The general thought the cartoons were funny and asked for both of them.

In the late summer of 1941 the division loaded into trucks and headed for the swamps of Louisiana to join the rest of the Third Army in mock battle against the First Army, from the east. These were the biggest U.S. military maneuvers ever held, involving some half a million troops: more than twice the size of our entire army a year earlier. If the Germans or the Japanese had any spies watching us, they must have laughed their heads off. Our War Department was drafting men and mobilizing guardsmen and reserves faster than they could be equipped. Some of our artillery pieces were stovepipes mounted on wagon wheels. Many machine guns were carved from two-by-fours, and numbers of in-

One of several cartoons kidding the division commander, Major General William S. Key. I can't remember the exact reason for this drawing, but it had something to do with gasoline rationing.

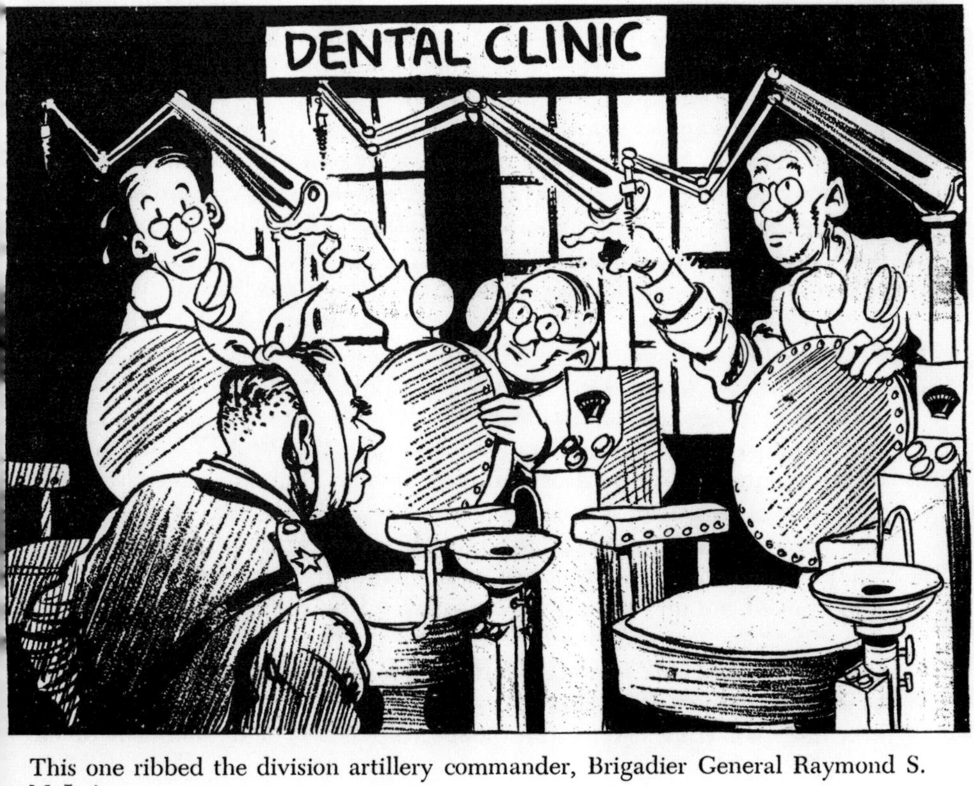

This one ribbed the division artillery commander, Brigadier General Raymond S. McLain.

fantrymen still carried painted wooden rifles which appeared to have been borrowed from color guards in high-school football parades. From time to time military aircraft were to be seen, including a few biplanes which looked like retreads from the Lafayette Escadrille. William T. Piper sent an airplane salesman named Bill Strohmeier in an olive-painted demonstrator from the Cub factory in Lock Haven, Pennsylvania, to try to convince the army that the machine would be good for artillery spotting and liaison work. Strohmeier dropped little paper bags of flour on soldiers' heads. It was hard for a man covered with Pillsbury's best to deny he'd been bombed. The Cub was accepted.

Colonel Harrison, no mean salesman himself, told division headquarters that the *News* staff, though unable to publish a paper in the piny bogs, should function as a sort of press agency, gathering material about individual soldiers and sending stories and pictures to their home-town papers. They gave us a pickup truck, with bench seats and a canvas cover in back, and a driver named Jack Church. Riddle and Pepper, of the original staff, were still with us, but the editing was taken over by Joe Stocker and Don Robinson, both draftees with professional backgrounds on the Oklahoma City papers under Harrison. We got a new reporter named Johnny Waddell, a round corporal on a small frame, with a big heart, a self-deprecating sense of humor, and an unquenchable thirst for beer. He became my favorite model. Johnny was sympathetic about the fact that I had always had trouble drawing wrinkles in clothing accurately. As long as I provided a bottle of beer for a prop, he would hold any pose until I got all the wrinkles down on paper. He acted the part of rifleman fixing a bottle of beer on the end of his rifle. He was a carpenter sawing with a beer bottle. Once he was an unwed mother waiting hopefully outside the soldier-father's tent with a wailing beer bottle cradled in his arms.

Our photographer on the *News* at that time was Private First Class A. Y. Owen, another *Daily Oklahoman* alumnus. A shy fellow who studied judo in his spare time, he used his muscle to wield a Speed Graphic as if it were a Leica. He was continually sneaking up on soldiers and trying to get pictures *Life* would buy. He often made it, too. The magazine paid him five dollars apiece. I agreed with A. Y. that this was pretty chintzy of Henry Luce and his famous journal, considering that I got the same price for a drawing from a single newspaper. However, I also agreed with him that he probably needed *Life* more than the magazine needed him, that *Life* knew it, and that *Life* knew he knew it. Once A. Y. talked me into posing with a rifle and helmet, poured a bucket of water over me, superimposed a negative of the moon, underexposed the print to make it look like night, and sent it to *Life* as a portrait of peacetime preparedness. They fired it back at him with a note explaining that rain does not come out of the moon. Undaunted, and unknown to me,

Owen sent it to the Phoenix papers with my name. They cropped the moon and printed me looking all brave and wet, upsetting my mother no end, because I had been telling her I was keeping regular hours and was being careful not to catch cold.

One day Don Robinson, Jack Church, and I were cruising around in our truck, Don in the back with his typewriter on his knees and me in front with my sketchbook, when we came upon a scene from my childhood. Almost an entire regiment of the 1st Cavalry Division was moving across a large field a half mile ahead, on horseback, with the sun glittering on its weapons and its guidons fluttering.

"My God," said Jack, stopping our machine with a jerk that almost cost Robinson his typewriter. "I never thought I'd see a sight like that outside of the movies."

"It's not real," Don said.

I started to explain about the 1st Cavalry and how I seemed destined to keep running into it. I was so anxious to prove myself an authority on the subject that I forgot the obvious: a unit of that size in a war zone would have scouts and outriders all over. I also forgot that the 1st Cav was on the "enemy" side. A horseman popped up alongside us, three more hemmed us in on the other sides with carbines leveled, and we were captured. I found myself enjoying the situation. Don, however, was trying to get some copy mailed and was all business. He pulled out a green armband and told the cavalrymen we were neutral press. The rider in front of us brought his horse alongside to see what further proof we had, if any. This move was a tactical error. Don hollered at Jack, who jammed the truck into gear and roared away.

We learned that a cavalry charger full of oats is much faster in his lower gears than any army truck. They couldn't stop us, but they could and did ride in circles around us for the first quarter mile or so, whooping and emptying their carbines at us. Blank cartridges use wads to hold their powder charges; at very close range the wads emerge as projectiles and hurt like hell. By the time we got up to fifty miles an hour and began to pull away, the troopers had dealt out the punishment we probably deserved: our ears were ringing and our hides were stinging.

The maneuvers were the mounted cavalry's swan song. Actually, their mechanization was already well along, with most units already in jeeps, armored cars, and trucks. We had been lucky enough to see one of their last big horse shows on the day we got shot up. It was worth the pain. In fact, I got my favorite cartoon of the entire war from the experience. Sitting in our office tent that night with a little breadboard I had bought as an easel on my knees, trying to think up cartoons to send out to the papers, I made a rough sketch of an ancient cavalry master sergeant, with hashmarks to his elbow and a beer-barrel gut, standing beside a jeep which had broken off its left front wheel in a rut. Covering his eyes in

Some maneuver carto

This one puzzled the
Medicine Man.

A lot of my gags still had a distinctly civilian flavor.

"Could I borrow a ton of sugar?"

"*Willie, you left a ring around the edge!*"

Here Joe is still an Indian and Willie still looks like Johnny Waddell.

"*O.K.—it's a swap, if ya throw in yer tin hat.*"

his was no empty gag. Much of our "artillery" s still made of lumber, tars" of stovepipe, etc. army was a long way rom combat readiness.

anguish with one hand, the old horseman had drawn his service pistol and was about to put a bullet through the radiator.

I kept learning over and over that real-life experiences were necessary to my drawings. When I begged off field trips during maneuvers and hung around the "office" more than a few days, my mud stopped looking wet and my pen-and-ink warriors lost authority. When a dogface carries a rifle upright at sling position, he hooks his thumb through the juncture of stock and leather. What about when he slings it muzzle down in rain? It would not be so comfortable to stick a thumb where the sling joins the other end of the forepiece from the stacking swivel—and yet it doesn't look natural to have the guy hold the strap elsewhere. How did I hold my own rifle? I couldn't remember. Embarrassed, I had to go borrow somebody's weapon and find out. If a drawing lacked authenticity the idea behind it became ineffectual, too. This was especially true in the infantry, where a man lived intimately with a few pieces of equipment and resented seeing it pictured inaccurately. Once I drew the safety ring on the wrong side of a hand grenade hanging from a man's belt. It was a tiny thing, and I couldn't find a razor blade to scratch out the detail for a correction, so I was tempted to let it go. In the end, though, I signed my name backward and asked the engraver to reverse the whole drawing. I never regretted it.

The best things I got out of going afield, however, went beyond technical details for drawings. One day in a swamp I stumbled across the Medicine Man. He had dismantled his rifle, immersed the receiver end in a gallon of boiling water over a Coleman stove, and with a rod and patch was swabbing out an accumulation of wax and primer fouling from the blanks he had been firing. Even allowing for the fact that he was working with a hot and greasy chunk of metal, his greeting to me was less than effusive.

"What you been doing?" he grunted.

"Oh, I've been working."

"I saw something with your name on it in a Shreveport paper. You drew a fighter airplane crashed in a big pile of pots and pans behind some chicken wire. The pilot was climbing over the fence with a stupid look on his face and a couple or three civilian women and kids were looking at him."

"Did you think it was any good?"

"They must have left the caption off."

"There wasn't any caption."

"I guess I didn't get it, then."

"What the hell?" I said. "What do you mean you didn't get it? There was this big scrap drive, see, and the pilot made his contribution, you might say, without really meaning to."

"What scrap drive?"

"If you'd been around any of these little towns lately, you'd know they've got a big aluminum collection going all over the country. There's a shortage for building airplanes."

"No kidding." He looked apologetic. "I guess we been in the woods too much."

I spent the next few days with K Company, got my feet wet a couple of times, and went back to the press section with a pocketful of ideas. Not one was directly related to anything I had seen or experienced, but all were about the infantry, none were contrived, and the Medicine Man told me he understood most of them.

My first book was published in Louisiana that summer. A couple of Texans in straw hats, seersucker suits, and two-toned shoes drove up to our tent one day in a big Oldsmobile and asked for me. I remember I was sorting some field-artillery sketches, and those fellows had me charmed from the moment they said my fame as a soldier-artist had spread all the way to San Antonio, where they ran a modest publishing house called Universal Press. They wanted to print a souvenir book of my maneuver drawings. Colonel Frank Duffy, the 45th Division's judge advocate general, obligingly drew up a contract for us. Robinson and Stocker excused me from my turn at mimeograph cranking and envelope licking. I got a three-day pass to Shreveport, and Church drove me to a motel at the edge of town. At the end of two days and two nights I had finished some three dozen cartoons and sketches. I felt they weren't quite enough but had run out of money for room rent. The Shreveport *Times*, which had used a number of my drawings during maneuvers, let me set up shop on the big table in the paper's editorial conference room. One more day and part of a night later I had completed the book, which I named *Star Spangled Banter*. My only excuse for the title is that I was tired. The editorial staff found me happily sacked out on the table next morning, helped me mail the material to San Antonio, and gently pointed me in the direction of the 45th Division. Universal Press worked fast. The maneuvers had only a few weeks to go, but before we started packing for the trip back to Barkeley copies of the book began turning up. It was a handsomely printed paperback, priced at twenty-five cents, with an introduction by Reg Manning in Phoenix. I was nineteen years old and suddenly I was watching people with their noses buried in a book I had published. The fact that I didn't hear another word from Universal Press and never learned where they mailed my royalties hardly hurt at all. A couple of months later, the Camp Barkeley post exchange, which had taken on a large consignment of the books, told me they had a couple of hundred unsold copies on hand and asked what to do with them. I sent them out to everybody I knew and solved my Christmas-gift problem that year.

Sergeant Don Robinson, an Oklahoma City reporter who became a fine editor and nursed the *News* through the war.

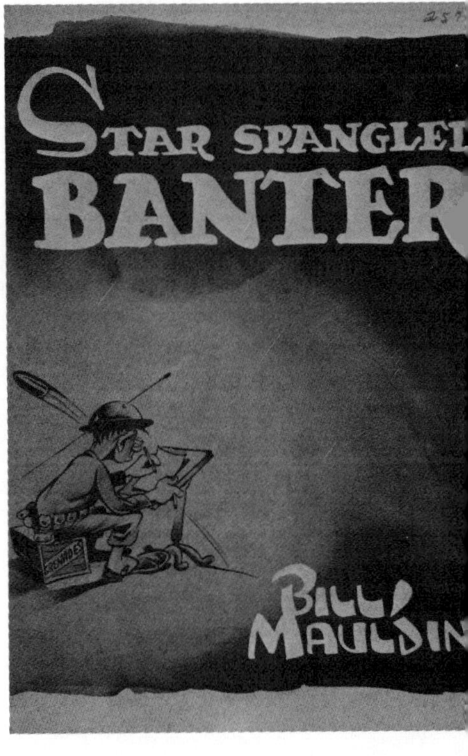

My first published book, at age nineteen. I'm still waiting for my royalties.

More constructive work. I did a series of editorial cartoons on security. They were reproduced as posters around the division.

The first cartoon of the cavalry sergeant killing his crippled jeep. It was published two inches high on the back page of *Yank*.

One of several subsequent renditions of the same idea. Each was labeled "redrawn by request." It was my favorite cartoon and I was determined to put it across.

6

The real war started for us a few months after maneuvers. I was spending a weekend pass in Abilene's Wooten Hotel, wearing my sharkskin suit, and was joined at breakfast in the coffeeshop by Don Robinson, in his pin-striped blue serge. The division's chief of staff, Colonel James Styron, came in sporting a casual ensemble of flannel slacks and tweed jacket, stopped by our table, and asked if we had heard of the custom of rising when a senior officer entered a room. On our feet, one of us—I think it was Don—said we didn't realize the rule applied in mufti. Styron told us that the question would be henceforth academic because the Japanese had bombed Pearl Harbor, for the past fifteen minutes ours had been a nation at war, and we had all better report back to camp and get out of our civvies, which we would not be allowed to wear again for the duration.

As I look back on it, our country's situation was not good, and you'd think that as military men we'd have been the first to realize it. Germany had taken all of Europe and was deep into Russia and North Africa; the Japanese looked invincible in Asia and had now destroyed our navy. Our army was still of puny size and not exactly tuned to fighting pitch even after Louisiana. A lot of our artillery remained in the fake stovepipe-and-lumber stage. Cartridges still had to be rationed on the firing ranges. You'd have thought we'd be preoccupied with these matters. I understand our West Coast forces were somewhat shaken, with a Japanese invasion considered imminent, but a thousand miles or so inland our main concern was finding cardboard boxes in which to mail our civilian clothes home. The first sergeant of the division headquarters company announced that any suits found on the following Saturday inspection would be thrown "straight in the insinuator." My own topkick in K Company said he planned to give the Salvation Army any nongovernment threads he turned up. It's hard to believe nowadays, with the military establishment practically owning the national economy, but we used to let our defenses get into pitiful shape between wars. Then, when something like Pearl Harbor occurred, we didn't even have sense enough to get scared.

One immediate effect of the war was a sharp increase in the number of local weddings. Nature always seems to step up the mating instinct when killing is afoot; in Abilene apparently our libidos grasped the situation ahead of our brains. Since maneuvers my girl in town had been a Hardin-Simmons University sophomore named Norma Jean Humphries, from Toyah, Texas. A pretty brunette with freckles and a high scholastic record, she was a premedical student intent on becoming a doctor, not a cartoonist's constant companion. Over the weeks, I sent her flowers and gradually convinced her that a smart girl could do both things. In February, 1942, at the age of twenty and a half (Jean was eighteen), I forged my father's permission on a marriage certificate, and Jean and I joined a long procession of other couples on their way to the division chaplain, who was probably the busiest man in the outfit at that time. He knew me personally, and wasn't too busy to warn me that if I was up to some funny business and that wasn't really my old man's signature, under Texas law the union could become legal within a short time anyway, and I wouldn't be able to sneak out of it, minor or no minor. I was genuinely outraged at the suggestion. Having come from a broken home, I said, I was not a trifler about such matters.

My father, then working as a steamfitter in a California shipyard, was pleased when I told him about the forgery. Knowing I was a crafty penman who could duplicate either parent's signature, he took it as a sign of fealty. Actually, I wasn't playing favorites; it simply seemed to me that this was a father-son matter. As for my mother, she arrived on the next train after the wedding, spent a couple of days looking the bride over, and went home, apparently satisfied. My brother, Sid, who had recently become a married man himself, sent his congratulations and the news that he had gotten a medical discharge from a naval boot camp and was riveting airplanes in San Diego. My grandmother was delighted to learn that Jean was a premedical student; after all, half a doctor in the family was better than no doctor at all. My infantry captain said he hoped this new development did not mean I was going to start expecting a promotion.

We intended for Jean to continue at college, and for a while she did.

As for me, a whole new life started. We lived in a rented room in town. Division policy at the time was to give all married men class A passes, which meant we were free to leave camp when off duty. However, because of stepped-up wartime training activity, the rule about getting back in time to stand reveille in the morning was reinforced. Before, I had thought five o'clock was a terrible time to get up. Now it had to be 3 A.M. in order for me to catch the bus—and I learned that it is much harder to get out of a double bed at that hour than a single one. Meanwhile, my work on the newspaper had expanded to a whole half-page of cartoons weekly, which meant a session at the drawing board almost every night after the infantry let me go.

"If you aren't careful," said Captain Fred Stoft, our new officer in charge, "you'll be a burned-out has-been before you're old enough to vote."

Possibly out of pity for a perishing cartoonist, or because Stoft couldn't think of a way to fill that half page after I was gone, division headquarters pulled rank on K Company's command. I was given more time on special-duty status, and was promoted to private first class. Since I was still infantry property, the rank had to come from that unit's table of organization.

"You've cost me a third-cook's rating," the captain said, bitterly. "It's going to raise hell with morale in the kitchen, you goddamn quartermaster fugitive."

"He's full of crap," the Medicine Man comforted me when I told him I felt awful and wanted to give the stripe back. "He didn't pull it off anybody's arm, did he? He was hoarding it. He thinks he's a watchdog for the U.S. Treasury. It serves him right to lose it."

My wife wasn't unhappy about it, either. Since all of my outside income from the *Daily Oklahoman* reprints and most of my army pay was spent on our room rent, she had been working after school in an ice-cream parlor and bringing home quarts of the stuff for supper. Now she was able to quit her job, devote the time to her homework, and buy hamburgers, which stuck to our ribs better than frozen skimmed milk.

Jean and I both had grown up under hard enough circumstances so that we had a strong instinct for salting away whatever money we could. In our case this amounted mostly to pennies and nickels, which we kept in a Woolworth's china pig with a slot in its back. Part of Jean's "dowry" had been a large, decrepit alarm clock with a puny bell which belied its size and, worse, sometimes failed to go off at all. Our intention was to buy a reliable clock as soon as the pig was full. About the time the beast would begin to feel pregnant when lifted, I would wake up next morning half an hour late and smack the errant timepiece with the flat of my hand, whereupon it would jingle apologetically. I would leap into my uniform while Jean dumped the pig's contents into a handkerchief and

"It's the only way we can make bed check since this marryin' boom started."

Married life inspired a new line of ideas. The address was ours in Abilene.

Another fake "redrawn by request." Living in town made me hate the bus lines.

"No news, fellas, just 'Garden Beautiful' asking do I wanna renew my subscription."

The Elks sponsored a national cartoon contest to encourage letters to soldiers. I won second prize, $200, with this effort. It was by far the biggest money I had ever made.

tied it up. At the bus stop there were always two or three taxis waiting for us tardy types. The trip to my company took about half an hour and cost four dollars; I spent the time counting the money out of the handkerchief and making little stacks of coins so I wouldn't have to wait at our destination while the driver sorted chicken feed. We never did get to buy a new clock in all the months we lived in Abilene.

During the week married soldiers were a pitiable lot, but on Sundays life became beautiful. Abilene was not a bachelors' town. All the women were taken or spoken for. A stag in uniform could stand around on a sunny holiday and watch the couples stroll, or he could go to the drugstore, get a pint whiskey prescription for a nickel (this was how one got around the Texas dry laws), wrap the bottle in a paper bag, insert a straw from the soda fountain, and take a long walk. If he felt gregarious he could start a fight. The MPs took a dim view of such behavior because they appreciated and wanted to perpetuate the town's unworldliness, so the miscreant was almost guaranteed a free ride back to camp and a night in the guardhouse.

In the early spring of 1942 the 45th Division was included in the plan for the invasion of North Africa and was sent by train to Massachusetts for a summer of maneuvers and amphibious training. Our wartime departure from Abilene was a contrast to our peacetime arrival, when we had whooped and hollered and the city had turned out to greet us. We left in the dark, subdued and grim. Everybody pulled a lot of guard duty on the flatcars. Railroads are the best way to move large military units but they are vulnerable to sabotage, and at first we took the danger seriously, most of us resisting the urge to ride in the cabs of the lashed-down trucks and manfully pacing our cars as we barreled through the sooty Midwest and industrial East at fifty miles an hour in twenty-degree weather. The sleeping cars ran out of washing water early in the trip and I'm sure most people who saw us pass in daytime thought we were the first all-black division. Finally, at night when it got colder and the train seemed to go faster, we took to climbing into the trucks to avoid frostbite. This was risky. It was easy to fall asleep on the cushions. Theoretically a man could be executed for that in wartime. If they had shot all of us who were caught napping in the cabs of those vehicles the division would have been decimated before it ever got overseas.

I remember one cold afternoon when I was on a flatcar during a long stop on a siding in Pennsylvania. I stood at the end of the car, my rifle with fixed bayonet slung on my shoulder, trying to look alert and soldierly for the benefit of a gaggle of farm kids who stood behind a fence looking up at me. Their mother came out of their house a quarter of a mile away and crossed the field toward us, carrying a basket. It held a pot of coffee, a stack of paper cups, and a sack of cookies, doughnuts, and sandwiches.

She handed the basket up to me, told me to help myself, and asked me to pass it along to the other cars. As we started to move out, I asked her how we could get the basket and pot back to her, and she told us to keep them.

"God bless you," she said.

I had been in the army for a year and a half and we had been at war for several months, but I believe that was the first time I enjoyed the rather special feeling a soldier is supposed to get about the people he is presumably in uniform for. The lady's act was one of simple generosity: she might have done the same for a section crew repairing the siding on a cold day. But she wouldn't have blessed them, would she? I felt nine feet high. She was my country and she was worth all the soot and chilblains.

In Fort Devens I was spending my nights with the boys again, but the living was better. For the first time the division was in barracks, with grass underfoot instead of mud. For our Indian soldiers the biggest advantage of New England over the Southwest was that they could walk into saloons and drink legally. This was still forbidden to them at home because of the old notion that, ounce for ounce, redskins became crazier than whites on booze. Considering the rotgut they used to get from shady traders, the story might have been true. A poisoned savage was more likely to stagger than a white who was merely drunk. The bars of central Massachusetts were suddenly full of copper-colored soldiers. Nobody had got around to telling the nervous citizens that an Indian in the 45th was likely to be better educated and more civilized than the average New England WASP. The Medicine Man, whose sense of humor was eventually to be literally the death of him, couldn't let this sort of opportunity pass. My friend was in a Fitchburg bar one night with some tribal cronies from various parts of the 3rd Battalion. Taking note of the fact that all the civilians in the place were staring, the Medicine Man pretended to be drunker than he was. He stalked over to the juke box, selected "The Eyes of Texas Are Upon You," which was sweeping the country at the moment, and invested a nickel.

"All right, I want every loyal citizen in this place to stand at attention during the playing of the anthem," he announced, drawing his pocketknife. "Any citizen who wishes to remain sitting may do so, earless." They all stood until the last note died.

"Now I will admit that I am from Oklahoma and I hate Texas," he confessed. "I would like to buy all you loyal citizens a drink." He did, too. The Fitchburgians went away agreeing that the Indians were still as mysterious as the Pilgrims had found them.

Another Indian episode in Massachusetts involved a girl named Ann Michaels, who worked for a local radio station and beamed a reveille-time program each morning at Fort Devens and another army post to the east called Camp Edwards. Ann was a cheery girl who brightened our mornings even as we winced at her radio name: Devvie Edwards. Don Robinson had become friendly with her. One day he brought her to Devens, where she became enchanted by an Indian dance group, organized and directed by Major Lee Gilstrap and Sergeant Arnold Woodall, the division public-relations staff. Devvie, or Ann, suggested that the redskin image might be helped if the group appeared on her show. Gilstrap, Woodall, and Robinson agreed. Unfortunately, the dancers were volunteers, under no compulsion to get up a couple of hours ahead of what they considered an already-unreasonable reveille. All but one refused. This lone Indian was a big, mean-looking specimen, with scars which made him look especially savage. He had been grunting at Ann in monosyllables, according to Don, and she was more than a little afraid of him. What she didn't know, and what Don would have told her if the brave hadn't gouged him in the ribs, was that her Indian was the only egghead in the division whom the Medicine Man considered his superior in English literature. On the morning of the broadcast the whole division was tuned in—even those who didn't have to get up at reveille.

"Uh, soldier . . . brave . . ." Ann started.

"Call me soldier."

"Well, I'm glad you could make it."

Silence.

"You're sure you're not a chief or something? You look pretty fierce to me."

"No. Simple brave. Call me soldier."

"O.K. Swell. Now, how can I put this? I would like you to talk about the dances you do. You understand? Maybe you could tell us what they mean."

"As I see it, the dances are a series of progressions," the soldier said. Here I quote Don Robinson's own account: "He then delivered a learned lecture on the history and meaning of the Indian dance form, and concluded by comparing the narrative elements in the Indian dance chant and action with those in Chaucer's *Canterbury Tales.*

" '*Canterbury Tales?*' asked Ann.

"The Indian unhesitatingly recited a substantial portion of the Prologue, thereby clarifying his point and dispelling a myth recently believed in Massachusetts about the cultural level of the American aborigine in the twentieth century." *

At Fort Devens we took off our thunderbird shoulder patches, presumably so the enemy wouldn't know where we were until we jumped him in

* *News of the 45th,* University of Oklahoma Press, 1944.

Sketches on the troop train.

Player on left is Don Robinson; on right, with hand in pocket, Bill Barrett.

sketches were made on the flatcars. It was too damned cold.

Africa. We turned in our World War I style tin hats, which resembled soup plates, and received the latest pot type. At Cape Cod we practiced clambering down nets from ships into boats, then jumping out of the boats into the water. Because of the shroud of secrecy which kept everybody outside New England from knowing who we were and where we were going—even the War Department in Washington lost track of us once and thought we were still in Texas—publication of the *45th Division News* was suspended. This created a certain amount of panic among those of us who still belonged to line companies. Although fully aware of the value of my infantry background and associations I had never given up the idea of eventually getting transferred permanently to the paper's staff and had lately maneuvered myself into spending more and more time behind my drawing board, which the G-2 boys had kindly brought along with their office gear. In K Company the captain had recently told me that I was now referred to as the Unknown Soldier. Not only was I becoming invisible, but nobody had been able to figure out a job for me in case they should find themselves stuck with me in combat.

Then suddenly somebody in Washington moved a pin on a map and we were taken off the North African invasion lineup. We sewed back our shoulder patches, the *45th Division News* was back in business, and everybody relaxed. To my astonishment, I found myself feeling a certain letdown. Esprit has a way of sneaking up on the worst of us, and anybody who knows the army is aware that esprit usually involves one's immediate comrades, not one's flag or whatever high principles dragged it into its current battle.

"You're a victim of mixed emotions," the Medicine Man told me. "It's like watching your mother-in-law drive off a cliff in your new car."

"Mauldin spends so much time at division headquarters that his arches are coming back," the platoon sergeant remarked. "Join us later this week when we sneak up on New Hampshire, walking through poison ivy all the way, with full equipment and half a canteen each."

I invaded Boston instead that Friday. The local office of Scribner's, the book publishers, agreed with me that a volume of war cartoons might indeed become a best seller someday soon, but I didn't strike them as the most likely author. The *Christian Science Monitor* looked at my stuff with some interest, but the editor to whom I talked felt that my soldier characters were too sardonic. I didn't help matters by lighting a cigarette in his office. Nobody had warned me that one doesn't do this at the *Monitor*. The editor suggested I try the *Harvard Crimson*. At the *Crimson* I found appreciation but was told that they couldn't use contributions from nonstudents.

"Contributions, hell," I said. "I'm trying to sell the stuff."

Finally, I struck pay dirt at the *Herald*, which bought a full-page color layout of soldier cartoons for twenty-five dollars, and at the *Globe*, which used some single panels. Looking back on it, I'm amazed that I got in to see any of those editors. I had reached twenty, but looked a sallow sixteen, with a cigarette usually hanging from my lip, and squinting eyes which people keep telling me were sullen in those days. "I thought maybe you had stolen that uniform," a Scribner's man told me, years later.

On weekend passes I went as far afield as New York and Washington, trying to peddle my stuff. I was armed with letters from Walter Harrison telling anybody it might concern how good and authentic my soldier cartoons were. In Washington Congressman Mike Monroney from Oklahoma, a former newspaperman and loyal follower of the 45th Division, tried to get various publishers interested in me. Part of the trouble was that publishers are not often available on weekends. Also, the war was new. Even *Yank*, the new army weekly, was chary about publishing my drawings. They ran a few, but the cartoon editor complained that my characters were too unsoldierly. When I challenged his credentials as a military expert, he wrote me a tart letter saying *Yank* was getting sick and tired of this sort of criticism. According to him, the staff spent half a day every week drilling on Governors Island, which was a hell of a lot more soldiering than I was likely to see in a divisional public relations office.

In the fall of 1942 the division was ordered to Pine Camp, New York, a frigid spot near Watertown and the Canadian border, for arctic training. I believe the new plot was to send us to occupied Norway. Of course, we didn't know that at the time, any more than we had known for sure about Africa, but it wasn't hard to make educated guesses. Before leaving Massachusetts, the *News* staff heard from Walter Harrison. He wasn't coming back to the 45th from staff school but was being assigned to an active sector of the Pacific war, which made us feel better for him, because the salty little weekend colonel really wanted to soldier. By this time most of our senior National Guard officers had been replaced by regulars. Even the good-natured General Key, who hadn't minded being kidded in cartoons, was relieved by Troy Middleton, a professional, who was called from retirement for the job. This purge upset the division at first—after all, a National Guard unit gets to be a sort of social club—and there were mutterings about "The West Point Protective Association," but it all turned out to be justified by the 45th's combat record. Indeed, Middleton himself, after eventually leading the division through a distinguished beginning in combat, went on to become a corps commander.

Harrison's farewell letter noted my cartoons for the Boston papers, which had been sent to him, then reminded Robinson and Major Gilstrap not to let me worm my way completely out of the infantry.

"The bat-eared bastard is busting with ambition and really knows what's best for him," he wrote, "but he is essentially shiftless in things that have

Massachusetts and its coast fascinated southwesterners in the division.
Our Indians fascinated the New Englanders.

"We do it with dogs back in the States—on a somewhat smaller scale, of course!"

Yank encouraged my penchant for dumb gags. These two are typical of what the cartoon editor considered military humor.

"I haven't the heart to tell 'em we got bunged up this way at the roller rink."

no immediate bearing on the work he likes to do. He will slither out of the reality of K Company and into being a full-time gag man if you don't keep an eye on him."

The colonel mentioned with some pride that, while he was in Washington waiting for assignment, he had learned that the *45th Division News* had attracted some attention among morale specialists, and that the army was taking a serious look at the idea of authorizing similar operations for other divisions. Hot damn, I thought—any well-rounded table of organization for such a journal as ours will have to have a place for a cartoonist. I shared the colonel's pride and said a little prayer for the project. Imagine a sergeant-cartoonist in a military T.O., and me as the precedent setter!

"The whole idea is terrible," said Robinson. "What makes us click is lack of status and insecurity. The fact that we can be dissolved and sent back to our units at any time keeps us on the ball and our product sharp."

Don needn't have worried. Right up to the end of the war, during his entire tenure as editor, he saw to it that the position of the *45th Division News* remained as precarious, and therefore its condition presumably as sharply honed, as it had been at the beginning. Even after Troy Middleton became a faithful reader and devotee of its editorial policies, the paper managed to stay on thin ice.

By this time the *News* staff had undergone a turnover from transfers and discharges. Riddle, Pepper, Waddell, and Owen were gone, along with Sam St. John and Merle Tannenbaum, who had been with us briefly at Barkeley. The new reporters were Fred Sheehan, a jaunty character from Throg's Neck, Long Island, and Bill Barrett from Cleveland. Both were experienced reporters from civilian life, and both had spent enough time in soldiering after being drafted to know the army. They not only fitted into the *45th Division News;* they largely built its tradition after their arrival. George Tapscott, a former copy boy from the *Daily Oklahoman,* had just realized his ambition to graduate to staff photographer when the draft caught him. Now he was going to get a chance to use his camera full time in the army and was beside himself with joy. Like me, all these men were still members of line companies on temporary assignment to the *News.* If Don's theory about insecurity creating quality was right, we were going to put out a hell of a paper.

In Pine Camp we learned to dig foxholes in ice (we never saw the actual ground there) and how to survive in thirty-below-zero weather, with brisk winds across Lake Ontario driving the frost factor down to about eighty below. As I recall, the technique was to burrow into a snowdrift, pull up your collar, and shudder violently until relieved by your replacement. It seemed wasteful to send a whole division such a distance to learn shivering.

Although I had told Jean to stay in Abilene and learn how to get rich practicing medicine just in case, she had quit college and joined me. We rented a room in the home of a hospitable Watertown family for a reasonable sum, plus an agreement on my part that I would help stoke the coal furnace. This made sense; it was no trouble for me to lay on a couple of scoops on my way to the bus at 3 A.M., and it meant the family didn't have to bank the fire at night and wake up in a cold house. I heard they bought an automatic stoker first thing after the war. In most ways domestic life in Watertown was almost like Abilene again. The evenings were great, the early rising hours were awful, and the town's friendliness belied the bitter weather. I even managed to spend a lot of hours hanging around the Watertown *Times,* which used a few cartoons and considered my offer to send back some exclusive stuff from overseas. I decided I liked the people, could get used to the weather, and would like to build up a readership here in case my relationship with the *Oklahoman* didn't work out after the war.

In February, 1943, the division moved to Camp Pickett and Camp Patrick Henry, Virginia, to practice more amphibious landings and stage for the invasion of Sicily. Jean and I hadn't realized how lucky we'd been in our past dealings with civilians around army camps. Whereas we had been able to rent nice rooms in Abilene and Watertown for less than fifty dollars a month, the crummiest quarters in Virginia were twice that amount—when you could find anything. Luckily, my specialist's rating, stolen from K Company's kitchen, had been converted to a sergeancy under new army rules of rank. We finally rented a room in Blackstone from a surly woman who eyed my new chevrons and demanded a hundred a month, which about summed up my pay and allowances. *The Daily Oklahoman* was still reprinting me faithfully and depositing a weekly five-spot in the bank, so we fooled our landlady and ate.

"Let's get a few things straight, sahjent," she said one day when I complained about the lack of hot water in the bathroom, which served four upstairs bedrooms, each of which housed a soldier and his wife. "I don't like the ahmy," she said. "I 'specially don't like your ahmy." (I assume from this that she meant the Yankee army, although you could have cut the Southern and Southwestern accents of most 45th Division troops with a knife.) "As long as I'm stuck with you, I'll get whatever I can and put out as little as I can. Do I make myself clear?"

As embarkation time grew nearer and security tightened, the division's married men received orders almost with relief to send their women home. I haven't reminisced much in these pages about Jean or my brief time with her. Like many marriages contracted in wars, ours came to grief quickly after the homecoming. Although Jean belongs in these pages because she's part of them, I still find our relationship a difficult subject,

As we did amphibious training on Cape Cod, my humor remained frivolous but became occasionally pertinent.

45th's Card Ready Soon

Bill Mauldin's 45th Division Christmas Card will be sale at all PX's in the division area by early next week, it v announced Friday.

Fifteen thousand of the cards have been ordered initially, and more will be ordered when these run low.

The cards will sell for two cents each. The price is made possible because of the quantity ordered. (One outfit here last year paid several times this amount for cards, being unable to make a quantity purchase.)

POSTAGE FREE

Cards will be on good quality paper, and the envelope is included in the price. Christmas cards, these and all others, may be mailed free by service men if they are of standard size.

A reproduction of the Mauldin Thunderbird card is carried with this story. The card is 4⅞ by 4 inches — the size illustrated. The card will be printed in color.

In the original announcement of the cards last week, it was stated that profits would go to Army Emergency relief. As the 45th Division News has turned the project over to the post exchange, the News will derive no profit. The post exchange is offering the cards barely above cost, and any profit will be handled in the usual manner — being returned in dividends to units in the division.

FIRST 45th CARD

Sgt. Bill Mauldin, cartoonist who designed the card, has drawn for The 45th Division News more than two years. His cartoons appear regularly in several daily newspapers, also, and appear often in YANK.

Advance reports indicate the sale of the cards will be great. Many soldiers are planning to send the cards to lists of 20, 50 or more friends and relatives.

Although this will be the third Christmas the division has spent n service, no division Christmas ard has been offered before.

More public relations work. I was trying hard to solidify my position.

At Pine Camp, New York, where temperatures got to thirty below, my work began to take on some form and relevance.

ne Camp, N. Y.

"That's all for this morning, men. Dismissed . . . I said DISMISSED*!"*

even after all these years, and even in this time of open-drape reminiscences. Jean was a good sport about the short rations and most of the general hardships of a low-ranking soldier's wife. In fact, she had a sort of high-spirited gumption which armored her for the life. I saw something like this quality later in many infantry soldiers. It enabled them to bare their teeth in a half grin and meet situations head-on; without such capacity a person in rough circumstances soon finds himself hanging on by his fingernails and then going under.

Jean's vulnerable side was her loneliness. In many ways this was what drew us together, and it was responsible for driving us apart. As long as I got home from camp on the right bus everything was fine. If I had to stop by the *Division News* to pick up some unfinished sketches for homework, or if I had to check something in or out with K Company's supply sergeant, and was half an hour or an hour late, chances were Jean would be waiting at the bus stop in a sort of panic, which was touching at first, but it could quickly turn to rage. If I went away for a few days on training maneuvers, which I might have avoided through my work on the newspaper, she felt competitive with the army itself. As for my cartooning, she understood my ambition and the necessity for doing work at home even when it encroached upon the little time we had, but she was distressed if I seemed to her to be unduly absorbed in it. At these moments I became the one who felt threatened. My drawing had become my Rock of Gibraltar. With it, I was still convinced the world might be mine. Without it, I felt like an insignificant jerk.

What a combination! A frightened, stubborn girl and an unformed young man whose only sense of identity so far was in his drawing hand.

7

As the 45th Division prepared to ship out for Europe, it was trained to a peak. It might even have been a bit overtrained. It often turns out that the real thing is nothing like the book. In the infantry, it also happens that officers and noncoms who are real crackerjacks in maneuvers and on the drill fields sometimes turn out to be battlefield duds, whereas many of the slobs and troublemakers earn medals. There's no way to predict these things. One of our regimental commanders, a West Pointer with an outstanding academic record and an exemplary garrison career behind him, made a speech to his troops shortly before embarkation, exhorting them, in a bloodcurdling manner that General George Patton himself would have admired, to go and slaughter the foe without mercy.

"I want a regiment of three thousand killers," he roared.

On D-Day in Sicily some weeks later, when directed to capture a vital enemy airstrip from which fighters were attacking the beachhead, this same officer held up his advance because a scout reported "mysterious figures skulking in the brush." The once-ferocious colonel was found, wringing his hands at the rear of his regiment, by Brigadier General Raymond McLain, the division artillery commander and a National Guard officer, who took it upon himself to relieve the man of his command on the spot. McLain then walked with the lead scout of the lead company to the airstrip and directed the attack from a vantage point in an olive tree until the Germans shot him off his perch. The regular army colonel went home in disgrace and was promoted shortly afterward. In fairness, it

"AWRIGHT—COME OUT AN' LOOK FER YASELF IF YA DON'T BELIEVE IT."

must be noted that McLain himself ended up with three stars.

When the division finally embarked on what turned out to be the largest convoy ever to cross the Atlantic (the Sicily invasion fleet), the staff of the *News* was assigned to Hold 4-D of a troopship named the *James O'Hara*, or the *PA-90*. The fact that our billets were three feet below the waterline on the port side of a vessel assigned to the port flank of a huge convoy in waters containing U-boats hardly bothered us at all at first. The main thing was that we hadn't been sent back to our units. As long as we were together we would find a way to survive and justify our existence.

Hold 4-D was jammed to the ceiling with layers of humanity. The only way to stretch out on your narrow canvas bunk was to slither aboard edgewise (there were about fifteen inches of headroom before you encountered the sagging butt of the man above) and kick your barracks bag, which shared the bunk, onto a neighbor's territory. If he was asleep he wouldn't kick it back. The whole ship was crammed this way belowdecks. The only promenade space above was roped off and placarded OFFICERS' COUNTRY, so that the troops spent all of their time below except when bucking a chow line. Our convoy took the sunny route, toward the Azores, which meant the ships soaked up heat all day, and shower facilities were limited. We were all aware of each other's presence.

Even so, living three feet below the waterline and hearing the slap and gurgle of waves against the steel plates had a certain soporific charm for the first few nights of what turned out to be a twenty-six-day voyage. During the day there were various diversions, including multi-level poker games, with the dealer flipping cards to players two and three bunks above and below. Every hold developed its champion: eventually these all met and held finals, so that all of each ship's money almost invariably ended up in the pockets of one man. I shunned the gambling and busied myself with getting out my ink bottle and doing caricatures on fatigue jackets. My price had gone up to fifty cents and these were mostly fresh clients: the *45th Division News* staff had shipped with a bunch of combat engineers. I decided two rich men would be getting off this ship and only one would be a gambler.

Another redeeming feature of our early days at sea was that the navy cleverly worked out a system so that troops who so desired could get exercise and fresh air without encroaching upon Officers' Country. Incredibly complicated routes were laid out between each hold and the soldiers' galley, winding up and down ladders, in and out of passageways, and occasionally popping out onto some odd corner of the deck itself, so that a man in line actually caught glimpses of sea and sky. The dispensation of food was timed and the routes were planned so that if a soldier wanted to eat three meals in a day he was on his feet for at least fourteen hours.

A shuffling ship is a happy ship.

I contented myself with eating once a day (I was a heavy smoker in those days and didn't care about food), sleeping, and knocking out caricatures. Robinson, also a spare eater, spent his time lurking around the ship's officers, lobbying for use of a mimeograph machine to start a paper. Sheehan was torn between the excitement of the gambling—which was quickly settling down to a few serious, high-stake stud and crap games—and the chow line. Barrett had chosen a full-time career in that line. Tapscott, whose cumbersome Speed-Graphic equipment had been hopefully packed (along with a box of my drawing materials and everybody else's typewriters) among the division headquarters' office gear, was in a bad state because he was hungry, yet he hated to walk and was too restless to sleep. Finally, he got hold of a gun somewhere. A guard-house lawyer type among the engineers assured him that his special-duty status as a photographer relieved him of his Hippocratic dilemma (George was a combat medic by classification and technically obliged to remain unarmed) and he would be free to defend himself against the Hun wherever we landed. Now he spent his time happily polishing the weapon.

As I stood in the supper line late one morning, enjoying a moment of sunshine and calculating that we must be passing about north of Bermuda, I noted that *PA*-90's position was still on the convoy's left side. Every imaginable kind of vessel was on our right—transports, LSTs carrying LCVPs, antiquated liners, seagoing tugs, and cargo ships—all stretching as far as you could see. To the north nothing stood between open water and Hold 4-D except an occasional destroyer knifing along on patrol. Normally, I wouldn't have made much of it in my mind. None of us had yet adjusted below our necklines to the idea that a real war was going on somewhere. We knew about the submarines. We just hadn't *felt* our knowledge yet. Then the squawk box cut loose four feet from my ear. There was a sick whistle which always precedes naval broadcasts from Above, followed by the captain's voice:

"Now hear this. We are entering an area of considerable enemy submarine activity. All personnel are cautioned when loitering on deck [ha!] to stay well away from the rail at all times. Torpedoes strike just below the waterline and anyone at the edge will suffer severe flash burns."

That, I reflected, is nothing compared to what we'll get in Hold 4-D. The captain went on to say that there was a shortage of experienced personnel in the crew. This was no surprise to the soldiers aboard. Except for a handful of petty officers the entire crew, including the junior-grade officers, appeared to be barely out of diapers, and one of our favorite diversions had been watching them fall over each other on duty. What got my ears up was the captain's request for army volunteers to help man anti-aircraft guns.

"We don't expect air activity this far out," the captain said, "but if the crews start working together now they will be ready when they're needed. We only want men already familiar with the twenty-millimeter gun."

"You've never been near one of those things in your life," grunted Robinson, when I reported to him that I felt my duty lay above the deck from now on, especially at night. I was certain Hold 4-D would get clobbered while I slept.

"He said familiar, not qualified," I shot back. "I've drawn that gun three or four times, and I must have studied dozens of pictures of it."

"I'll bet he's more familiar with it than those kids in the sailor suits are," said Sheehan. I marked him in my mind as assistant gunner as soon as there was an opening.

It was delightful on deck. The sea was smooth as glass as we glided along at about ten knots so we wouldn't lose the slow boats. Days were spent fussing with the gun and getting sunburned. Nights were nice, too. As the stars came out I would stretch out on a couple or three inflatable life belts and tell the young sailors lies about life in Juárez. On my third or fourth day as a 20-millimeter gunner Robinson came to my station (I never left it except for trips to the head, which I executed at flank speed).

"They're going to let us print," he said, grinning.

"Print what?" I asked.

"A paper, for God's sake. Get your head out of that ammunition drum. We're back in business."

"I don't believe it. How can we distribute the *News* all over a moving convoy?"

"It won't be the *Division News*. It'll be the ship's paper."

"What'll you call it? *Anchors Aweigh?* How about *Now Hear This*, with a daily guest column by the officer of the deck?"

"I wish you and your ack-ack gun every happiness," Don said, turning away. "Who needs cartoons in a mimeographed paper?"

"Where'll we print it?"

"In the corner of the officers' wardroom, where the mimeograph machine lives. You'll be well away from flash burns if a torpedo gets us, and you'll have a crack at the lifeboats. We have to work at night, when the wardroom is empty, but you can still spend your days up here tracking gulls."

My luck runs in streaks. Not only was our paper (complete with cartoons) a daily success, but the captain turned out to be remarkably tolerant of our flippant editorial policy. The troop commander, an old 45th Division colonel, was already used to us. I had never cut drawings into stencils before, but quickly got the hang of it. My first target was Officers' Country, my second was the chow line, the third drawing was about the shower facilities, the fourth about the thick layer of grease on the galley duckboards, and so on. I regret that I didn't save any.

And then, as my cup was already running over, I met George McCracken. George was a cook in division headquarters. Before this voyage I had never eaten his food—he worked in the officers' mess—and I barely knew his name. His specialty was baking, and he preferred working at night. This was lucky for him, because his assignment on *PA*-90 was to cook for his own officers in the navy officers' galley, and the navy cooks wanted him out of their way in the daytime.

It was lucky for me, too. One morning about two o'clock as I scratched at a stencil on a table I became aware of a presence at my shoulder. It was George, in his white kitchen garb, puffing on a cigar. He gave me a start, because he seemed to have risen through the floor. From where I was sitting both entrances to the wardroom came within my peripheral vision.

"Bother you if somebody watches you work?" he asked.

I assured him it didn't. Then, since I felt like taking a break anyway, and night people tend to be congenial, I lit a cigarette and told him about an art teacher I'd had in Chicago who had cured our class of kibitzer shyness by taking us on watercolor sketching trips around town, where we would attract onlookers like flies. Most public kibitzers are pretty inconsiderate, too, crowding right up on you and asking stupid questions. The art teacher had taught us a handy trick. You have to work very fast on watercolors, getting on each fresh brushload before the previous one dries. This means loading your brush with water and pigment and quickly flicking it, which gets rid of the excess and shapes the point. When people move close, you simply start slinging paint around. It looks totally accidental and you can develop accuracy with a little practice, splattering the pests and leaving the innocent untouched.

George McCracken thought this was real funny, and asked if I'd like to join him for a cup of coffee and maybe a piece of pastry. I couldn't imagine anything better. This had been one of those days when I had missed all of the snake dances to chow. One of the sailors on the gun had shared a sandwich with me, but it hadn't been much. I rose from my table to go with George, but he told me to wait till he made sure his galley was clear. The navy is much tougher than the army about trespassing. Then I saw how the cook had arrived in the wardroom. A few feet behind me was a hand-operated dumbwaiter, about two and a half feet square, with its supporting rope running right through its middle. George scrunched Yoga-like into this tiny cubicle, grasped the rope, and grinned out at me.

"If I don't send it right back for you it means somebody's down there," he said. "Just wait." He fed the rope through his fingers and started down with amazing speed. I suppose he could have used the ladder legally but found this easier, or more fun. Or maybe the navy cooks had told him it was strictly forbidden to ride the dumbwaiter. It came back immediately. Aside from a momentary claustrophobia halfway down the shaft, when I felt as if I had been buried alive in a shoebox, I made the trip with no strain. The thing must have been counterweighted, because the rope took very little pull.

McCracken fixed me up with coffee and cake, but first he insisted on hors d'oeuvres—consisting of a huge T-bone steak, medium rare, and a baked potato with sour cream.

"George," I said, on my way back to the dumbwaiter, "if there's anything I can ever . . ."

"If you get a chance sometime," he said, "how about making a quick drawing of my face to send home? You don't have to—just if you get time someday. Look's like this ride's going to last for a while."

Shades of Hillbilly Larry! One of the nicest things about cartooning is the way you can revive the barter system with it. It's the only way to do business: no wholesalers, middlemen, or agents. In the two remaining weeks of our voyage I worked on a watercolor sketch of George for a few minutes every night. Naturally, he had to pose, and the best place for this was down among the steaks and ice cream. When the portrait was finished, it showed George with his head through a porthole of *PA*-90, with his cook's cap jauntily cocked on his head. When his family finally got it, they must have wondered about the significance of the halo over the cap. Meanwhile, some of my shipmates began to wonder how it happened that I was missing every chow line, yet was visibly gaining weight.

I mentioned earlier that our convoy consisted, substantially, of the Sicily invasion fleet. Naturally, we didn't yet know that was our destination. The most popular and educated guess was that we were going to Southern France. The landings in North Africa, which we had missed a few months earlier, had recently ended in a total Allied victory over the Afrika Korps. The last German stragglers were still being picked up, and we Americans, who like to simplify our thinking about our wars, assumed that the enemy was now on the run everywhere and that we had arrived barely in time to pick up a few souvenirs as we mopped up in Europe. When we went ashore for a few days at Arzew, near Oran on the Algerian coast, to get our land legs back, there were mutterings from a few of our more gung-ho types, especially in the rear echelons, that they hoped the 45th would be able to get a little piece of the action before the armistice.

Our particular little group of insecure soldier-journalists were preoccupied, as usual, with whether we would function in what we considered our most useful capacity—or would join our old outfits, whose dust we could see in the distance as they practiced forced marches with full equipment. We stayed out of sight as much as possible, drinking wine in the village of Port-au-Poule and studying native Frenchmen and Arabs.

"Don't ask foolish questions. Th' schedule calls for calisthenics. We'll start with th' left eyelid."

By the time we arrived in Africa the Arabs were used to dealing with Americans and tangerines cost their weight in gold. We got revenge by selling them our mattress covers, which we no longer needed, for thirty dollars each.

"No, thank you. My mother says I'm too young to smoke."

The former were a sour lot, much like the Virginians we had just left, and we would probably have despised the Arabs except that the Frenchmen treated them so badly we began to feel sorry for them. The Arabs were easily the sorriest human beings I had ever seen or imagined. Some were so emaciated under their robes—made of mattress covers sold to them for exorbitant sums by American soldiers—that they looked like formless spooks flapping around a graveyard. Local French police levied a fine of five dollars for running over a child with a truck and twice that for killing a goat or a donkey. I suppose property damage made more paperwork. Under those voluminous Arab rags and behind those running sores there was often a powerful streak of pride, too, which our people chose to interpret as sly malice, because an American finds it hard to imagine a proud man who doesn't even have a decent pair of shoes to his name. Every soldier could tell you about a friend whose friend was found murdered for his boots, with his balls cut off and stuffed into his mouth. I never heard the story at less than third hand, but I suppose it must have happened a few times. I also heard of Arabs being used for target practice by troops riding past in trucks, and I suppose this happened a few times, too.

One afternoon I failed to duck around a corner in time and was assigned to stand guard among some headquarters tents outside Port-au-Poule. The weapon assigned to me was a 1903 Springfield, which fortunately was not loaded, since the chamber and barrel were so fouled with desert sand and beach mud that it would have been more dangerous to stand behind it while firing than in front of it. I had barely taken my post when I saw an Arab youth, about seventeen or so, emerge from between two tents with a barracks bag dragging behind him. From the bulges I could see it was full of shoes. We stared at each other for a moment, then I gruffly told him, by voice and sign, to drop the boodle. He grinned at me with a "No spikka da English" shrug, and started for home.

If you must stand guard with an empty weapon, an old Springfield, with its bolt action, sounds the most authoritative. All you have to do is work the action as if you're throwing a round into firing position. Its clicks and snicks are especially loud if the bolt is full of abrasive material. Who's going to stick around to see if you've really got brass in there? That crazy kid did. Not wanting to be shot in the back, he turned around, still with a grin, laid the bag down (he didn't drop it), and spread his arms wide to give me a clean crack at his chest. Mind you, at that time in that place he really expected to be killed, and he knew I was within my legal rights. It was my first experience with someone who really had nothing to lose. It was disturbing. When he saw that I was either chicken or had no ammunition, he picked up his burden and resumed his journey.

"Goddamn that lousy Mauldin: some son of a bitch got my shoes," a voice cried from a tent a little later. Other voices soon joined in. I was

For a while, being overseas was like being back on maneuvers.

"I gotta hand it to ya. I didn't think that buried treasure rumor would work."

saved by the fact that I could show the rifle and prove my impotence against the small band of three or four knife-bearing marauders I described. Most of the anger was then directed at that dumb son-of-a-bitching lieutenant who issued empty weapons as if we were still back in training, not out here among a bunch of bona fide cutthroats. I couldn't have taken a shot at that boy if I had been holding a loaded and well-oiled Tommy gun and my life had depended upon it, but I kept that fact to myself.

8

We invaded Sicily on July 10, 1943. On July 9, Nature, after having let us ride for a month across a becalmed Atlantic and a glassy Mediterranean, chose this time to brew us up a gale-force storm. You wouldn't believe a land-locked body of tepid water could behave so violently. Every man on board our ship (and all the sailors, as far as I could tell) got sick, but the ones who really suffered were aboard the stubby LCIs and other landing craft. Those vessels had made the crossing empty but were now pregnant with men and equipment. Many were trailing barrage balloons. The huge gasbags were supposed to be riding a thousand feet or so above on steel tethers to discourage dive bombers from coming down among us. Now the cables were stretched out almost horizontally, with their rubberized sausages gyrating and flapping among the whitecaps, while the crews frantically tried to reel them in. Most were secured; some broke loose and soared away. It didn't matter: no enemy pilot in his right mind was flying that day. Whatever element of surprise we achieved with our invasion was undoubtedly because no sane army should have been afloat that day, either.

For a man who is susceptible to motion sickness—as a child I used to throw up even in automobiles—I did pretty well all day. Having eagerly volunteered to resume my anti-aircraft job when we reboarded the *PA-90* I had plenty of refreshing wind and spray in my face, plus the fascinating sight of our mighty armada, tossing like so many corks, to keep me from thinking about personal queasiness. Then I made the mistake of going down to the head near Hold 4-D for a simple piss, which could have been performed from my station to leeward with nobody the wiser, in that wind.

The instant I stepped into the head I was undone. It was a big compartment, triangular in shape, about thirty feet long, with a glazed tile floor and dozens of toilets along the sides. At each fixture was a soldier—sometimes two soldiers—facing the bowl doubled over, in convulsions. Not all of them were hitting the toilets. Some of them were even falling into toilets. The floor was slippery with bile. When the ship dove headlong into a slough, I slid on my feet clean across the compartment, caromed off a structural member, and as the bow rose I slid all the way back again, still in a standing position, without having moved a muscle. If they have skating rinks in Hades they must be like this. A sidewise roll of the ship slammed me into a gagging pair sharing a toilet, and the three of us went into a sorry heap on the floor.

I will not add more paint to this picture, other than to say it must have taken me five minutes or more to claw, slide, and scramble on hands and knees back to the exit. Now the ship seemed to have gone into a permanent nose dive. The only handholds were on plumbing fixtures and people. A man would get almost within grabbing distance of a door, leaning at an incredible angle like a Mack Sennett drunk, only to be seized by somebody from behind and go slithering all the way back, taking along everybody else on the way. Multiply this scene by thousands, remember that our infantry invaded Sicily against heavy opposition the next day, and never again let anyone speak to you of the innate softness of the American soldier. Slobs we all certainly were for a while there, but not effete slobs.

The wind died that night; but not the sea, as our retching forces gathered off the Sicilian coast. Sometime after midnight Don Robinson staggered to my perch under the 20-millimeter gun.

"You joined the army, not the navy," he said in a gruff voice, which surprised me. "Time to go down and get your equipment together for the landing."

I wanted to say goodbye to my faithful navy ack-ack crew. However, those who weren't leaning over the steel coping were hanging greenly onto it. Obviously, this was not the time for sentiment. Sailors seasick enough to ignore the dangers of flash burn at the rail couldn't be expected to get ceremonious over the departure of a transient gunner. I left quietly with Robinson. The first thing I noticed when we got back to our hold was the absence of Sheehan and Barrett. Their gear was gone, too. I began to get a feeling in the pit of my stomach which transcended seasickness.

"An engineer captain took them away," Tapscott said, looking at me with tragic eyes. "They're with a landing party which is going in ahead of the infantry to look for mines and act as guides. They had your name, too, but we all said we didn't know where you were."

I thought of all the McCracken steaks I hadn't shared with those nice guys.

"It was bound to end, anyway," Don said. Things had been uncannily quiet, except for the slosh of waves and the creak of the ship, but now the naval bombardment of the shore had begun.

"What was bound to end, Don?" I asked, at the top of my voice, with my hands cupped around my mouth. He leaned to listen, with his own hand cupped behind his ear. We looked like two old men having a political discussion, as everybody else remaining in the hold bustled about and shrugged into harness of various sorts.

"This crazy idea that we could wade ashore and publish a newspaper and go on as we were. Goddammit, Mauldin, we're soldiers now, and we'd better face up to it."

"Everybody topside," a voice thundered through the amplifiers. "All army personnel on deck. Stand by the nets."

"Holy Jesus," somebody said, "we're gonna climb down into boats in this slop?"

"In this slop we might find ourselves climbing up into boats," Don retorted. He grinned wanly at me. He had made a funny in the face of fate.

"They had no right to take our guys," I said.

"Of course they did. The only reason they didn't take George or me is that he's a medic and I'm listed as head of the section. They know who we are and they know damn well we aren't going to be putting out a newspaper in that mess." He nodded in the direction we assumed to be land and I visualized a village with a printing press being flattened at that moment by a giant high-explosive shell.

"The captain told me I could have the boys back after the landing," Don said. "I got the feeling he meant I would get a boxful of pieces."

"Damn," said George, "I didn't know anybody ever went ahead of the infantry."

The sun was well up when the three of us went over the side into our boat. Don hadn't been kidding about the possibility of climbing up the net instead of down in that sea. On each wave the landing craft was rising and falling at such a rate that we had to time our arrival very carefully to avoid jumping as the boat started down, which would have meant a long drop. Such precision was not easy when the guys above were stomping on our helmets. Fortunately, we had been trained to hold the vertical ropes of the net, otherwise everybody's hands would have been stepped on and half the invasion force would have drowned. As it was, I think it was a miracle there weren't more accidents that morning.

Acoustically, there was a hell of a war going on as we chugged and pitched our way toward the beaches of Sicily. The navy had lots of firepower and was shooting as fast as it could reload. I remember catching a glimpse of a heavy cruiser a couple of miles away as it let go one of those broadsides we'd heard earlier. The belch of fire and smoke was majestic and the clap of sound when it reached us was awesome, but what impressed me most was the way that giant, floating steel island seemed able to coordinate its fire with the rolling effect of the waves so that its shells presumably landed where they were aimed. The sound of tons of projectiles tearing overhead reminded me, for some reason, of the logging train which used to come down the steep grade past Mountain Park with all its brakes locked and screeching.

None of this heavy stuff was landing on the beaches, which were already secured, but was in support of the 45th's infantry, now working its way inland. There seemed to be little return artillery fire, although the Luftwaffe was around in some force, strafing the men landing supplies on the beaches and making occasional runs at the ships. It turned out that one of the reasons for the lack of enemy gunnery was a Hearst correspondent named Mike Cinigo, who went in with an early shore party and stumbled onto a command bunker of the Italian coast artillery. While his army companions rounded up the resident brass hats, Mike, who is of Italian descent, picked up the phone, just for the hell of it, and ordered all units to hold their fire until further notice. Miraculously, it worked. The Italians had gotten pretty sick of the war by then, anyway.

Most of our naval bombardment in support of the infantry was being directed by radio from ground observers and from a few small spotter planes, including several antiquated, amphibious biplanes, made of cloth and wire, which had been launched by catapult from our larger ships. A sleek Messerschmitt got onto the back of one of these potbellied relics and began pumping bullets into it. The enemy pilot's main problem seemed to be keeping his propeller out of the tail fabric of his victim, whose top speed was probably around a hundred and fifty miles per hour. Our navy pilot came in a shallow dive right down among the landing craft, either in desperation or because he was already dead. He passed a few hundred feet to our right as we watched, goggle-eyed, over the side of our heaving boat, and then he went in with a great splash. I remember thinking how German war machines always looked more deadly (and usually were) than ours. Don admitted later that he, too, was having abstract thoughts. The whole thing was just too much like a movie. Our musings were interrupted by a second, even bigger splash, followed by the billowing smoke of burning gasoline. The Messerschmitt had hit the water practically on top of the debris of the navy plane. All of us—apparently including the German—had been so transfixed by his kill that we hadn't seen a camouflaged Spitfire stalking the predator. The friendly avenger, now so low that he had to thread his way among the nearest warships, executed a little victory roll as he climbed out past the larger ones, one of which had lost its chick. The Germans might have made meaner-looking killing equipment, but when it came to gestures nobody could touch the British.

In all this excitement, most of our boatload had forgotten about seasickness. We waded ashore in pretty good shape, Don with a briefcase and pistol, Tapscott with his pistol hidden somewhere, and me with a musette bag full of drawing supplies and my own pistol. Whichever way our careers were headed—war or journalism—we were prepared. We were almost afraid to think about our reportorial staff, as we walked across the narrow beach and saw that in spite of "light" opposition it hadn't been beer and skittles for those who had gone in earlier. The sand was chewed up and cratered. Here and there were strips of cloth showing the way past mines (this was why the engineers had gone). Some of these murderous devices had been discovered the hard way. The twisted hulk of a jeep was still smoking over a crater. The wreckage was soaked with blood. To me the war still had a movielike quality, but it was becoming more 3-D every moment.

We were near Scoglitti, a fishing village south of Gela, on the right flank of the 1st Division. In Gela the 1st had found the Germans waiting in force and were having a hell of a fight. The 45th was running into serious German opposition, too, as it pushed further inland. One of the reasons our landing had been comparatively quiet was that most of the defense in our sector had been by Italian troops, who had met our men with something less than ferocity. Most of them seemed to want to explain that they had kinfolks in Detroit. Right now hundreds of them who had surrendered were crowded into great clumps among the dunes, so that the place had something of a Coney Island look. One American would be standing guard over a hundred or so. Because we could think of nothing better to do, and wanted to look as if we knew what we were doing, Don and I headed for Scoglitti to look for a printing press. We didn't find one, but we did discover a fresh group of about three dozen Italian infantrymen who wanted to surrender to us personally. Don told their spokesman (who said he'd lived in Chicago) that we were too busy, and pointed out the direction of the last big collection of prisoners we had seen. The men seemed slightly hurt that we didn't want to take them in at gunpoint, but they shrugged philosophically and trotted off where they had been told. In Scoglitti we also found a couple of engineer officers who told us that Sheehan and Barrett had been killed, along with most of their landing party.

"You hear about the wastefulness of war," said Don, who was inclined to make philosophical noises when overcome with emotion, "but it doesn't

P.W.
ENCLOSURE
"WELL, IF IT AINT 'SLINKY' COSTELLO, 'KNIFE' RANDUZZI, AN' 'BABY-FACE' STAMPIONE! REMEMBER ME, BOYS? I'M DAT THICK-HEADED FLATFOOT FROM PRECINCT SEVEN..."

Author (below) fraternizes with Italian soldier by disabled German tank. Whatever enthusiasm Italians might have had for the war had long since evaporated.

mean anything until something like this happens. They were fine newspapermen and they'd have been great someday."

I had admired Barrett, a taciturn but pleasant young man who liked his work and applied himself seriously to it, and I shared a bond with him in that we were the only married men on the *News*. But the one I would miss most, I decided, was Sheehan, an ebullient cuss who had quickly mastered the art of thumbing his nose at the chickenshit side of the army without inviting rancor or retaliation.

Well, a lot of people were being killed that day. We decided the best memorial to the boys would be to put out the first Allied newspaper on Axis soil in World War II. The nearest possible printing facilities, we learned, would be in Vittoria, a larger town a few miles inland. Walking in that direction, we met a three-quarter-ton weapons carrier packed with infantrymen. The driver asked us for directions to the nearest aid station. Suddenly, I noticed something about the men in the truck. They were all gray-faced, each was clutching some part of his anatomy, and all were bloody from head to foot. It might seem strange that this last detail wasn't immediately discernible, but we were all wearing dark woolen uniforms,* and for some reason red does not show up sharply against olive drab. Even the driver appeared to have two or three holes in his torso. They said they were a patrol which had been shot up, had found their unit gone when they returned, and had commandeered the vehicle. We gave directions and offered to drive, but they said they had come this far without help and could make it the rest of the way. It seemed an almost childish pride and stubbornness until you realized it was what was holding their heads up. Some of those guys looked as if they would have been a lot more comfortable lying down in a ditch back where they'd been hit and dying. As they drove off I recognized a man in the back as a friend of Sheehan's from E Company of the 180th Infantry. My God, they were from my regiment! Now the war got even more real.

A little later we ran into Clark Lee, a correspondent we knew, who had just come out of Vittoria. He had gone there in a jeep with a driver, had left the vehicle for a moment, and had come back to find German soldiers making off with his transportation and his soldier. Vittoria would have to wait. We found the division command post and started to settle down for the night, first digging shallow slit trenches between the roots of an olive tree. We were told by our friends in G-2 that the 45th expected German paratroopers to try to cut the division off from the beach, since our lines

* The U.S. army had a theory that in midsummer in Sicily voluminous wool would be more comfortable than scanty cotton. This sort of thinking might have been fine for Arabs, who face frigid nights as well as scorching days, but was not shared by any of our allies or enemies in Sicily, all of whom wore light clothing with short sleeves and legs.

of communication were now stretched pretty far. The command post, being about halfway between the front and the beach, seemed likely to be in the drop zone. We dug a little deeper between the roots of our tree.

Around midnight we heard the planes start coming: a throbbing drone which bespoke waves of them. You could hear them slow as they began dropping the parachutists. Then you couldn't hear much of anything, because every gun in the navy cut loose at the planes. We could see flashes nearer at hand and realized that even our army truck drivers had opened up with the heavy .50-caliber machine guns mounted above their cabs. Planes began falling, and chutists died by the hundreds in their harness before reaching the ground. The drop had been foiled. The only trouble was they were our own paratroopers. They were supposed to go to Gela to help the hard-pressed 1st Division. Instead the planes had brought them where Germans were expected. A final irony would have been if the enemy had jumped over Gela that night. They'd have probably been received with open arms.

Finally, there were no more friendly paratroopers for the navy cannoneers and army sharpshooters to kill. The noise died down, except for sporadic rumblings and cracklings toward Gela and inland, and we all went to sleep in our little slit trenches. At dawn we awoke to grimness: trees here and there festooned with ribbons of nylon, and little knots of parachutists picking up the remains of their friends. I had learned my first practical lesson about war: nobody really knows what he's doing. It could be that Robinson, Tapscott, and I were the only men in that divisional headquarters area with clear intentions for the day. As we struck out on foot for Vittoria (the Germans *had* to be out of there by now) we passed more airborne men forming up on the road. All looked a little dazed. A few hours earlier they had been keyed up to land on the coal-scuttle helmets of the Hermann Goering division. Now they found themselves in our rear echelon, with worse casualties than if they'd reached their objective, and faced with the embarrassment of having to walk into battle. All because of some jerk of a navigator who was probably stirring ice cream into his coffee right now back at his African airbase. Our hearts went out to the troopers as we walked by them, but we didn't try exchanging any pleasantries with them.

In Vittoria, the first Americans we saw were two riflemen from the 179th Infantry, escorting six German soldiers to the rear. The prisoners could have been models for a Wehrmacht recruiting poster: they were in their late teens, healthy and neatly turned out, with real jackboots. They were the only natty Krauts I saw in the entire war; the probable explanation is that they were from the Goering division, which was fighting the 45th as well as the 1st, and considered itself at least as elite as an SS outfit. The six youngsters were marching briskly, in perfect step, with hands locked behind their heads and big, defiant grins on their faces. Our two dogfaces shambling alongside looked like, and probably were, Oklahoma plowhands.

"It's hard to tell who won," said Tapscott.

"You can tell by who's carrying the guns," Robinson replied.

A couple of blocks farther we found another pair of our infantrymen, armed to the teeth, draped with bandoleers and grenades, drunk as lords, with their flies open, displaying a brace of limp and rather stringy-looking sex organs to an assortment of young Sicilians of both sexes. The children didn't seem shocked: they were politely attentive. If the conquering army wanted to show off all its equipment it behooved the public to pay attention. (So far the public didn't include any adults. They were behind shutters, looking us over.)

The next American we met, a little way down the street, was the 45th Division's provost marshal, a normally beet-faced major who had turned purple as he stared at the exhibitionists.

"Robinson! Mauldin!" the major barked. Tapscott had ducked behind a building. He was quick at summing up tactical situations.

"Sir!" we replied, respectfully, then watched with horror as he pulled two MP armbands from his pocket.

"Put these on and go arrest those two drunks. They're stragglers and they're disgusting." He pointed to a building. "Bring them in there to me. Or drag them in. I don't give a shit if you have to kill them."

"That last part is easier said than done," muttered Robinson, as we closed on the culprits, who unslung their rifles and watched us come, passing their wine bottle back and forth. A moment before we had been journalists on our way to a publishing venture. Now we were deputy sheriffs on Main Street at high noon. We both wore pistols but weren't about to touch them. After all, as Don pointed out later, these were our subscribers. As soon as we deemed ourselves far enough away from the captain we slipped off the hated armbands. That helped. Although our friends ahead kept their rifles in hand, they lowered the muzzles. I remember that in spite of my apprehension my cartoonist's brain couldn't help registering the fact that, since the boys had neglected to tuck in their members, we were now faced with four sagging weapons, not two.

"Come on, button up, will you?" Don said. "I can't talk with a man who's trying to pee."

The men started giggling. The little kids, who had taken cover behind a low wall as we approached, emerged and started laughing, too. This infuriated the man who had the bottle. He threw it at them. It hit the wall; by the time the last splinter fell to the ground our audience had vanished again. At this point I would have abandoned the whole project, even though we were under direct orders. Don was a more responsible sort.

He was also persuasive. He recited the Articles of War to the soldiers, making up a few statutes as he went along, and pointed out the alternatives to a peaceable surrender. He even invoked the underworld, pointing out that every element of Sicilian society was cooperating with the Allies (this turned out to be true in regard to the Mafia) and that there would be no place for a couple of fugitives to hide—especially guys who had shaken the very foundations of Latin morality by shameful exhibitionism before small children.

"All right," said one of the men, "we'll go with you. But no surrender. We keep our rifles and you walk in front of us."

The major must have been watching our strange capture. When we led our "prisoners" into the courtyard of his building he stepped in front of them, disarmed them both at once with a two-handed grab, dropped their weapons, then knocked them each sprawling with open-handed slaps that sounded like gunshots. He was a brave man to handle two mean soldiers that way, even drunk ones. As for them, they were hardly deserving of charity, considering that they had deserted their company, which was up ahead fighting right now. Still, Robinson and I felt in no position to pass judgment since our contribution to the war effort so far had been to eat some K-rations which might have gone to waste otherwise. As the major took his now-passive charges inside by the scruffs of their necks, we folded the MP armbands, laid them on the wall under a large piece of masonry, where they probably rest to this day, and ducked around the corner. There we found Tapscott, who had been lurking there through the whole performance. He was still shaking his head in wonderment and pity at two jerks who had been in the army as long as we had and didn't know enough to get off the tracks when we heard a train whistle.

We found a printing shop in town. It was shuttered, like everything else, but we rounded up a few civilians in the neighborhood and sent them to find the owner. We learned as we went along later that in the first hours of any town's capture, before the people learned that with all our thundering bombs and awesome equipment we were mostly slobs at heart, you could get almost anybody to do anything with a snap of your finger. If there was any hesitation, it could be cured by whipping out a pad and pencil, writing out a requisition, and signing it "Eisenhower." The victim would give you whatever you wanted and go away hopefully clutching his *carta.* This was a dirty trick, to be played only on suspicious people. Some scoundrels in our army even broke open Monopoly sets from Special Services supplies and passed off the money for a few days as "Sicilian occupation currency."

The printer showed up early in the afternoon, with a couple of typesetters. They managed to contain their joy at the news that they would produce the first American newspaper on Axis soil, but they seemed willing enough. Don studied the ancient flatbed press, decided on a three-column format and a two-page, single-sheet edition, which would avoid folding problems. Besides, we didn't have much to say. Pictures or cartoons were out of the question. There were no photoengravers in Vittoria. As Don sat at a table and began writing in longhand about how the American and British armies had successfully landed in Sicily, it occurred to me that since the demise of Sheehan and Barrett the most useful thing I could do was to run out and gather some copy. Tapscott, whose camera, had he been carrying it, would have been as useless as my pen, offered to join me, but Don kept him to help get the typesetting started.

We had agreed that broadcast news from England or the United States would be our only voluminous and reliable source, and that the most likely place to get it would be aboard one of our ships. As I started the long hike back to the beach, I was intercepted by two Italian soldiers coming out of an orchard. One was carrying a carbine with a nasty little needle-type bayonet folded along the barrel. The bolt was open to show his peaceful intentions. His companion was pushing a bicycle loaded with their baggage. They told me they had been trying for two days and a night to surrender. Each American they had met had been *simpatico* but too busy. (There were few language problems with Sicilians and southern Italians. Every group of two or more had a member who spoke English, more or less.) I took the time to escort them back to the provost marshal's office, then confiscated the carbine and bicycle. There was some argument about the vehicle, until I assured the prisoners that it was in the same category as an enemy truck or tank, and asked them if they had ever seen a bicycle in a stockade. I clinched it with an Eisenhower requisition. The half hour or so I had lost was quickly made up as I pedaled toward the beachhead with the carbine slung across my back.

Hiding the bike in some bushes behind a dune and carrying the gun as bait, I looked for a cooperative landing-craft crew. I had heard that sailors were great souvenir hounds. Sure enough, the very first LCVP pilot I approached pounced on the weapon, fondled it like a ten-year-old with his first Daisy BB, and whisked me out to his mother ship. I explained my mission to the officer of the deck, who showed me to the radio shack. Meanwhile, my gig waited at the foot of the ladder, possibly because I had kept the carbine for insurance. The radio man not only let me listen to a variety of news broadcasts but gave me a sheaf of dispatches that had been copied.

Back at the ladder, I found my boat driver practically in tears. The damned fool had told the O.D. of our bargain and had been reminded of an edict from the bridge that all souvenirs capable of shooting or exploding would be confiscated.

"All right, sir," the sailor said, suspiciously, "just let me have the pleasure of throwing it overboard right now."

"Never mind; I'll see that it's disposed of." The officer held out his hand and I gave him the gun. "Now get this man back to shore," he snapped. "Did you get what you were looking for, soldier?"

"Yes, sir," I said, refraining from adding that it looked as if he'd gotten what he wanted, too.

"That thieving son of a bitch," the sailor mourned on the way. I looked more sympathetic than I felt. Obviously this boy had just begun his life in his country's service, and would have to learn things the hard way. I did offer him one small comfort by saying it was an odds-on bet that the carbine would eventually end up on the wall of the captain's cabin.

I lost my bike to enemy action halfway to Vittoria. There had been a sharp decrease in German air activity over our crowded beaches and supply roads after we had captured a couple of their advance fighter strips and put them to our own use. Even so, the Luftwaffe managed to sneak in a strafing or dive-bombing sortie from time to time. Traveling on foot, I had been sharply aware of this and ready to dive into the ditch at any time. However, pedaling down a country road on a sunny July afternoon makes a war seem less real, so that my main concern became not getting run over by speeding trucks. When I heard an airplane engine, I thought it was a ground vehicle with a loud exhaust somewhere nearby, even though the road wa empty at the moment. Then I saw dirt dancing in front of me; a shadow passed by, and suddenly I looked up with the same belated, unbelieving shock a dumb chicken must feel when a hawk makes a pass at him.

It was an elderly Stuka dive bomber, flying low and slow to be inconspicuous among the dunes as it made its way home from the beach with empty bomb racks. Its crew just couldn't resist a bit of sport when they saw that bicycle. As he went by at about ninety miles an hour, the machine gunner in the back seat swung around for another crack at me, I finally stopped gawping and headed for the ditch. Riding the bike had made me forget the war; now the war made me forget I was riding the bike. I hit the dirt in a tangle of spokes and bent rims. When the evil black bird had gone I abandoned the wreckage and walked to the printing shop, arriving with my bundle of news no more than two hours after I had left.

Don had a surprise for me. Inside, working with a typesetter and roaring in frustration as he kept learning over and over that the Italian alphabet has no k's, w's, or y's, was Fred Sheehan.

"Goddamn it, Don, you told me to turn m's upside down for w's and now we're outta m's," he complained.

"Noted," said Bill Barrett, who was at the table converting Robinson's longhand, which the setters couldn't read, into hand-printed letters which

45TH Division News

JULY 13, 1943 VITTORIA, Sicily VOL. IV

DANCE IN DIRT CAPTURES PRISONERS

Early in the invasion, when you didn't know whether the next foot of beach belonged to you or to the enemy, Ist, Lt. Thomas E. Akers and his driver, Pvt. Weaver went on a reconnaissance. They fouud themselves in Scoglitti, but the soldiers they saw were Italian!

" Oops, „ said the lieutenant. when he realized his spot, " Turn around, Weaver.„ They retreated until they fo-

TEN MAJOR CITIES OURS

Along an arc of about 100 miles on the Sicilian front the Allies have captured at least 10 important to wns and ports, and smashed seven Axis counter-offensives, an Allied communique has announced to the people back home

Gen. Montgomery's Eighth Avmy sped for Catania after taking Syracuse, and plans going on to Messina straits -

SOVIETS HOLD THEIR GROUND

The greatest battle in history, raging 14 days on the Russian front, has left the lines about as they had been.

German claims to capture of 38 miles ot Soviet territory mentioned no names of places, and the Russians said no serious breech has occurred.

Russia claims to have taken toll of 2,500 tanks and 2,068 planes in 14 days.

Our first effort.

lfway through the front page ran out of *w's*.

POPOLO DI 45 TH

This, so far as we iow, is the first United ates Army NeWspaper be published in the iropean invasion. We ppe it is. The Division ews was the first pa-er of the " National mergency, „ and this ew " first „ was /our nbition.

Don't blame vs if it n't our best effort. We, ke you, have been bom-d, straffed and sniped . We're printing in a icilian print shop whe- the printers don't iow a word of English, d the press must be n, ' temporarity , by nd.

We'll print as often s we're able.

We also ran out of electricity.

From **News of the 45th**, by Sergeant Don Robinson with art by Sergeant Bill Mauldin they couldn't understand. Also, he had been scratching out all words containing k's or y's and thinking up substitutes. "From now on, no m's either," he muttered. "Tell me we're out of e's too, and we can all go home. Without e's you've got no English."

Our heroes looked bedraggled but they were alive.

"How'd you find them?" I asked Don.

"They found us. They asked for the print shop, figuring we'd be here."

For a while that evening we left the shipboard news with the printers (who found the typing somewhat easier to follow) and celebrated the resurrection of our reportorial staff with wine and K-ration cheese. Late that night, or early next morning, we got the worst of the kinks out of the type, locked pages one and two into their forms, and printed three thousand copies of the *45th Division News*, working by lamplight and turning the press wheels by hand, since the power station had been bombed off the map. (Most of our printing was done this way in the smaller towns during the next few weeks as we followed the 45th across the island. At one point Barrett observed, as he nursed a blister, that if every writer had to set his type by hand and crank the press, he would turn out leaner, better prose.)

Our first printing bill in Vittoria was four dollars and fifty cents, including overtime. Everybody put in a dollar bill except Tapscott, who had been wrung out in one of the shipboard games. He searched his pockets and was able to find two quarters.

"I'm almost ashamed to pay so little," Don said. "Can't we raise it to ten?"

"Typical American," said Sheehan. "You just got here, and already you want to spoil it for the other publishers."

The division was pleased to get the *News;* although the paper was not up to our usual standard in size, typographical excellence (try turning m's upside down for w's and see how it looks), or content (the absence of photos by Tapscott and cartoons by Mauldin was conspicuous, to say the least), it served its main purpose. In the first few days of a large battle, rumors get started. Not all are harmless. This is especially true if your top leader is a flamboyant nut like Patton, who commanded all the Americans in Sicily. We were ready to believe anything about him. One story which made the rounds was that he had to be evacuated in a strait-jacket because he had learned that a large German Panzer force was coming across the shallows at Messina to kick us back into the sea, and he had worried himself sick about what this would do to his reputation. It's an interesting tribute to Walter Harrison's concept of a military newspaper that when our little rag reached the soldiers the rumors died. Because we had never been considered the voice of officialdom we had our credibility. Our readers assumed, correctly, that if anything newsworthy had

From **News of the 45th**, by Sergeant Don Robinson with art by Sergeant Bill Mauldin

Wherever a newspaper office opens, the actors come.

"You hear that, Ferdinando? Th' invasion is over! You ain't a enemy no more!"

happened we would have printed it.

As the 45th Division battled northward, the *News* staff followed closely. We had to. We had no means of transport except our thumbs; even bundles of our printed papers had to be delivered by hitchhiking, and sometimes by foot. We didn't mind. Anybody who keeps close contact with an infantry division in combat regards all forms of exercise in the rear echelons as healthful and pleasant. Besides, we were feeling good—even cocky—about our initial overseas publishing effort.

Working with printers gave us an opportunity to get to know local people as we went along. The Sicilians seemed to be an odd mixture of warmth and reserve. It was unthinkable to them not to ask us home, individually and collectively, for a glass of wine, a cup of coffee, or even a meal, after working with us all day, often turning the wheels of the presses shoulder to shoulder when the power was off. Yet, when one or several of us would be seated with the host's family, there was usually some strain in the air. Part of this was a language difficulty, of course, even though we were all picking up a fair brand of pidgin Italian. Mainly, though, I got the feeling that our problem was being in uniform. Sicilians have been run over too many times by too many armies. As Americans we had several things going for us. Hardly a family on the island lacked a relative or two in the United States. Also, we were kicking the Germans out. The people regarded them as cold fish. When we were invited to a home, we always took a gift of canned rations. Still, it was fairly clear, no matter how hospitable they tried to be, that they wished we would leave (and take our damned bombers and artillery with us). We felt better about all this when we learned that the Italian army wasn't very welcome in Sicily, either, and that Mussolini had never dared set foot on the island in his entire career as head of state.

Caltanisetta, a fairly large town almost exactly in the center of Sicily, had been important to the Germans as a supply hub. We had bombed it heavily. It was the first really messed-up city I saw in the war. If we hadn't learned there was a good press in town, with intermittent electricity, the *News* staff would have gladly passed Caltanisetta by. Half the buildings in the middle of town were piles of rubble, much of it still smoking. Atop each pile a cluster of civilians frantically dug and poked for relatives, possibly hoping in some cases that they wouldn't be found. The bodies had already begun to stink in the mid-July heat. Growing up in the American Southwest, I had been used to the odor of dead creatures, ranging from run-over rabbits to worn-out horses, but in war I quickly learned that nothing can quite equal the pungency of decaying humans.

There are many special smells about people in war. In a village near Caltanisetta, residents had lived for many days in their cellars because of the bombing, perspiring heavily from heat and fear. When they came boiling up into the streets as we passed, there was a powerful stench of wet and rancid wool, accompanied by lesser, more subtle odors. Animals can smell fear in people: if enough frightened people are crowded together, surely another human being can detect the scent. The Germans had abandoned a storehouse of wheat. Somebody from Allied Military Government broke down the door and began rationing the grain, one helmetful to a person. There was plenty for everybody, but these people had gone underground without supplies and were ravenously hungry. I think there was a smell about this, too. Sweet, little old lady types were rolling on the street and clawing at each other for places in the line, and grown men were knocking children down. I was pressed into service, along with several other passing soldiers, to try to keep order, but the people mobbed us, too, even though we brandished guns. Along with discovering new odors, I saw that nothing is more powerful than hunger.

We set up shop in a municipal building. Next door was the Caltanisetta opera house, which had acres of gold leaf on the walls, half the roof gone from a direct hit by a five-hundred-pound bomb, and plaster dust all over the velvet seats. The director's offices befitted the rest of the building, with inlaid tables and great, overstuffed sofas. When we discovered a passageway between the municipal building and the opera, we took over the sofas for sleeping. For a while we had an interpreter—an aging singer-actor who hung around the building and agreed to work for rations. His English was terrible and we learned that his Italian was almost as bad, but his price was right.

While Robinson organized the nearby printing shop and the rest of the staff thumbed its way to the front, I poked into the ruins of the local police station. I had noticed what appeared to be a motorcycle handlebar sticking out of the rubble. It turned out to be a single-cylinder Moto-Guzzi in running condition. There were only two problems about this bike. One was that I didn't know how to ride it, and the other was that on the gas tank was the sign POLIZIA. The first was simple. I did know how to ride a bicycle, the Guzzi was a light machine, and it was simply a matter of learning how to operate the gears and clutch. By early afternoon I had it broken to saddle, having suffered only a skinned knee and knuckle.

As for the ownership, this resolved itself later in the evening, after I had moved the machine into the office and was rubbing out the insignia on one side of the tank while the interpreter worked on the other. The chief of police arrived, affectionately patted the bike on the saddle and thanked me for having found it. He said it was the only mechanized equipment the force owned. I said, through the interpreter, that this made his sacrifice all the more poignant. What sacrifice? he wanted to know, and I said the contribution the Caltanisetta police were making to a free press. The interpreter handled this nicely with gestures. I borrowed

Robinson's typewriter and typed up a very formal-looking receipt, which declared that he would get his motorcycle back at the end of hostilities and made it all the more binding by signing it "George S. Patton."

I used the bike locally for the next couple of days, running out to supply dumps and hauling back cases of "five-in-one" rations (so-called because they would feed five men for one day or one man for five days) lashed to the rear fender. This built up our food supply and gave me the feel of my new machine. Every time I rode back into town the chief would be waiting for me, wringing his hands and pleading for his bike back. I kept reminding him that Italy hadn't surrendered yet, that we were still technically enemies, and that my side appeared to be winning. He always retreated, grinning and looking conciliatory. (I never met a cop of any nationality who didn't quail before conquerors. They probably think they are thus preserving law and order.)

The real reason I wanted the motorcycle was to get myself to Palermo, the capital, a city large enough to have a photoengraving shop. The *45th Division News* was still being published without my drawings and I regarded this as an ominous situation. How long could I justify my existence as merely an assistant publisher and a ration scrounger? Only until I Company found itself in desperate need of replacements, I figured. Using for drawing paper the backs of eleven-by-fourteen-inch portraits of Mussolini and King Victor Emmanuel which I removed from the opera office walls (photos of these worthies, which were always printed on high-quality double-weight paper, provided me with a steady source of paper for the next several months), I belted out a couple of cartoons one night and set out early next morning for Palermo. Sheehan and Barrett had told me the city was already ours or due to fall at any moment.

As the Moto-Guzzi purred northward, blowing the last of the bomb dust from its innards, I found the countryside was mine. It was an eerie feeling. Sicily is a small island; two great Allied armies were battling across it, and yet aside from an occasional blown bridge and the fact that villagers scuttled out of my way, not knowing if I was an advancing American or a retreating German, I could have been a tourist on a prewar summer day. Approaching the outskirts of Palermo, I found things more normal. A tank column of the 2nd Armored Division was parked along both sides of the road. A grimy fellow with a star on his collar leaned on a jeep, smoking a cigarette.

"Excuse me, sir," I said. "Is Palermo clear?" Normally, I would have sought information from someone of lesser rank, but he seemed a young and friendly brigadier.

"Clear of what?" he asked. I noticed several heads popping out of nearby tanks, then I did a double-take as I saw that every man had at least one star on his collar. Some had as many as three. Apparently, I had

ee the town has been occupied three days . . .”

From **News of the 45th**, by Sergeant Don Robinson with art by Sergeant Bill Mauldin

We compared photographs with the Jugoslavs.

stumbled into a staff conference of underage generals.

"Clear of MPs, he probably means, you meathead," growled a major general. "He's AWOL, he's swiped a bike, and he wants to hit the poontang trail before they catch him."

"No, sir," I said. "I've got business in town."

As I hastened on my way, I saw more men with stars, including one with at least seven stuck to his helmet, and it finally dawned on me that these were Italian army stars, a standard ornament on the lapels of all enlisted men, and identical in appearance to those of our generals. The tankers had taken them from prisoners or found them in a supply dump.

To hell with asking questions, I decided. As long as I was riding down the road between rows of American tanks I figured I was safe. Besides, their turrets were unbuttoned, a sign of tranquillity. I put-putted into Palermo this way, noticing that few people were in sight and most windows were shuttered. Either they were expecting the Germans back, or were waiting to see what sort of liberators we were.

A 2nd Armored Division MP at an intersection directed me to the city hall, where I found Allied Military Government headquarters. Charging a local carabiniere with the job of watching my machine, which still bore legible traces of ownership by the Caltanisetta carabinieri, I went inside to learn what I could of photoengraving facilities in the city. Luckily, one of the first AMG people I met was Colonel Charles Poletti, a former lieutenant governor of New York, and a man not insensitive to the needs of journalists. He had just taken charge of a war-torn city of half a million or so hungry, panicky souls, and he took time to listen to the problems of a cartoonist looking for an engraver so he could get his work printed in an obscure divisional newspaper.

Poletti took me to a line of civilian men applying for interpreters' jobs. This was highly desirable work, since it led almost directly to food and supplies, and it attracted many people who couldn't even speak English. The colonel found one who could, and who also claimed he knew a photoengraver. My man, who appeared to be some sort of middle-aged civil-servant type and was dressed in a pin-striped suit with lapels to his ears, arranged himself on my back fender, using as a cushion the musette bag which contained the remnants of a five-in-one ration and the two cartoons I had prepared on the backs of the portraits. I could hear them bend and crackle furiously under this treatment, but it was too late to do more than trust the durability of the Roman photographic paper.

We found the engraving shop shuttered and deserted. Upon going to the rear, we saw why. A big bomb had wiped out everything but the front wall of the building. Neighbors told us that the engraver, fearing bombs, had moved his equipment to his house in the suburbs several days before the shop was hit. They gave us the suburban address, but advised us that we were probably wasting our time, since the house had taken a bomb in the same raid that got the shop. They seemed to find this amusing. We made our way to the house, which had two walls and half a roof. The owner was in his yard, tinkering with the lens end of a huge old copy camera. There was no sign of his family, if he had one, and I tactfully didn't ask. That bomb had done quite a job.

Fastrelli, the engraver, spoke a little English, which took the strain off my interpreter, and we were able to communicate fairly well. I produced my two cartoons, by now dog-eared, dusty, and sweat-stained, as well as crumpled, and asked if he could make a two-column cut of each. He pointed at his camera, held up a set of the little screens used to make half-tone engravings of photographs, and said that was all the equipment he had left. It was easy to believe. The yard was a welter of broken glass, twisted metal, and wood splinters.

"It is hopeless," he shrugged.

"Too bad," I said. "I would pay a good price."

"You *pay*?" He looked at the conqueror incredulously.

"Sure."

"Well," he allowed, "maybe with a little acid and zinc we could do *something*. No line engravings, you understand, but maybe halftones."

Getting the acid was easy. Leaving the interpreter, Fastrelli mounted my back fender and directed me to a warehouse. He banged on the closed metal shutters until a man let us in and sold us two glass carboys of nitric acid, each containing about five gallons and wrapped in straw. As we gingerly picked our way back through traffic (the town was now coming alive) with Fastrelli perched on the bottles lashed to the fender, it occurred to me that a pint or two would have done the job—I hadn't forgotten my engraving lessons at the Abilene *Reporter-News*—but the price had been right, and what was wrong with putting a man back into business?

Finding zinc to make the plates wasn't so easy. Fastrelli said it was a high-priority item. Then he had an inspiration. We rode to a village in the hills above the city, where we found a coffin maker. Wooden caskets of all sizes and descriptions stood in rows inside and outside the shop. The better ones were lined with zinc. The proprietor said he had none of the metal left and was outraged at our suggestion that he remove the lining from one of his masterpieces. The issue was settled when I bought a whole coffin. The maker tore out the lining with his own hands, bent it into a loose roll, and tied it across my handlebars. There was enough zinc for a hundred cartoons, but again I felt Fastrelli deserved fringe benefits. So far, my outlay for acid and metal was ten U.S. dollars.

Back in his yard, Fastrelli showed himself to be a genius at improvisation. Normally, a photoengraver uses arc lights. We used the sun, which by now was getting pretty low. Lacking the chemical called dragons' blood to coat the zinc, we concocted a mixture of our own, containing India ink, among other things. Fastrelli had been right: line engravings were out of the question. But by dark we had created two acceptable halftone cuts, and if I could get them back to Caltanisetta I would be back in print.

After negotiating briefly and settling on a price of one dollar apiece for the engravings, plus the materials, Fastrelli invited the interpreter and me to stay for supper and the night. The eating part was agreeable—it had been a long day since breakfast—and became enjoyable as we combined my canned goods with tiny tomatoes and other items from Fastrelli's garden, plus some good wine. However, I did want to get back, even though it meant riding blacked-out roads on a machine which was still not completely under my control. The interpreter said he would stay with the engraver and look for a more conventional employer in the morning, so I paid him two dollars—my cash outlay was now up to fourteen dollars but worth every cent, I felt—and took off into the night with my precious metal two-column plates buttoned inside my shirt pocket.

Half an hour later, my good manners cost me my transportation. Stopping at AMG to thank Colonel Poletti, I parked in front of the building and again asked a carabiniere to guard the machine. The colonel was busy so I left a note for him. Outside, there was no sign of the policeman or the bike. I had to admit to myself that there was a certain justice in a Palermo cop's theft of a motorcycle which had been stolen from a Caltanisetta cop, and besides, the Moto-Guizzi had served its purpose. I caught a ride in a truck headed south, and next day the *News* went to press with Mauldin cartoons.

We got word that the division brass was pleased with the overseas *News*. We stayed out of everybody's hair, we put out a readable paper, in spite of production difficulties, and we had credibility. A tangible sign of headquarters approval was the assignment of a leaky amphibious jeep to the *News* staff, with a driver named Irving Richtel. We called him Rico. Like most of us, he was a refugee from the infantry—in his case the 157th Regiment. Rico immediately realized that he had a vested interest in the success of our newspaper, so that he became a rare bird in the annals of military jeep drivers: he was friendly, willing, and able. We couldn't say so much for his machine, which we called a seep, after an abortive attempt to make it float. The only thing that could be said for amphibious jeeps was that their heavy hulls made them ride better.

We moved to Palermo and applied to AMG for quarters, going through channels for one of the few times in the life of the *News*. A British officer in charge of billeting gave us an entire schoolhouse in the center of town. We were a newspaper, weren't we? The building had about thirty rooms, which the officer hoped would be adequate for our staff. If not, we could have the small department store next door. We assured him that the schoolhouse would do for the moment.

A day or so later, we returned to our billet from a scouting expedition for downtown printing and engraving facilities and found the British officer waiting for us. He had learned the true size of our staff and had moved fifty liberated Jugoslav partisans into our schoolhouse with us. Captured and brought to Palermo by the Germans as labor troops, they were lucky to have been abandoned by their captors rather than shot, which was the usual German practice with guerrillas, who had no legal rights.

"They're really an incredible bunch of chaps," the Britisher told us. "They don't look like much now, but they were pretty solid citizens at home. That one over there was a Diesel engineer, I understand. There are schoolteachers, electricians, carpenters—they're all intelligent, well-educated professional people. Remarkable."

"Who's going to take care of them?" we asked, staring at our new roomers, who looked about as remarkable as a pack of drowned rats. The Germans had not been kind to them.

"At the moment, AMG can't do much beyond billeting them. I was rather hoping you chaps might think of a way to provide for them for a few days. From what I've seen, you don't have much else to do."

Rico had an inspiration. We had been given a number of signed, blank requisition forms to provide ourselves with necessities from various ration and supply dumps. This was very irregular; it amounted to a blank check with all sorts of possibilities for black marketeering, but they trusted us at division and so far we hadn't let them down. Now we did a little swindling, by adding a five to the six on several of the forms so that we were able to draw stuff for sixty-five men. Rico made the rounds of the dumps in his seep and returned with a mountain of blankets, clothing, and rations. Just for the hell of it, he had also accepted several hundred contraceptive kits. The Jugoslavs, deeply moved by all this, filed by to thank us, one by one, as Richtel issued the goods, including the little kits. From these the men removed the bars of green soap—powerful stuff to kill crabs—and took turns using the bathroom in the school principal's office, until everybody was deloused and shining, if a little bloodshot in the eyes from the soap.

That night we had a party. One of the partisans found a broken electric record player in a closet. Borrowing Rico's pliers and screwdriver, he fixed the player. Another man fussed with the wiring in the building for half an hour and we had power. Two partisans disappeared into the streets and came back with armloads of records, including some old Caruso opera songs which were probably collectors' items. Others went out and came

"Stop shootin' at him, ya idiot! Wanna give away our position?"

This is one of the first two engravings made in Palermo on the coffin zinc. Note the edge of a nail hole above the airplane's wing.

back with wine, bread, and cheese. All this was accomplished without spending any money. One tough-looking young man who turned out to be a mathematics teacher disappeared during the festivities and brought us an entire roll of tickets for *Intermezzo,* with Ingrid Bergman, playing at a nearby civilian theater. Robinson caught this Jugoslav returning one of our .45 pistols to its holster. The fellow admitted he had held up the box office. He wanted to give us something we might enjoy.

Toasting time came. The partisans had stolen a lot of wine. We got into long, complicated salutes to Roosevelt, Marshall, Eisenhower, Robinson, Richtel, Tapscott, Mauldin, Sheehan, and Barrett. Finally, it occurred to me that we should reciprocate. I lifted my cup to King Peter of Jugoslavia. A silence ensued. What the hell? Peter was their king, wasn't he? Realizing that I was embarrassed, these Communist disciples of Tito slowly got to their feet and solemnly toasted their king, whose guts they hated and whom they regarded as a collaborator with the enemy.

"I told you your political savvy was on a par with Little Orphan Annie's," Robinson whispered to me. "You're goddamn lucky they didn't throw you out the window."

After a few days a Jugoslavian liaison officer arrived to take away our friends, who had begun to look almost human with a little flesh on their bones from our rations. Their departure was the occasion for another party. At one point, I toasted Tito, which brought forth a roar of applause. The officer made a little thank-you speech to us and said the men would go to North Africa for outfitting and would shortly be dropped by parachute back into Jugoslavia. They are probably all dead now.

9

Now that the *News* was more or less comfortably established I had little excuse not to get out and see more of the war. The 45th Division had some of its bloodiest combat in Sicily toward the end of the campaign, pushing eastward along the north coast, where the Germans were fighting a ferocious rear-guard action while evacuating the bulk of their troops across the Strait of Messina into Italy. By now the royal Italian government was thinking of surrendering to us, but Mussolini's Fascists and the Germans made it clear that even if this happened they intended to delay our triumphal entry into Rome as long as possible.

Although I mostly hung around the infantry when out in the field, I developed a complex about going back to K Company. It probably started one day when I arrived at my old outfit a few hours after the Medicine Man had been killed. He had flushed a German rifleman out of a foxhole with his bayonet (apparently he had fixed the bayonet to his rifle just for this particular purpose, since infantrymen seldom used the things in combat) and had chased his victim across a clearing between some German and American positions. The pair had run back and forth for a while, the frantic German scurrying like a mouse and the big Indian cat loping behind, jabbing lightly at the enemy's rump as a goad, laughing his fool head off. Both sides stopped firing and stared in astonishment at the weird chase until the Medicine Man tired of it and skewered the German, whereupon the other side blew him apart. Since he could have safely shot the German in the first place, maybe he was just displaying an Indian's macabre sense of humor. Personally, I suspect it was the Medicine Man's way of having a fit of combat fatigue.

Most of my friends in K Company were getting killed in more prosaic ways, by impersonal, random rounds of mortar, howitzer, or machine-gun fire. The 45th was a well-trained division and lost its men in dribbles, not floods, but the dribbling went on day after day. It's much easier to see this happening to strangers rather than your old friends. Besides, I had a special sense of guilt because I had been conniving for several years to end up with a sketchbook in my hand instead of a weapon. It could be argued that this was a sensible allocation of talent, since I was a hell of a lot better with a pencil than with a gun. But I knew that nine out of ten guys getting killed out there were also better at doing something else than getting killed. My guilt was compounded by the fact that when I did visit K Company my surviving friends were proud to see my stuff in the paper and not a bit resentful. One of the things that always distinguished the infantry for me was that you seldom saw a man who had been in that sort of combat for long bitching and groaning about the fact that some other guy or branch of service had a better deal. If he saw a bomber passing overhead with its crew headed for warm billets and cold beer, he would not snarl in envy but would sigh in appreciation. So I was based in Palermo, huh? How was the tail? They made me feel awful.

Getting to the front in any twentieth-century ground war imposes certain other emotional strains on the visitor. The problem involves transition from safety to danger, and everything becomes relative. For example, a regimental command post hardly ever suffers casualties, but almost everybody in those CPs wears a helmet, and from there you can hear most of the fireworks. An unknowledgeable visitor there might well imagine himself to be in the middle of the action. Most VIP and movie-star tours end at regimental CPs, from whence the luminaries return home and tell how they've seen the war. Battalion CPs are something else. They are generally within howitzer and heavy-mortar range, and you can get hurt there. But not often. To a soldier heading rearward from the real front his battalion CP is a haven. Moving forward from battalion to company, you get within range of bullets, which is a hairy thought, yet strangely enough the war gets quieter (unless, of course, there is an enemy barrage going on, in which case you took a wrong turn back there or got some bad advice). The reason it gets quieter is that it has become more personal. Enemy artillery pieces and your own are about equidistant from you and expend a surprising amount of ammunition simply shooting at each other, so that most of it is usually going over your head and booming in the distance. The important thing from here forward is to have a few acquaintances. Even though I often avoided K Company

I tried to confine my visits to units where I knew people. One of the most fatuous and puzzling notions common among many inexperienced civilians and rear-echelon brass hats who actually get to the front is that the infantrymen up there are going to be solicitous about their visitors' welfare. If you are a stranger blundering your way toward a clump of enemies in a bush, the average dogface in his hole will assume that you know what you're doing, or that you are a souvenir hunter. Besides, it might be useful to him to see exactly where the fire is coming from when they shoot at you. If he knows you, on the other hand, he realizes you're an idiot and might holler a warning at you—unless it means exposing his own position. Before he'll do that you have to owe him a lot of money. Why should he feel otherwise about all this? His ass is on the line all the time, every day. You can leave any time; he can't.

Anyway, when you do head for the rear, with your notebook full, you are amazed as you pass this point and that one that you could have felt such a growing nervousness as you advanced by them earlier. By the time you're back at a regimental CP you feel as secure as if you were back in the States. Yet if you come back next day the same trip will scare hell out of you all over again. Sheehan, Barrett, and Tapscott, who spent more time at this sort of thing than I did—and didn't share my advantage of being able to choose units to visit, since they had to cover the entire division—all admitted at various times that they often found it easier on their nerves to stay in the lines than to go back and forth. It isn't just a mental thing, either. Any study of casualties among war correspondents will show most of them hit in transit, not at the actual front.

Up to now, our publishing overhead had been ridiculous. We lived off ration dumps and paid printing bills out of our own pockets. I don't think any had exceeded fifteen dollars. In Palermo, however, we were putting out a bigger paper on more sophisticated presses, with Tapscott's pictures and my cartoons running up engraving bills. Rico had an idea. I had told him about my book-publishing venture in Louisiana. He convinced Don Robinson that a Mauldin cartoon book of the Sicilian campaign would be a hot item among the troops as a souvenir. While I gathered my material and made some new drawings, Rico went around to the regiments taking orders. Within a week, *Sicily Sketchbook*, a small paperback of about two dozen pages, was off the presses and sold twenty or thirty thousand copies throughout the division at twenty-five cents apiece, including a mailing envelope. This got us out of hock to the printers and carried us well into the Italian campaign.

My first son, Bruce, was born that summer as the Sicilian campaign was ending. I read about his birth in a letter while riding with Rico through a village on the north coast. Elements of the 45th had taken the town not long before; as we entered, it had the usual bleak look of

Jean, with Bruce, right, who was born while I was in Sicily, and his brother Tim, born after the war.

"Yessir, I got my Purple Heart—nossir, I ain't married—yessir, my blood is type 'A'—if I got any left after all these questions."

recent "liberation," with drawn shutters and deserted sidewalks. Sicilians have been liberated too many times to be hasty about welcoming the latest conqueror before sizing him up through a crack in the curtains. Now, as I sat in the seep in a slightly dazed condition, reading details about my child, I became dimly aware of windows and doors suddenly banging open, and of excited villagers thronging about us, jabbering and hollering in what appeared to be joy.

"Jeezus, something big must have happened," Rico said.

"Damn right," I said, showing him the letter. When a mustachioed old boy gave me a tearful, garlicky kiss, it seemed entirely appropriate, and I kissed him back. At some point Rico got near a radio and told me the news had just broken that Montgomery had entered Calabria with two British divisions, and Italy was formally withdrawing from the war. Even so, I kept on accepting congratulations from everybody as a personal thing. Why not? I was twenty-two years old, a father, and the author of a best-selling book of cartoons.

The Roman government's surrender did little to upset German strategy; if anything, it simplified things for them. Now they could defend Italy without the Italian army underfoot. The 45th and the rest of the Allied units began staging for the Salerno beachhead. The *News* closed shop in Palermo and we went into bivouac with the division headquarters company. It wasn't bad, tenting under the olive trees, and discipline in that particular outfit had never been Spartan, but still it chafed a little to be reminded that we were back in the army after our independent life of the past few weeks. Around headquarters there was always some damned lieutenant or major who felt he should be saluted. Rico tried for the hundredth time to seal the cracks in the battered seep, although nobody could figure why he wanted it to float. Sheehan and Barrett gathered fresh anecdotes to lighten the pages of the next issue (there was no doubt in our minds that there would be one), Tapscott fussed with his camera equipment, Robinson started a book about our adventures so far for the University of Oklahoma press, and I suddenly got sick.

My ailment was sand-flea fever, a short-lived but virulent thing which put me into a field hospital near Palermo. Three days later, wobbly but recovered, I asked for a ride back to my division. Naturally. Where else would I go? To any soldier his unit becomes his family and home after a while. He might hate it sometimes, but that's where he belongs, and when he has been sick or hurt and in the hospital for a while, you would think the U.S. army would see the sense of sending him back to his outfit. In my own case, of course, it was unthinkable to go elsewhere.

There I was, almost within spitting distance of the staging area where my friends were loading up for Salerno, and there I was told, to my unbelieving horror, that I was no longer a member of a unit but a "casual," subject to reassignment anywhere. I learned later that this was common practice: the army's way of being impersonal. A man was a unit, a statistic. If a company was supposed to have 170 men, only the number was important. Any 170 would do. Later, in Italy, time after time, I ran into men who hid minor wounds and ailments to avoid being sent to hospitals and ending up as casuals. A man was safer staying with his friends. He could get killed in some new outfit, full of strangers. In my own case, there was a fine, budding career at stake, as well. Along with several other protesting convalescents, I was loaded into a truck and sent to a replacement depot.

"Why are you guys in such a hurry for another beachhead?" asked the lieutenant who checked us in.

That night I fell in with a group of diehards and plotted a breakout. The depot was indistinguishable from a prisoners' stockade, with a high wall on all sides and guards on the wall. After considering and rejecting a half-dozen plans, we decided the only sensible way was the spectacular one. About twenty of us went over the wall simultaneously, in a rush, and told the guards to go to hell. Since it wasn't really a prison, exactly, and they weren't actual MPs—merely casuals like us who had been dragooned into guard duty—they didn't shoot, although they did wave their weapons at us and return our obscenities.

I caught one of the last of the division's boats to leave for Salerno. It was an LST, loaded with ammunition for the beachhead. After we were under way I was told that along with the other stragglers aboard I would be allowed to work off the price of my "ticket" by helping to unload the ship. To my amazement I found Don Robinson also aboard. He had hit a snag on his book and had been dawdling along at a mere eight thousand words a day, so preoccupied that the rest of the company had pulled out from under him, leaving him typing alone under the olive trees, and he had had to run to catch this boat.

By the time we arrived at the beachhead below Salerno, the desperate part of the battle was over and the fighting had moved inland, but the Luftwaffe, which had a habit of being officially destroyed and then resurrecting itself, was out in force, trying to clobber the supply ships, and a number of P-38s, Mustangs, Thunderbolts, and Spitfires were working hard to frustrate them. A couple of destroyers were frantically racing about laying down smoke screens to hide us, but the stuff seemed to cling to the surface, leaving our superstructure showing as a target and making the air unbreathable for us. We were glad to note that there were plenty of other LSTs unloading, which provided a variety of targets.

It became a long night. The attacks kept up, but we could no longer watch, because we were busy in the hold. There were monstrous stacks of 155-milimeter artillery projectiles, piled like cordwood, each weighing

"Thank you, sir—all we needed was somebody blowin' his horn."

A typical landscape in Sicily and Southern Italy. This cartoon shows I was not always anti-MP.

upward of a hundred pounds. There were mountains of 105-millimeter shells in wooden crates, three to a box. There were mortar shells and cases of grenades. The method of unloading was simple: we were anchored in deep water a half mile from shore with our huge clamshell bow doors open and the ramp down in the water. A procession of DUKWs, or "ducks," big brothers to our amphibious jeep, chugged out to us, drove up the ramp, took on their loads, and chugged back to shore. I don't know why most of them weren't swamped, because the water was slightly choppy and when loaded these monsters had only about an inch of freeboard.

I have never been involved in a working party where there was so little malingering. We knew that we would not get ashore until we had finished. There were only about a dozen of us, and there must have been four or five hundred tons of high explosive to handle. Even some sailors pitched in and helped. We weren't hit once, although the LST was rocked a few times, either by bombs aimed at us or misses aimed at other craft. Once we were bracketed by two of them. Oddly, although everyone was nervous and tense, I don't think anybody was truly scared. The situation was something like standing in a forest fire with a suitcase full of fireworks: fear seems a rather inadequate emotion. Finally, it was done. As dawn began to break, we loaded ourselves into one of the ducks, and set out for Italy.

We went ashore at Paestum. Don Robinson, who had a taste for ancient history, had made an avocation of trying to improve my mind as we made our way through Sicily, pointing out this ruin and that and explaining its significance. Now, as we hitchhiked toward the 45th's sector of the front, he told me about Paestum, a veritable treasure trove of classic Greek ruins, but his heart wasn't in it. Mainly, we were looking at a lot of modern corpses. If we had felt a little sorry for ourselves while unloading ammo a while back, we got over it as we surveyed the grisly beachhead scene. The Germans had almost thrown our forces back into the sea. We passed a field where a company from the 36th Division had dug in and been overrun by a Panzer outfit. German infantrymen riding on the tanks had jumped off and slaughtered the men in their holes, some with bayonets. Many bodies were still there. A little farther on, we passed a coffin which had been blasted out of the ground by a bomb. The lid was askew. From within, an old man, withered but still with flesh, stared at us with empty eye sockets and a horrible, toothy grin.

As often happens when you wander around footloose in a moving war, we missed our divisional CP and found ourselves caught up with a battalion from the 157th Infantry, which was cautiously moving up a mountain road. It turned out that we both knew the captain of the lead company, and while we were asking directions from him, one of his scouts came back and led us all to a farmhouse by the road. The corpses of two Italian men lay in a courtyard in front of the house. Three shiny brass Mauser cartridge cases lay ten feet from them. The courtyard had a gentle slope; from each man a little rivulet of blood coursed downhill for about twenty feet. It was still moving slowly, so they hadn't been dead long. From inside the house came a moaning sound. We found three women, two of them widows of the men outside. The other was the wife of a third man, who sat slumped in a chair, barely alive. It was the woman who had been moaning, not him. He had been hit in the throat, the bullet going in just above his breastbone and coming cleanly out between his shoulder blades. All he could do was bubble.

The women, who had been in a state of shock, suddenly let go their emotions when they saw us, and began screaming and wailing and kissing our hands as if we had saved the situation. I lit a cigarette and offered it to the wounded man. As Robinson observed afterward, it hardly seemed appropriate medicine for a man with a hole in his pipes, but the farmer took it with a gray little nod of thanks and it seemed to perk him up a little. I left him the pack. Although the captain sent the scout out for a litter to take the man to the aid station, I doubt if he survived. The women told us the shooting had occurred half an hour earlier. They had thought the last of the Germans had pulled out, but suddenly two young riflemen had showed up, called the three couples outside, and asked the farmers and their wives if they knew their government had pulled out of the war. The Italians had said, of course they knew it. Very well, the soldiers had said, we just want to be sure that when you ladies are living in peace behind the enemy lines you won't forget your old friends and allies. Then they had butchered the men, tipped their forage caps to the women, and departed.

Not all the natives felt like kissing our hands. As we made our way over the hill to division we passed through a little mountainside village where the entire population, some thirty or forty people, were gathered in the square. We said, "Bon giorno," and they said nothing; they simply stared balefully at us. Then we saw the body of a little boy. He was horribly shot up, and laid out on a large stone, almost like a sacrifice on an altar. Although the people were clearly not in a chatty mood, we felt compelled to ask what had happened. One of our fighter planes had made a single strafing pass over the town, and this was the only casualty. There is no way of knowing whether the pilot thought he saw a legitimate target or was just being exuberant, but as far as the village was concerned that man had come all the way across the ocean for the express purpose of killing that child. That is the attitude villagers everywhere take when war comes to them. I don't blame them. We Americans fought our wars in a much more innocent frame of mind in those days.

While Don and I were still in the 157th regimental area, we came upon a scene which always comes back to my mind when I see television comics portraying stereotypes about World War II: the Germans, of course, being blockheads who march over cliffs at orders from their monocled officers, and the Americans being laconic, freewheeling democrats at heart. We saw a patrol bringing in two prisoners: a young German lieutenant with a badly mangled and gangrenous leg, and a private from the officer's platoon. The lieutenant told us he had been left behind because he was too sick to move. He said the soldier had volunteered to stay and look after him until they were both captured.

In the heat of war, especially a fast-moving invasion, there were no money-back guarantees about letting oneself get captured. Even against an enemy who was supposedly committed to following the rules, a lot depended upon the mood of the man to whom one surrendered. If he had just lost his best friend, or if he was in a hurry and couldn't be bothered with prisoners, he was likely to shoot. This was a reality of combat known to both sides. The two German captives were obviously veterans who knew it, too. Therefore, the soldier's act of devotion was not just a gesture, or a way to get a free ride out of the war. It was interesting to note that the 157th dogfaces who brought the pair in were impressed to such an extent that they were carrying the officer with gentle solicitude and had given cigarettes to the soldier.

"Stop and think," Don said to me. "Did you ever know an officer you'd do that for?"

"Sure. Walter Harrison," I said.

"I mean company grade, not headquarters colonels."

I had to admit, with some horror, that there were few. We had all heard stories of American officers being shot in the back, of course, and possibly some of these were true, though I didn't know of any cases that could have been authenticated. Personally, I couldn't think of any lieutenants I hated, exactly, but there sure as hell weren't any for whom I'd have risked my skin.

"We just never got over the fact that a guy named Von Steuben helped train the first American army," Don said. "Our military hangs on to some of its Prussian ways even after the Germans have recognized them as obsolete."

For a while we hung around the outskirts of Salerno like buzzards and watched the British and Germans fight over the town, but when it became obvious that neither side was getting anywhere, Sergeant Robinson succumbed to the pounding of ink in his veins, squared his shoulders, and led his men where duty lay. Within hours we were set up in a relatively undamaged shop and Don had rounded up some reluctant printers. Barrett and Sheehan were loaded with 45th Division copy they had picked

"Hit th' dirt, boys!"

"That's our mountain team."

"Dammit, ya promised to bring rations this trip!"

"Yes, we've sent our quota to the rest camp. . . .
This is the company commander speaking!"

This scene shows why I switched from fine to heavy brush lines, and from grays to stark blacks and whites. It not only showed the mountain war more accurately, but made for better reproductions from local engravers and printers.

Photo by John Phillips

"What's funny about horizontal foxholes?"

up during the past few days, and they had got the latest BBC international news from a British battalion radio operator. One item stated that His Majesty's troops had taken Salerno. We corrected this to read that the town was *being* taken by *Allied* troops. This was tit for tat. BBC had a habit of crediting British with their own Eighth Army triumphs, and "Allies" with American scores.

Then, while Rico set out with the seep to distribute our product, we looked around for an empty apartment. These weren't hard to find, since many of Salerno's residents had found the suburban air more to their liking for the moment. We took over a large flat on the second floor of a building across the street from the printer. A smaller apartment next door contained a grand piano. That place will always be memorable to me as the scene of a fastidious rape. Toward midnight of our first day there, I was alone with the piano, picking out tunes with one finger by candlelight with a blanket over the window, when there was a knock, accompanied by a small barrage of mortar fire into the next street which dropped ceiling plaster all over the piano and me. The floor was already littered with plaster. At the door was a grimy British infantryman, festooned with bandoleers and grenades, and a pretty Italian girl who couldn't have been more than fifteen, although her charms were ample.

"Hello, Yank," the soldier said, grinning. He went to a cupboard, rummaged around until he found a lace doily about ten inches in diameter, delicately spread it over the plaster in a corner and placed the girl's rump upon the doily. I will have to define the rape as statutory, since there was no struggle from the victim. In fact, she smiled at me as they left. I tried to get back to my music, but my heart wasn't in it. I kept looking at the doily and thinking what a gentleman the guy had been not to get plaster on the girl. The British might be decadent, but they were delicate.

Next morning when I was alone in the apartment working on a cartoon, the most godawful domestic squabble I had ever heard broke out in the alley below our window. There was a crashing and screeching and roaring, followed by more hollering and a couple of thuds. I stepped out to our balcony and saw, directly below, a skinny, mustachioed young buckaroo beating hell out of his wife, a hefty girl about half again his size.

The battle was not altogether one-sided. The girl had no boxing ability, but she was a slugger, and from time to time her husband walked into a roundhouse and went on his fanny, only to bounce up and pepper her with a barrage of rights and lefts. Once he got her down and kicked her in the stomach. This man was clearly out of control and didn't give a hoot where or how he hit her. One of the most shocking aspects of the whole thing, to me, was that the combatants had a large audience of neighbors, male and female, all of whom were enjoying the spectacle and hollering encouragement or abuse at one or the other. The claques seemed about evenly divided, and a couple of ancillary slapping matches broke out between husbands and wives in the audience, but these didn't amount to much. I stared, horrified, for a couple of minutes, and then began yelling down from my vantage point directly overhead. I was only about ten feet away, and in good voice, so I did attract some attention from the people, who were not used to hearing English spoken in these affairs. But then they must have decided that I had merely joined the husband's claque and ignored me as another fight fan. The husband and wife never noticed me at all. She was bleeding from the nose and both eyes.

I went back into the room, grabbed somebody's M-1 rifle, and reappeared on the balcony, lining the husband up in the sights. We were a safety-minded crew and kept our weapons empty in quarters, but I'll swear if that piece had been loaded I'd have been tempted to shoot the guy. The effect of the empty rifle was just as good. There was a gasp from the crowd, which melted into doorways and around corners. The panting battlers looked up at me. The husband's eyes grew big as saucers and he dropped to his knees, covered his head with his arms, and began begging for mercy. Not so the wife. Wiping her bloody nose with her skinned-up knuckles, she marched across the alley, reached up, and grabbed the rifle's muzzle. I snatched it back to safety, and stood there dumbfounded as she screamed at me. Happily, I couldn't understand most of it, but I got the idea. She was telling me what she thought of people who interfered in private family discussions, punctuating her lecture from time to time with a grunt as she made another lunge at my weapon. Slowly, the husband uncovered himself, got to his feet, and stared at his woman with love and pride. When she had finished with me, this magnificent hunk of wifehood turned her broad back on me, took her husband's arm, and led him away. The people in the alley went back to their affairs and I went back to my drawing board.

10

As the American Fifth and British Eighth armies charged up the Italian boot, the Germans fought skillful delaying actions and used the time gained to dig into a defense line across the peninsula, between Naples and Rome. The key was the mountain range around Cassino, where nature had arranged the topography in such a way that a resourceful defender could hold out against almost any odds. In fact, the Cassino area was famous in war colleges all over the world as near-perfect defensive terrain. It was true, and the Germans were plenty resourceful, so there we bogged down. It would have been a bad winter at best—one of the coldest and wettest in Italian history, with constant snow and freezing rain in the mountains and seas of knee-deep mud in the valleys—and the ordeal of our infantrymen was compounded by poor management in many cases. At a time when rifle companies were hacked down to platoon size by casualties, trenchfoot, and pneumonia, there was no rotation system, so that for every dogface suffering in the hills there were ten "support troops" getting fat in Naples and working union hours in the rear. As Churchill once remarked, our military peacock was mostly tail. Just about the only way the combat man could get out was to be carried out.

The *45th Division News* became part of the Neapolitan scene, settling in a building on the Via Roma in Naples, near a small printing shop. We were probably somewhat more aware of the contrast between front and rear than the average clerk or quartermaster because our work constantly

"How ya gonna find out if they're fresh troops if ya don't wake 'em up an' ask?"

Our money-making Christmas card.

Our full-page, full-color Christmas cartoon.

took us to and from the 45th, which was dug in around Venafro, east of Cassino. Each of us came back from every trip forward feeling both grateful and guilty about being spared from those freezing-wet foxholes and those deadly-accurate German 88 guns and mortars, and it was probably a good thing, because our work reflected our feelings. Our paper took on a new character. Light anecdotes gave way to irony. It was during this period that Willie and Joe became ragged and grew beards. The reason infantrymen at the front wore beards that winter was that supplies had to be carried up the steep slopes by mule and man back, so that there wasn't even enough water for drinking, let alone shaving. Besides, beards kept faces warmer, and helped camouflage them at night.

About the only sign of war in Naples was the daily air raid. Skillful as they usually were at the game of war, the Germans were unimaginative time-clock punchers in some of their activities. They would get into the habit of shelling a crossroads or bombing a town at certain hours and minutes of the day, and would get so predictable that you could time them down to the last sip of coffee or drag on a cigarette before you climbed into your hole or went down to your cellar. They sent planes over to raid Naples harbor every evening at precisely five-fifteen. People literally set their watches by it. At five-oh-five the anti-aircraft people would light up their smokepots, and by five-twelve the city would be choking in a dense, acrid white cloud. At five-fourteen the guns would start firing in the suburbs, you would hear the drone of the engines, and at five-fifteen the whole thing would come to a crescendo directly overhead, with machine guns chattering, 40-millimeter cannons thumping, and the big 90s roaring.

Interspersed with this clamor were irregular thumps and crumps as the planes dumped their loads at random around town and got the hell out of there. They seldom hit the harbor. We knew this because we were only three or four blocks away from it and considered it the safest area in Naples. In fact, they never knew what they were hitting under that thick cloud, and I doubt if they cared. They had orders to go bomb Naples harbor, at exactly five-fifteen, and they could faithfully report home that they had done their best. If they had ever been sent out ten minutes early they could probably have sunk everything in the harbor, because the defenses got into the habit of punctuality, too.

Although the scattered bombs caused little more actual damage to the city than did our own dud anti-aircraft shells crashing back down on our heads, most Neapolitans were terrified of the raids and spent a great deal of time that winter huddled together in dank shelters and tunnels. A louse could walk miles over warm bodies without having to touch ground. Since lice transmit typhus, Naples soon had the beginnings of a

"Th' yellow one is fer national defense, th' red one wid white stripes is fer very good conduct, and th' real purty one wid all th' colors is fer bein' in this theater of operations. . . ."

"Straighten those shoulders! How long have you been in the Army?"

"Th' hell with it, sir. Let's go back to th' front."

It was during this period that Willie and Joe took on their final identity.

"Them buttons was shot off when I took this t sir."

terrible epidemic. One day there were a dozen cases, a week later a thousand. For the soldiers there were shots. These were so effective that the army had only a handful of mild cases, mostly among men who neglected to take the second and third shots in the series.

For the civilians there was the newly-invented DDT. Nobody knew in those days that the stuff was a menace in its own right. At the time it seemed a miracle from heaven. Gentlemen and stevedores, prostitutes and proper ladies lined up and opened their clothes without a blush to be sprayed from head to foot with the white powder. I remember dusting a two-ounce can of DDT over myself every day during the epidemic, so that I always looked as if I had been working in a bakery. One day I dusted a dog belonging to one of the printers, holding a newspaper under him to catch the bugs. It sounded like rain on a tin roof. Whatever the dangerous residual effects may have been, there is no doubt that DDT prevented a major tragedy in Naples. Within days after the dusting started the epidemic was over.

Looking back on it, I suppose Naples was my favorite Italian city. Of course, it was spectacularly beautiful, even with all the damaged buildings and sunken ships cluttering its harbor, which was its best landscape feature. But best of all I liked the Neapolitans. As in Sicily, working with local people in the printing shop gave us a chance to get invited to their homes and meet their families in a relaxed way denied to most American soldiers. Unlike Sicilians, Neapolitans seemed at ease with invaders.

"We've been picking foreigners' pockets in wholesale lots for centuries," one of our engravers said. "If the Germans ever let you get to Rome, you will find the people there very self-righteous. They will tell you not to lock anything up: 'We're not thieves like those Neapolitans.' Then they'll steal your shirt from under your coat. In Naples we tell everybody to put a pin through his money pocket. We are open, honest crooks here."

On my way to this man's home for dinner with his family one night, I walked through a maze of narrow, crowded alleys, stopping occasionally to watch domestic squabbles or to extricate myself from mobs of persistent ten-year-old pimps. (At one point during our occupation of Naples there were eighty thousand registered prostitutes, probably three times that many unregistered ones, and each must have had four little brothers.) Under my arm was a canvas musette bag containing a flat can of beef stew from a five-in-one ration, several cans of C-ration, and three or four tiny foil packets of instant coffee. The bag was buckled when I started and still secure when I arrived at my host's apartment. Also, I had kept it tightly under my arm the whole way. Even so, along the way somebody had managed to unfasten it, remove the stew and coffee, and buckle it again, all without my knowledge. I respect professionalism in any endeavor.

Acquisitive as they might have been in a material way, I found Neapolitans—and southern Italians in general—very warm and generous in human affairs. A drunken soldier who passed out on the street was sure to be rolled, but if he looked uncomfortable the next passer-by would rearrange his limbs, or even roll up his jacket and put his head on it. As the military occupation of the city grew older thousands of nice Neapolitan girls shacked up with rear-echelon clerks, made their meals, washed their clothes, got pregnant by them, and asked only to be reassured from time to time that they were loved. Naturally, most of these girls had matrimony on their minds. Married American soldiers with shack jobs found it easy to lie to their mistresses in these matters, and groups of them would sit around a beer in the Galleria laughing about the gullibility of their broads, then complaining in the next breath about the cynicism of the conniving Neapolitan male.

Actually Neapolitan larceny had a lilt, like the local music. Thieves stole with style. Born artists, they also knew when to stop. The trouble with a great many crooked Americans in Naples was that they had no such sense of restraint. Immediately after the city became the main supply port for the American Fifth and British Eighth armies, providing dock facilities for unloading weapons, vehicles, clothing, ammunition, and provisions for some half a million men, the pilferage and black marketeering rose to levels which were to be approached only after a quarter of a century, in Vietnam. Literally thousands of U.S. troops became involved, some of them deserters working full time and others on a moonlight basis. Imagine yourself back in that time as a Neapolitan grifter with a family tradition of mild skulduggery, accustomed to eking out a delicate living, enough to keep pasta in the kids, with meat twice a week. Out of nowhere come hundreds of ships loaded to the gunwales with fresh beef, canned fruit juice, beautiful leather boots, warm jackets, fluffy blankets, sleek machines, beer, whiskey, wool underwear, cotton mattress covers, and cigarettes. So many cigarettes that if you lit them all in one puff Vesuvio herself would expire with envy. Consider that these ships were manned by merchant mariners, highly-paid civilians, members of a union that demanded extra-hazard money for going into any war zone, whether the dangerous Murmansk run or the comparatively placid Mediterranean. Their pay was in U.S. currency, worth about six times the official exchange rate for military scrip. They got air-raid bonuses every time enemy aircraft, even single ones, appeared over a harbor in which their ship was anchored, regardless of whether the mariners were aboard or ashore multiplying the bonuses by six. (The Navy crews who had to stay on deck manning the anti-aircraft guns somehow missed out on the bonuses.)

Consider further (you are still thinking as the meek little Neapolitan hot-cameo peddler and postcard dealer) that waiting on the dock to take all the tons of goodies out of the hands of the mariners are U.S. quartermaster troops, many of whom have been brought up to believe that free enterprise was invented by Jay Gould and have been told by certain prominent sports celebrities married to movie stars that nice guys finish last. Swell the ranks of the quartermasters by some combat veterans who came to Naples on rest leaves and for various reasons forgot their way back to the front. Finally, take stock of the fact, you self-deprecating, shoulder-shrugging, gold-toothed hustler of the back alleys, that you forgot more about larceny before the age of ten than the average American thief working the battered docks of your hallowed city could hope to learn in his pampered lifetime. Clearly, the overfed jerks need leaders. For a man of your stature to refuse a call to greatness would be an impertinence.

Hard-working American boys under Neapolitan guidance achieved miracles. Long convoys of trucks, manned and guarded by crew-cut youngsters from such places as Brooklyn and Broken Elbow, led by jeeps bearing U.S. lieutenants and majors with personal papers and requisition forms in order, relieved freshly-arrived ships of comestibles, dry goods, or both. (They didn't take ammunition if they could help it. Fortunately for the war effort, it wasn't very marketable, so most of it got through to the front.) Sometimes these convoys had MP escorts. The procession of trucks would take a shortcut through a side street or alley, emerge empty within a few minutes, and go back for more. Sometimes the vehicles themselves disappeared, having been dismantled on the spot for future sale as spare parts.

At one point late in 1943 supply officers in the field estimated they were receiving only about two-thirds of what was being shipped to them from the States. Even this figure is misleading, since with only salable items being pilfered, if one-third of the gross supplies were missing, then higher percentages of the best food, cigarettes, and clothing were going on the black market. Infantrymen in the mountains, enduring the wettest, coldest winter in Italian weather records while fighting one of the nastiest wars in military history, suffered from trenchfoot because they couldn't get boots to keep their feet dry, pneumonia because they couldn't get jackets and blankets, malnutrition (literally) because even the miserable types of combat rations then being issued were in short supply and had to be doled out—and to top it off, they were denied the comfort of a smoke. Most good cigarettes went on the black market. When the infantry got any at all, they were usually ten-cent-per-pack brands such as Wings and Twenty Grand. Possibly all this explains why some of the boys decided to get lost themselves in Naples.

"Just gimme th' aspirin. I already got a Purple Heart."

Presiding over this mess was an American major general in command of what was called the Peninsular Base Section, which included Naples and its harbor. A tidy soul, the general cared less about what was going on in the alleys than about how his streets looked. Trickling back from the front were occasional infantrymen on four-day rest leaves. There weren't many of them, since most units at the front were woefully under strength and often stayed in the line for weeks without relief. About the only way a soldier got a rest leave was when his commander decided the man was on the edge of a physical and mental breakdown. Naturally, when he arrived in Naples he was a mess. His shoes were muddy, his clothes were filthy, torn, and often bloody, he needed a shave and haircut, and you could smell him a block away. He also needed to get drunk and get laid.

The dogface seldom achieved the last two aims. The general of Naples had worked out a neat scheme for keeping these apparitions from the front off his orderly streets. His MPs met them as they entered town and hauled them off to jail, where they learned that the sentence for wearing unshined shoes, unpressed trousers, unbuttoned shirts, beards, or long hair, or any combination of these things, was exactly four days in jail. Having paid their debt to society, they were shaved, showered, and released to return to their foxholes.

I drew many outraged cartoons about this for the *45th Division News*, getting away with it because not many people outside the division saw the paper, and as far as our own brass was concerned, they were so upset about the Neapolitan situation that no editorial expression was too strong for them. The general in command of Naples was creating a serious morale problem. A year earlier, the same base section officer had run a similar show in a North African city. Terry Allen, commander of the 1st Infantry Division, had become so infuriated by chickenshit jailing of his soldiers that he had turned his whole division loose in the city one weekend and had filled the hospitals with MPs, thereby cleaning the situation up, at least temporarily. A number of our field commanders in Italy were tempted to do the same thing, but unfortunately the Germans were holding all their attention at the time. Our little paper had to say it all. Some of my cartoons were so rough that even I worried a little that I might have gone too far, but Don Robinson, who had a sensitive ear where division headquarters was concerned, cheered me on. Sheehan, Barrett, and Tapscott, who listened with equal intensity to the soldiers in the field, also approved of what I did.

As Christmas of 1943 approached, our publishing funds were getting low again. Fred Sheehan came up with an idea. During that year the innovation called "V-Mail" had come into general use. Soldiers and their families could correspond on printed forms which were microfilmed, transported across the ocean, then enlarged and delivered. A single airplane could carry more mail than a fleet of ships. We printed a hundred thousand V-Mail forms, I drew a special 45th Division Christmas card which we printed on the forms, and we priced them at two cents each. The profit was about a cent apiece. We sold them all through regimental Special Services offices in a few days, used the money to publish a new cartoon book called *Mud, Mules, and Mountains,* and used part of the proceeds from that to put out a special Christmas issue of the *Division News* in full color.

This was probably our most ambitious venture so far. For the back of the paper I drew a full-page cartoon, painted it with a little watercolor sketching set I carried, and turned it over to our Neapolitan engraver. A week later, after much prodding on our part, he delivered the four-color plates and we went to press. The paper was a success in the division. We really felt we had done a little to brighten a miserable winter. Later, talking with the engraver, I learned what a remarkable thing he had done. Lacking a proper apochromatic lens and filters to make color separations mechanically, he had done most of the engraving by hand, working night and day. I think his entire bill was less than thirty dollars.

About this time the *Stars and Stripes* started reprinting my stuff from the *45th Division News.* The original *Stars and Stripes* was printed in Paris during World War I, and launched the careers of such journalists as Harold Ross, who later founded *The New Yorker,* and Alexander Woollcott, the writer and critic. At the beginning of World War II, several alumni of the old *Stars and Stripes,* including Egbert White, a New York advertising executive, talked the army into reviving the newspaper. White was given a colonel's commission and eventually ended up in Naples in charge of the Mediterranean edition of *Stars and Stripes.* (Unlike the original paper, the World War II version was printed in many different places because of the diversity of our war effort. At one point, more than a dozen different editions of *Stars and Stripes* were being printed simultaneously around the world. Each had its own staff and policies. There were other military publications, too, including *Yank,* which now had several editions, and the *CBI Roundup,* printed in the China-Burma-India theater of war.)

The Mediterranean *Stars and Stripes* had a daily circulation in the hundreds of thousands throughout the Fifth Army. It had taken over the entire building and production facilities of *Il Matino,* Naples' largest paper, in the Galleria on the Via Roma, a couple of blocks from our two-room office and quarters, and it compared to the *45th Division News* as the *New York Times* does to the *Village Voice.* The big paper was no stranger to us, having also been published in Palermo, and we knew

Photo by John Phillips

Author with a model.
Italian mountains were too much even for the redoubtable jeep.
It became a war of men and mules.

"I calls her Florence Nightingale."

"It's best not to speak to paratroopers about saluting. They always ask where you got your jump boots."

The cartoon above brought me a present from the 509th Parachute Battalion: a beribboned box containing brand-new jump boots. Having taken an editorial position on the matter, I wore them only when nobody was looking.

Photo by John F

several of its correspondents, including Ralph Martin, Milton Lehman, and Jack Foisie. I believe it was these "fieldhands" from *Stars and Stripes* who talked the paper into picking up my stuff. They had long been carrying on a private crusade to get the big daily to devote more of its attention to combat troops. It was trying to be a balanced newspaper, covering all parts of the army. Lehman, Martin, Foisie, and a few others strongly believed that the rear echelon had more than its share of benefits, such as the USO and Red Cross, plus regular access to the pleasures of civilization, whereas the newspaper was just about the only diversion available at the front: therefore, it should be slanted that way. They liked my cartoons because I drew almost exclusively for the infantry, with occasional stuff about artillerymen, engineers, and medics.

The campaign to infiltrate my work into the *Stars and Stripes* was bolstered when Will Lang, a *Time-Life* correspondent who was partial to the infantry, became interested in the *45th Division News* and got *Life* to run a layout of my drawings. Don Robinson was very generous in approving of the outside use of my work. He admitted to me later that the thought crossed his mind that I might get ambitious about joining the bigger paper, but when he noted that the first few drawings they reprinted were about the Naples MPs' treatment of infantrymen, he figured he was in no danger of losing his cartoonist. He was almost right.

One of the first cartoons showed a natty MP officer arresting a couple of dogfaces and pointing out numerous deficiencies in their attire. One of them says, "Sir, them buttons was shot off when we took this town." Another showed some doggies who had actually made it as far as the rest camp surrounding an MP at the gate. He is proudly explaining the decorations on his blouse. Every MP in town had pre-Pearl Harbor ribbons, theater ribbons, good conduct ribbons, and other colorful but meaningless junk. The average infantryman in those days had never seen a ribbon.

The commanding general of the Peninsular Base Section hit the gold-leaf ceiling of his baroque office. Apparently he had been chafing for some time about the *Stars and Stripes* letters-to-the-editor column, called the B-Bag, which had been forthright in airing gripes about everything from the cigarette shortage at the front—due to the black market—to the tyranny of the Naples MPs. Now these goddamned insolent cartoons were the last straw. He called in Colonel White and Captain Robert Neville, the paper's officers in charge, and Sergeant Dave Golding, the managing editor, and chewed them all out.

Of course, I had no idea at the time that I was stirring up such a fuss. I was used to indulgence from high places, and White, Neville, and Golding said nothing to me at the time about the confrontation with the general. As Golding admitted later, they found themselves in a bind.

"What we all liked about your stuff was its bite," Golding said later, "but who likes a bite that backfires?"

I was possibly saved by the Germans. Around Christmastime I took my sketchbook into the high mountains above Venafro to visit the 45th Division's 179th Infantry Regiment. Company I of the Third Battalion was dug into a ridge dominating a deep valley. This was a novel situation in itself, since our infantry in Italy seemed generally to find itself looking up, not down, at the enemy. I joined the crew of a light machine gun in their sandbagged hole. They lent me their binoculars and pointed out various German positions, including several only a little way down the hill. From one of these a small-bore mortar began laying occasional fire along our supply trail down the mountain. It was strictly harassment, since they had no observation, but the enemy knew every twist and turn in the trail. Up to then I had been thinking what a fine morning it was for sightseeing at the front. Sooner or later I was going to have to use that route.

We all tried to spot the mortar position. We could hear it plainly as they dropped each round down the tube. Finally an artillery observer on the ridge thought he had located the target and called in howitzer fire on it. When the dust settled, all was quiet. I thanked my hosts, gave back the binoculars, hopped out of the hole, and started sliding down the hill on the seat of my trousers, just in time to meet a fresh round from the German mortar. It went off three feet below the soles of my shoes with a white flash, then I couldn't see anything. They say that in a situation like that an old man thinks of his eyes and a young man grabs for his balls. I was young, and besides I was sure I was blind anyway. When my crotch felt all right, my sight began to return. My eyes were full of dirt. What had saved me was the fact that in sliding down the hill I was almost prone. My only damage was a ringing in my ears and a fragment in my shoulder. It burned like fury but was very small. The wound hardly bled.

Another visitor on that hill was the division artillery chaplain, a gutsy character with the unlikely name of Eugene Rector, who spent most of his time visiting forward observation posts. A fragment from the same round had hit Rector in the arm, badly mangling his elbow. He made a tourniquet of his handkerchief and walked with me down the hill toward the battalion aid station. I asked him if he wanted me to go ahead and send back a litter but he said they worked hard enough carrying legitimate cases without being bothered by us tourists. He probably lost a quart of blood on the way down that trail and his face was gray, but he never so much as leaned on me.

After treating Rector, the battalion surgeon dug out my tiny fragment, slapped on a compress, and told me to get a final dressing at the division clearing station. I did this on the way back to Naples, and when they had finished with me one of the aid men reached to a stack of green leatherette boxes and handed me one containing a Purple Heart. Thinking of Rector and his mangled arm, I was shocked. Personally, I had been cut worse sneaking through barbed-wire fences in New Mexico.

"Take it," the man said. "The rules say if the enemy draws blood, you get one. Besides, it might get you discharged quicker at the end of the war. That case fits real neat in an empty K-ration box if you want to send it home to your wife."

Sure enough, it did. I mailed it to Jean that night, and also drew a cartoon, which was easy since I am left-handed and the nick was in my right shoulder. I showed Willie at an aid station, with a medic trying to give him one of those boxes.

"Just gimme an aspirin," says Willie. "I already got a Purple Heart."

Next day, at *Stars and Stripes,* Golding showed me a letter from a soldier in the headquarters of the 179th Infantry, of all places. The writer wanted to know why the paper put the title "Up Front" on my cartoons. What did I know about the front? This was too good to let pass. The next "B-Bag" column printed the letter, followed by an editor's laconic note that I had just received the Purple Heart for a wound received while visiting Company I of Private So-and-so's own regiment. Although a reporter and an artist from the Mediterranean edition of *Stars and Stripes* were later killed in the course of the war, and there were more wounds among the staff, mine was an early one and good for the paper's image. Reprieved for the moment from the wrath of the Peninsular Base Section, I resumed my war on the MPs, and the *Stars and Stripes* began seriously thinking of taking me on full time.

"I've heard of million-dollar wounds, but that's the first one I've seen," said Rico back at the *News* billet. He had been urging me to go to *Stars and Stripes:* "the big time," he called it.

"Those bastards will ruin you. They'll corrupt you," Robinson assured me.

"It would be impossible to corrupt Mauldin," Bill Barrett commented in his inscrutable, ambiguous way.

A week or two later I was introduced to a WAC stenographer who had taken the minutes at a Fifth Army conference where field generals had met with staff and base section generals to work out some mutual problems.

"I'm not at liberty to tell you everything that went on," she said, "but your name came up."

According to the lady, the Naples general had complained again about the "B-Bag" and the cartoons, and suggested that concerted action be taken to purge the Italian campaign of the cancer of insubordination.

Maybe if enough generals griped, Ike would stop protecting us.

"Guess who stood up for you," my informant said.

I couldn't imagine.

"General Theodore Roosevelt, Junior," she told me. "He got up there and said your cartoons were saying what was on everybody's mind about the way infantrymen get treated in Naples. The other guy said you were inciting mutiny and Roosevelt told him you might be preventing it by blowing off a little steam for the boys."

"Did they take a vote or anything?" I asked, enthralled.

"No, they had a few other things to worry about, like the war," she said. "I hope this isn't going to swell your head."

It probably would have, if I had really believed her. While I was mulling over the story, I was told by Captain Neville that General Mark Clark, the Fifth Army commander, had called and asked for the original of one of the MP cartoons which had most infuriated the base section general.

"He's sending his aide down in his staff car to pick it up," Neville said. "That is, if you're willing to part with it."

"By all means," I said.

"He would be delighted if you would sign it for him," Neville added.

"No sweat," I replied.

"You realize what this means?"

"Yes, sir. It meant that WAC was telling the truth."

"Sometimes I get a feeling of unreality while dealing with you," Neville said. "What I'm trying to tell you is that Clark is giving you the Good Housekeeping Seal of Approval. It is his way of telling PBS to screw itself."

Within a few weeks I was officially transferred to the staff of the *Stars and Stripes.*

It was a wrench to leave the *45th Division News.* Working on it had not only been fun a lot of the time, but I think it gave us all a feeling of accomplishment. It had been the first and remained easily the best of the small unit weeklies in World War II. All of Walter Harrison's ideas were still in effect, and we had added a few innovations of our own. In the years since, especially while covering the Korean and Indochinese wars as a correspondent, I have been interested to note that divisional newspapers have become legitimatized to the point where there is even room on the tables of organization for a cartoonist. Don Robinson's forebodings about this might have been prophetic. Maybe the papers truly have become too legitimate. Most of the small ones I have seen in recent years have seemed tame in content. They even print pictures of commanders and speeches by generals. We never did that. We were a bunch of irreverent refugees from line companies, living and working from week to week and hand to mouth, with production methods that bordered on buccaneering a good part of the time. The result was a lively, readable, popular newspaper.

Ernie Pyle, the great Scripps-Howard correspondent whose dispatches were printed in every city in America, saw the "B-Bag" letter from the skeptical soldier about my cartoons and the editor's note about my wound. He interviewed me and wrote a column which started bringing syndication inquiries before my transfer was even completed. I had a serious discussion about this with Colonel White. Two or three other soldier-cartoonists were sold commercially—one had even managed to get a lieutenant's commission while working almost exclusively for a syndicate—and there had been no official protest. Whoever wrote the army's rules probably never dreamed that this sort of thing would come up. White and I agreed that the best course of action, and the one least likely to create repercussions, was to give the *Stars and Stripes* first publication rights to my work and to make it clear at all times that the army was my boss. What I did with my drawings later was technically my own business. White arranged for an agent in New York to handle all this, a contract was made with United Feature Syndicate (Pyle was also distributed by them) guaranteeing me $150 per week, and now I was not only successful but rich beyond my wildest dreams of avarice.

Just before moving to the *Stars and Stripes,* I made a final trip to the mountains in the seep with Richtel, Sheehan, and Tapscott. On the way back I developed a racking cough and a spinning head and was deposited by Rico at an army hospital in Naples at two in the morning. I sat there, along with a couple of other waiting patients, for three hours, getting sicker by the minute. The soldier at the desk told us the doctor on duty was busy screwing one of the nurses on duty. Finally, the young doctor, looking none the worse for wear, came in long enough to pop thermometers into all our mouths. I sneaked mine out and read 106 degrees.

"I thought that was fatal," I said to the man at the desk.

"Naw, you don't die till a hundred and eight," he said.

Meanwhile, the doctor had disappeared again, forgetting the thermometers. Dammit, I thought in my delirium, don't these people know who I am? Are they going to kill me now that I've hit the big time, before I can even enjoy it? Eventually, they admitted me and sent me up a couple of flights of stairs, where I passed out on a cot. I dimly remember a motherly-looking nurse fussing over me at one point, about the time my fever broke.

"Poor little shit," she said to somebody, thinking I was unconscious. "They're drafting them out of high school now."

The Galleria, which housed *Il Matino* and *Stars and Stripes,* was a glass-roofed shopping arcade several blocks square. The glass panes had all been blown from the arched steel framework during various Allied and German air raids, but no bombs had fallen directly on the arcade itself. Its marble-paved promenades and sidewalk cafés were now exposed to the rains, the shops had little merchandise, and the espresso was ersatz. Every whore and black marketeer in Naples either operated out of the Galleria or spent part of the day there. The place was jammed with Allied soldiers of every description: Aussies with their pinned-up sombreros, Free French troopers bargaining with boys for their big sisters while Moroccan Ghoums in striped robes bargained with the girls for their little brothers, Poles from the famous 10th Corps drinking rotgut cognac and trying to top each other's tales of personal woe and injustice, and American paratroopers looking for black-market jump boots—items of issue which they should have received free but which fetched $100 a pair and somehow never got to the front.

I was given a third-floor room overlooking all this, high enough so that when I felt like working I could close the window on the Galleria's sounds of commerce and glee, but low enough so that I could lean out and take in the show. I had explained to Neville and Golding that I worked best in solitude. They even looked the other way at my insistence on sleeping in my workroom instead of in the paper's requisitioned *pensione*. It was true that I was a nocturnal worker by choice and habit, and besides I thought it would be a good idea to establish myself as being slightly eccentric. I guess I really didn't have to work at that very hard. My room was furnished with a chair, a large table against which I leaned my drawing board (I held the other end in my lap), and a canvas cot. This last was by choice. I could have scrounged a comfortable bed from elsewhere in the building, but for some reason, which is still obscure to me, I have always liked two things the army offered in abundance: Spam and canvas cots. The fabric and the wooden framework in combination seem to have firmness and resiliency in exactly the right places for restful sleep. In my Naples office-bedroom the cot was against the wall opposite the window.

Although we were technically in the army, there was no nonsense about reveille, inspections, and so forth. Our first sergeant, Irving Levinson, a printer in private life, was also the head of our paper's mechanical department. Although he could be hard-nosed when the occasion demanded it, Irv's interest was in getting out a paper, not in military falderol. He had the right talents for publishing an army paper overseas: he was a scrounger and an improviser. Having talked several Stateside syndicates into sending the *Stars and Stripes* free color mats of their Sunday comics, Levinson found colored ink unavailable and invented a way to use army motor oil as a vehicle for the pigments. Our Sunday edition was a bit slippery to the touch, but the soldiers got to read *Blondie, Li'l Abner, Terry and the Pirates, Dick Tracy,* and other favorites in all their tinted glory. Irv and I got along well because I regaled him with stories of printing the *45th Division News.*

Directly across the hall from my room, a Galleria shopkeeper lived with his wife and two teen-aged daughters. The older daughter was a beauty, with long blond hair. According to her sister, who was a tattle-tale, she had been popular with several young German officers. She denied it, of course. Whatever the facts were, her hair was getting black at the roots—something you noticed about many blonde young Neapolitan ladies at that time. One night the girls got me to go to the shelter with them. When the raid began, and you could hear the flak marching closer as it followed the bombers toward the harbor, the younger daughter tapped at my door, explained that Papa was out of town, and asked if I would help them escort Mama, who always became hysterial during raids, down to the basement. I pulled on my trousers and obliged, partly out of neighborliness, and partly because I was developing big eyes for the half-blonde toast of the Wehrmacht. Most of the time I was a clean, reverent, faithful, devoted young American husband, who wrote to his wife practically every day, and I had resisted this temptress next door. But she was a dish; now her mother was hysterical, and I respected old ladies. What could I do?

Despite my charming companions, who clung to me through the raid, so that my left forearm had a cute, knobby little breast against it and my right triceps was pressed into an incredibly luscious and ripe mammary, I didn't enjoy the experience much. The room was crowded and sweaty, and close to panic at the end, when the building was rocked by a couple of near misses as the Germans jettisoned their loads and headed for home. However, as we climbed the stairs later, my spirits rose apace, my libido took charge, the little sister steered Mama homeward, and I led the beauty to my chamber. Somehow, the room didn't look the same as when I'd left it. The army blanket I had hung over the window as a blackout curtain was full of holes and flapping in the breeze. There was no glass left. Looking across the Galleria, we could see that the building directly opposite had taken a small hit—perhaps a 250-pounder—and the concussion had blasted my sash into a thousand high-velocity fragments. My cot, across the room, was cut to pieces and full of glass. Some shards were imbedded in the wall above it. By the time we got the broken glass out of the bedding Mama was at the door and the party was over before it started. I went to sleep musing that if I hadn't been trying to mess around downstairs I'd have been killed upstairs. There must be some sort of murky moral to all this, but it has always escaped me.

We had every shade of political opinion on the *Stars and Stripes.*

There were a few Marxists who tended to huddle and murmur together, plotting God knows what, and there were a couple or three militant right-wingers who were convinced we were on the wrong side of the war. It was about the same sort of staff you'd have found on any major New York paper of the period. The conservatives disapproved of me because I was rocking the boat with the Naples MPs. The militant left couldn't understand why I didn't lean more heavily on the Nazi aspect of the enemy. When I drew German soldiers I showed them very much like Americans: raggedy-assed and hollow-eyed.

I didn't like the Nazis but couldn't connect them in my mind with the ordinary German dogface. It seemed to me that most American soldiers felt as I did about this. I don't believe I heard the word "Nazi" used by an infantryman in all of World War II, nor can I remember combat types saying "Red" or "Commie" later in Korea or Vietnam. When our army shows prejudice, it tends to be racial, not ideological; we hear such terms as "kraut," "squarehead," "slope," or "gook." If such a lack of political passion is a failure on the part of our psychological-warfare branch, I'm all for it. It's bad enough to blame a man for parents he can't help having without also faulting him for leadership he was probably too young to help elect.

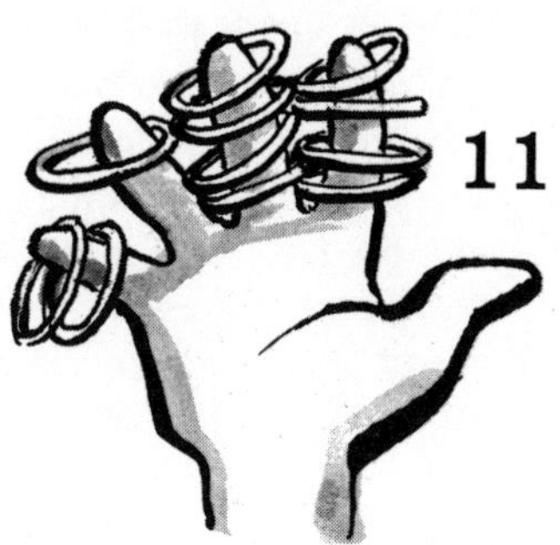

11

The war widened for me. I even became acquainted with the air force. It was fighting on two fronts: sending aircraft north and public-relations colonels south to convince the press that airplanes were winning an infantry war. One day, not long after I joined the *Stars and Stripes,* I was invited to a bomber base on Corsica, along with a couple of reporters and one of our circulation men. They put me in the co-pilot's seat of the B-26 which took us there and let me fly it most of the way. This was an enchanting experience. I had had one flying lesson in my life, in an Aeronca C-3, as payment for a poster I had done for an aviation school in Phoenix. On the ground at Corsica, I was startled to see our bomb bay open and disgorge case after case of Scotch whiskey. The booze was quickly trucked away and the plane was stuffed with cartons of fur-lined flying jackets and boxes of Ray-Ban sunglasses for its return to Naples. Our circulation man told me the bomber people had a simple barter arrangement with the British, who had plenty of Scotch but were short of warm coats and sunglasses.

We were taken to the officers' club. *Stars and Stripes* staffers were nearly all enlisted men—I still carried my sergeant's rank from the 45th—but with the air force this fact was apparently overshadowed by our status as journalists. At Corsica I learned that the air force's brand of press agentry can be self-defeating. I got so drunk on Haig & Haig that I could remember nothing of the visit, nor could the two reporters. I was later told that, during our week end on the base, several dozen raids were flown against the Germans, two B-26s were lost with all hands presumed dead, and one wounded plane with a hung-up bomb exploded on the runway about five hundred yards from the club where we were lolling, glassy-eyed, in our overstuffed chairs. Oblivious to it all, I was under the impression that all those guys did was drink.

Everybody's favorite air force public-relations officer was Major Jay Vessels, who ran an establishment called Villa Virtue, a requisitioned mansion in Naples' high-rent district on a bluff overlooking the harbor and Mt. Vesuvius. It was a grand place for watching air raids, being above the level of the smoke pots so you could see all the pyrotechnics. According to legend, a 90-millimeter anti-aircraft shell which failed to explode in the air during a raid landed just outside a bedroom of Villa Virtue and went off there, blasting out of bed two air force colonels and their girl friends. All suffered concussion and contusions; the colonels allegedly collected Purple Hearts, whereas the ladies got nothing but their fees.

"Not true," said Vessels. "That sort of thing doesn't go on under my roof."

What did go on under his roof was a nonstop poker game. The stakes were pot limit, with a twenty-five-cent ante and no limit on the number of raises. This was a most democratic game. Anybody could afford to buy a hand and look at it, but only a fool would stay in hopes of improving. With seven players—and there were always seven players at any hour of the day or night, with two or three people waiting for somebody to leave—and no raises or dropouts, a stud pot would be worth $3.50, including antes, when the second up-card was dealt. But for the third round, it would be worth $24.50, for the fourth, $171.50, and so on. Many people who should have dropped out didn't. Some of the most imaginative prose written in Villa Virtue was not concerned with war stories, but with expense accounts. The worst poker player I have ever known spent most of his waking hours in that game. He worked for a noted conservative Midwestern publisher. You could always tell when he was bluffing because he would sweat profusely. He messed up so many cards that the deck had to be replaced two or three times in a session when he played. He always got his losses into his expense account. One week he would report having bought a car on the black market to get somewhere on a story; another time he would say he had to bribe a high government official.

Ernie Pyle was one of the regulars at the Villa, with a room of his own where he worked and slept when not out in the field. Pyle worked about the same way I did: a week or two out gathering material, then a week or two putting it all on paper. Then he would unwind for a couple of days before going back to war. Some of his unwindings got pretty

City room of the Mediterranean *Stars and Stripes.* Extreme left, Howard Taubman. Next, with back turned, Peter Furst. Next, laughing, Bill Hogan, with Dave Golding. Right foreground, with backs turned, Joe Bailey and Mel Diamond.

Herb Mitgang in driver's seat. Bob Fleisher on back of jeep. Others are members of printing and circulation staff.

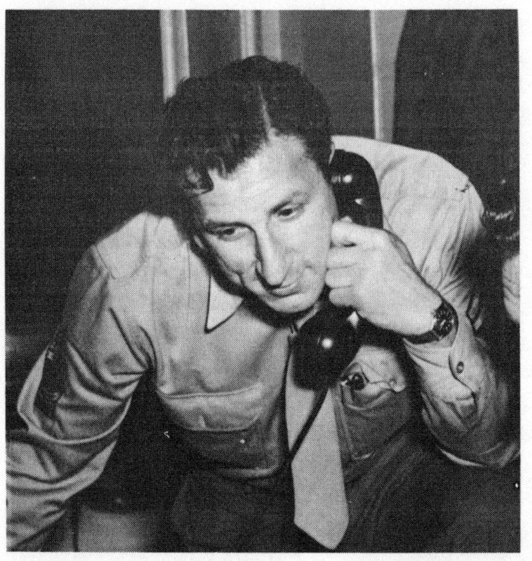

First Sergeant Irving Levinson, the mechanical genius.

Left, Sergeant Bill Estoff, the Syracuse bookie who specialized in getting people of trouble. Right, George, "The Real" McC a radio reporter.

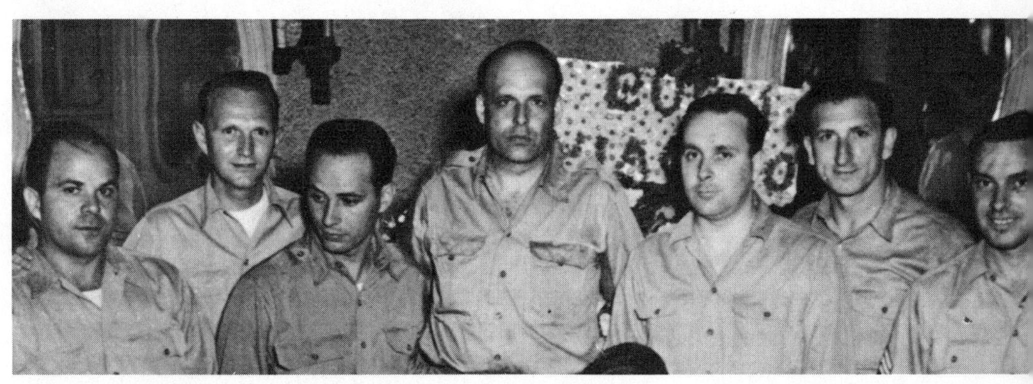

Bob Neville, center, during a revel in *Stars and Stripes* pensione, surrounded by staff members.

shaggy. I was in on the shank of one. While I was playing poker late one night, somebody observed that it was time to feed Ernie. Since I had dropped out of a hand, I was given a can of warm C-ration, a cup of coffee, and a spoon, and directed to the famous man's room.

There, on a cot, lay a tiny, wizened bundle of misery, with two sharp eyes peering out from under a bald dome fringed with gray hair. He thanked me for the food, and we got to talking. I asked him what ailed him, and he said he was sick from drinking bootleg Neapolitan brandy. I was horrified. I told him one of the stories going around about the local brandy being sold to us: that a suspicious customer sent a bottle to a friend in the laboratory at the 300th General Hospital for a chemical analysis and was told that his horse had kidney trouble.

"Apocryphal," Pyle said. "That stuff was poison, but it wasn't piss."

"Maybe not," I said, "but nobody in his right mind drinks it if he can get anything better. A man in your position can get Scotch, bourbon, or even real brandy if that's what you like."

"Maybe I just like poison," he said.

Maybe he did, I thought. I had heard from somebody that he had domestic trouble. Maybe he was trying to get killed internally as well as externally. Certainly if a bullet didn't get him that sort of booze would. The real reason didn't occur to me until I got to know him better. It was a simple theory, but sort of unbelievable at first. Ernie Pyle felt the war very deeply—or he felt deeply about the men in it. Working with them as he did, he identified with them strongly, and felt guilty because he was a civilian who could go back to his typewriter, leaving them in their muddy holes to be miserable and sometimes die. Well, if he couldn't share all their inconveniences, at least he could drink the same godawful sauce they got stuck with when they came back to Naples. If the army wasn't going to issue a ration of decent booze to the rank and file, Pyle wasn't having any, either. It's a miracle the guy didn't die right there in Naples. What he overlooked was that most people drank a few ounces of that stuff and went back to the rugged outdoor life, where it worked itself out of their systems in a few weeks.

I missed Richtel and the seep. Like civilian reporters and fellow staffers on *Stars and Stripes,* I now had to depend upon pool transportation to get to the war some forty miles north.

I have always been convinced that jeeps killed about as many people as any other weapon in World War II. The average army jeep driver was bad enough, but the ones who chauffeured the press were the least competent of all. The jeeps were delightful machines, as machines go, but they had to be driven with respect. They were small trucks, not sports cars, and they turned over easily. On my first pool ride for *Stars and*

Stripes, we ran over a woman in a village north of Caserta. The collision with the lady (who recovered, I learned), was my worst experience with pool drivers, but they kept scaring me, as well as wasting a lot of my time. Finally, remembering my Moto-Guzzi in Sicily, I went to a big ordnance depot in Naples and asked if they had a couple of motorcycles which had run over mines or been mashed by shells. What I had in mind was putting together the halves of two machines which had been hit in different places. I hadn't grown up hanging around those two mechanical geniuses, my father and brother, for nothing.

"Hell, we hardly ever get anything that was busted in combat," the man at the junk pile told me. "Usually it's drunk driving." I not only got the germ of a cartoon idea from this, but ended up with a slightly bent Harley-Davidson which I was told had run under the back of a truck, leaving its rider plastered on the tailgate. The ordnance boys lent me some tools and I got the thing running all right, though it crabbed slightly. During the next couple of weeks, I made two trips to the 45th on my bike. I would have kept on this way, except that as I became a better rider I couldn't resist becoming a smart-ass. I would retard the spark going downhill to make backfires, squirrel my way through convoys, and plow through mudholes at high speeds. One of these finally trapped me. It was an old bomb crater full of water. A kindly truck driver picked me up at the far side of the hole, helped me get the remains of the Harley aboard, and dropped us both off at the ordnance depot.

"Jeezus," my friend at the junkpile marveled, studying my machine and me. "Is there anything else I can show you?"

"How about a wrecked jeep I can fix up?" I asked.

"You need authorization for that," he said. "Everybody wants a jeep."

I wrote a letter to G-4 at Fifth Army headquarters, explaining my need for a broken jeep and assuring them of my competence to repair and maintain it. I didn't really expect anything to come of this. Meanwhile, the Anzio beachhead was established and I went up there by boat for a couple of weeks with my sketchbook, forgetting about wheels. When I returned, there was a message from the ordnance depot that my authorization for a "wrecked jeep" had come through, and it was waiting for me to pick it up.

The jeep was brand-new, fresh off the ship. On the bumper was a tiny license plate with my name and Willie's portrait. In the front seat was a manila envelope containing papers which assigned the machine to me, and a pile of trip tickets with my name in all the blank spaces, as motor pool officer, dispatcher, driver, and passenger. These trip tickets freaked out MPs at roadblocks all over Europe during the next year and a half. I learned later that the jeep was authorized, at least in part, by General Alfred Gruenther, who was then chief of staff to General Mark Clark.

Our relations with civilians in rural Italy ranged from comical to strained to poignant.

"Don't look at me, lady. I didn't do it."

The prince and the pauper.

Neville and Golding were doubly pleased about my acquisition. It helped solve part of the *Stars and Stripes'* transportation problem, and it was another message to Peninsular Base Section that my cartoons were not considered subversive by all the brass.

"Congratulations," my father wrote me from San Diego, "do you realize that is the first new car our family has ever owned?"

The boys at the ordnance outfit got out their torches and tools and helped me remodel the jeep. They removed the back seat, observing that no human being should ride back there anyway, and built a locker for my baggage and drawing materials. They put in leather seats from a wrecked Lancia, and when I told them the jeep's maiden voyage would be to Anzio, they welded half-inch steel plates into the floor as protection from mines. All this added weight, plus the fancy seats, made the machine ride as no jeep was supposed to. I took it out on the road and broke it in lovingly, then got into a line of vehicles at Pozzuoli waiting to board an LST for Anzio.

An MP waved me around everybody else and offered to let me board first. I demurred, since that would have put me in the back of the boat. I would then have gotten off last, and I had already found that the docks at Anzio were the most steadily-shelled targets on the whole beachhead. As I went back to my place in the line, I wondered why the MP had been so nice. Was it my leather seats? Then it struck me. I had paid an Italian lady to make a little khaki-colored cloth envelope to cover the license plate with my name on it. I was plenty proud of the plate, but didn't want to appear exhibitionistic at all times. The cover was about the same size and shape as the ones used to sheathe the stars on generals' jeeps when the old boys were not aboard. With my sergeant's stripes and my covered plate, it was easy to understand the MP's solicitude. I filed the gimmick for future reference.

The amphibious operation which landed the U.S. VI Corps at Anzio and Nettuno was supposed to chop off the Germans at Cassino to the south. Instead, it ended up taking much pressure off them, by immobilizing a large part of the attacking Allied forces in Italy. As hindsight proved, the Anzio landing was a shock to the enemy. We could have quickly taken Rome, thirty miles inland. Whether we could have held it is another question. The corps commander chose to be conservative. The invasion was successful and he didn't want to push his luck. So our troops dug in; the resourceful Germans recovered from their surprise, arrived on the scene, isolated the beachhead, and there the Allies sat for four months, swapping lead with them.

If you liked ironies, that beachhead was a cartoonist's gold mine for ideas. The Germans, sitting on the hills around us, had total surveillance, and nothing was beyond range of their artillery. It was one of those places where the rear echelon often found itself more under fire than the infantry. The waterfront, with its docks, was a prime target. Hospitals in the rear were constantly getting hit, although there was no indication that this was deliberate. A man would earn his Purple Heart at the front, get evacuated to the hospital, and pick up an Oak Leaf Cluster to his medal while lying on his cot. It got so bad that many men concealed illness or wounds to avoid being sent to the rear. The whereabouts of corps headquarters, in a wine cellar in Nettuno, was well known and perfectly zeroed in by the Germans: occasionally they managed to drop one right down the stairs and knock off a high-ranking type or two. One of their favorite tricks was to hit the officers' latrine. When you deprive field-grade brass hats of their leisurely morning bowel movements, you have created a serious morale problem.

The beachhead press billet was also in the resort town of Nettuno, just south of Anzio. The press villa had its own beach, a tiny Mediterranean cove in the back yard. It turned out to be one of the few spots immune from artillery. Anything with a high enough trajectory to drop over the sheltering villa didn't have the range. Although it was winter, the press beach was popular. A man could sit in the pale sun with his collar turned up and read magazines, or stare out at the splashes from incoming enemy shells rising among the barges and ships. I did most of my drawing there. At night we played poker in the cellar, and if German bombers were around we sometimes slept there. Bombs were about the only real hazard to the villa. One night, when Ernie Pyle was in residence in the penthouse, where he preferred to sleep and work because of the view, in spite of the exposure, the building was bracketed by two five-hundred-pounders during a German dive-bomber raid on the docks. The penthouse came down around Ernie's ears, and after the medics picked the splinters out of his skin, he joined the cellar dwellers.

I missed this incident, but was present during another raid, later in the spring, when we were beginning to push out of the beachhead. A number of reporters suddenly arrived from Algiers and points south to cover the breakout. Many of them had never been to the beachhead during its dark days, and of course this put them pretty low in the pecking order around the place. One night we were playing poker in the cellar with some of the newcomers when the building was rocked by a series of heavy bomb hits along the beach nearby. Some dirt fell on our heads, just like in the movies, and the candles flickered.

I remember I was sitting across from John Lardner, who, along with Jack Foisie from *Stars and Stripes* and a handful of others, belonged to the social elite of Anzio, having sweated through the great February crisis, when the Germans came within inches of pushing through to the sea. I looked to John for leadership. We had a problem. Our money was

". . . *forever, Amen. Hit the dirt!*"

A group of Anzio memories.

"I can't git no lower, Willie. Me buttons is in th' way."

in our helmets, which were in our laps. Should we pocket the money and cover our heads, or keep playing? Ordinarily, we'd have done the former. Lardner glanced at the kibitzers, not one of whom was wearing a helmet, although all were fingering them anxiously. They too were looking for leadership. As more dirt fell in our hair, we at the table reached silent agreement. We kept playing.

It was agonizing. The bombs kept falling, more dirt came down, the candle flames darted this way and that, and we anted and called and raised with every outward sign of coolness, even though we could hardly read our cards, much less make sense of them. I think we all rationalized to ourselves that if the cellar caved in the helmets wouldn't help anyway. Finally, though, it got to be too much. Lardner stood pat on a hand and emptied his helmet onto the table.

"I call," said Foisie, who later admitted he had something like a pair of sixes. He dumped his money into the pot and clapped on his tin hat.

"Me too," I said, on a bob-tailed straight.

The other players hadn't fooled around: at Lardner's move they had clapped their helmets on. Every one of them had money dribbling down around his ears.

My favorite outfit at Anzio was called the 1st Special Force, composed of volunteers from U.S. and Canadian paratrooper and ranger units. The group had been given special training in para-ski operations, explosives, sabotage, and so on, in Colorado, then had been scheduled to be dropped in Norway on what would have amounted to a suicide mission: to blow up vital hydroelectric plants, harass the Germans, and make nuisances of themselves until they were all killed or the war was won. Nobody had tried to kid them about which would have been likely to happen first.

This swashbuckling unit ended up at Anzio because after the Norway operation was called off nobody could figure out what else to do with them. The kind of men who are likely to volunteer for suicide missions do not make good spit-and-polish soldiers. They called their officers by their first names if they felt like it, they wore what they pleased and carried the weapons that suited them best. A couple of them were reputed to have been former bodyguards for Chicago gangsters. They occupied the extreme southern rim of the Anzio perimeter. It was the only quiet place on the whole beachhead. They had the Germans terrorized. Every night or so they would form up monster "patrols." Upwards of three hundred men would set forth toward enemy lines to see what fun they could have. One man would wear a bandana around his head and carry nothing but a knife and Tommy gun. Another might carry an old Springfield rifle because he liked its accuracy, while another, with a good pitching arm, would festoon himself with grenades.

The result was that the enemy lines grew farther and farther away

—as much as five miles, whereas most of the rest of the beachhead resembled trench warfare in World War I. The 1st Special Force, as a result, was able to live comparatively well. Nowhere else on the beachhead could you find men sunbathing alongside outpost foxholes. Using the survival techniques they had been taught they did some fishing with hand grenades and found buried wine casks by locating the steel hoops with mine detectors. Unfortunately, I wasn't able to use all of the material I got while hanging around that outfit. It was so wild it defied caricature.

I found myself playing guide on several occasions during this period when I was breaking in my new jeep by hauling it to and from Anzio on LSTs, as well as driving it back and forth between Naples and Cassino. In fact, I seldom had to travel alone. I had developed a reputation for getting around without taking unnecessary risks, either in traffic or around the war. Even so, one of my tours ended sadly. Gregor Duncan, a young New York painter and illustrator, had already established himself so thoroughly that he was assigned to *Stars and Stripes* as soon as he was drafted, and sent to Italy as a war artist. I was asked to escort him until he knew his own way around. It started out as a pleasant job. Greg was an entertaining companion, with a cheerfulness and serenity about him which I thought were mainly due to his huge artistic ability. I would take him for a visit of an hour or two with an artillery battery or an engineer platoon and he would fill whole notebooks with sketches in pen and chalk. Once I led him up the back side of a lone peak just south of Monte Cassino, called Mount Trocchio, where most of the Allied artillery kept its observation posts. It was a grandstand seat to the Battle of Cassino. In comparative safety, and with good glasses, you could hunker in a hole on the mountaintop and watch German paratroopers scurry from cave to rubble, and you could hear an artillery spotter call for a couple of rounds from a battery behind us, then hear the shells whisper directly overhead at the apex of their trajectory before sailing on into the battered town below. Greg wasn't too impressed with the fireworks. He was busy sketching the people involved: both friendly and enemy. He filled a dozen pages of one notebook with details from the huge cave on the back side of Trocchio's summit, where the artillerymen rested, ate, and slept. Everybody liked and trusted Duncan on sight. He was the only journalist I knew who had such immediate rapport with soldiers.

On our way out of the Cassino area Greg asked me to stop at a certain field hospital, and there I learned the real reason for his upbeat outlook on life. A pretty Red Cross girl came running out of one of the medical tents and hurled herself upon my friend with wild whoops of female joy. It was his wife, for God's sake. Not only had Duncan managed to be born

"I feel like a fugitive from th' law of averages."

"Wisht I could stand up an' git some sleep

"My God! There we wuz an' here they wuz."

with genius, and gotten himself assigned to the right job in the army, but he had ended up in the same theater of operations with his spouse. Whatever small machinations I had accomplished in getting myself where I was at that point seemed mighty puny all of a sudden. He got his wife excused from duty for the weekend and she rode back to Naples with us.

A few weeks later, after the breakout from Anzio had begun and it was possible to drive overland to the beachhead area, Duncan asked to ride up there with me for a few days of sketching. It was about a 150-mile, five-hour drive over battered roads. At the press building in Nettuno, I slept late the next moring, and got up to find that Duncan had sallied out with another *Stars and Stripes* man to watch the breakout battles in the northeast, toward the Alban Hills. An hour or two after that, while I was still at the press camp trying to decide where to go myself, we got word that the jeep in which Duncan and his companion were riding had taken a direct hit from an 88 shell and the artist was dead. Shortly after that, the surviving reporter returned to Nettuno with a broken arm in a sling. He said they were trying to pass another vehicle at high speed through an area in which shells were falling, and that the next thing he knew they were upside down in a ditch. The reporter didn't seem to be sure himself whether they had actually taken a hit or simply had an accident. The official story was that Greg was killed in action by shellfire. This was not unusual in itself; most vehicular fatalities in combat zones were listed as killed in action, especially where some reasonable doubt existed.

On the day Rome fell I picked up Fred Sheehan, my old *45th Division News* buddy, on the way into the city. We found that the best way to liberate a place is in your own jeep. As far as the girls were concerned, we were Don Juan and Casanova in a Ferrari. I was married and Fred was tired, but the pulchritude was overwhelming and we couldn't resist picking up a few loads of them and hauling them around in the triumphal parades. From the way they acted, we knew they had been on our side—at least since the night before when they saw the Germans leave.

Conquered cities are all the same in some ways. After entering a few, you learn who the real bootlickers of society are. Leading among them are hotel managers and police. The cops can always rationalize being collaborationists, but hotel people have no excuse. Fred and I drove to a small, new hotel a couple of blocks from *Il Messagero,* the city's largest paper, where I knew *Stars and Stripes* would soon be located. The manager came rushing out to meet us. We had a jeep, therefore, despite our disreputable clothing, we must be officers. Would we like a room? We certainly would. Nothing fancy—just a room with a view. We signed the register and were given a nice double looking out on the street. Fred went back to the 45th after a good night's sleep. I kept the room for two days, then the manager knocked on my door. His cordiality was gone. Was I an officer? No. Then I would have to leave immediately. This hotel was for officers and Red Cross only. As I crossed the lobby with my gear, the angry manager following to make sure I left the premises, I was hailed by a couple of Red Cross girls I knew, and a billeting officer, a major, whom I also knew. I kissed the girls and shook hands with the major. The poor manager was confused. What sort of illegal beast was I?

"Are you staying here?" the girls asked.

"No, I've just been thrown out."

"But that's silly—there's plenty of room," they said, looking at the major for confirmation.

"Sure; I don't see any reason why you can't stay—at least until the *Stars and Stripes* has billets set up," he said.

"Please, signore, please let me have your things," the manager said. "You can go back to the same room if you like."

He didn't know what was happening, but he was miserable. He grabbed my gear. I grabbed it back.

"No thank you," I snarled. "You said I wasn't welcome." I winked at the girls and the major and went out with flags flying. The truth is that with the Red Cross coming in I wanted out. No matter how good their intentions, those Red Cross females ran officers' clubs in their spare time, and I didn't want to live in an officers' club. I had learned the art of inverse snobbery.

After leaving Rome the Germans retreated rapidly across the flat country toward their next defensive line in the mountains above Florence. Soon the war was even farther from our offices than it had been while we were in Naples. My jeep had a standard rack for weapons on the lower part of the windshield. Although *Stars and Stripes* personnel usually had no reason to carry arms, I often carried an M-1 rifle in my rack. My rationalization was that I traveled alone a great deal off the beaten track in country that was not unanimously friendly, but I think the real reason was that I was a New Mexico boy who had not outgrown a fondness for shiny hardware. For a while I even had a Tommy gun—not the standard issue, but a beautifully made Chicago gangster model, with knurled walnut stocks and a pistol grip on the forepiece. It was a gift from one of the men in the Special Force at Anzio. With that thing I was surely the best-armed cartoonist in the world. After a few weeks I realized how ridiculous it was, took it out of the rack on the jeep, and replaced it with the rifle.

I only used the M-1 once. Milton Lehman, one of our more energetic combat reporters, hitched a ride with me one day to the 88th Division,

My new jeep. Above,
Gregor Duncan and his wife,
an, as Duncan and I took off
for Anzio on his last trip.

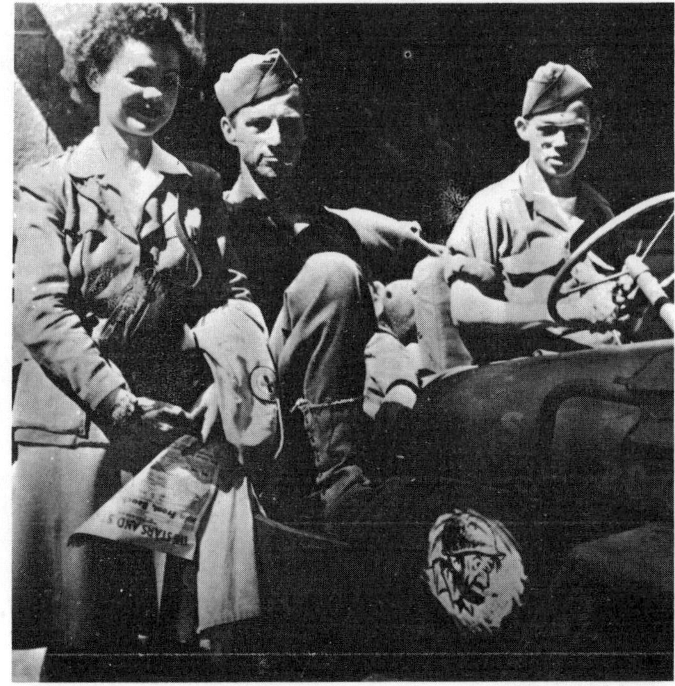

Photo by John Phillips

which was working its way up the west coast of Italy. A few miles behind the division, we came to a hillside village and were stopped by a crowd of civilians in the road. They had only recently been "liberated," and had that gray complexion and musty smell of people who have been cowering for a long time in cellars while a war rages over them. They also looked as if the food in the cellars had long since vanished.

They stopped us, they said, because they saw we had a rifle. A local nobleman, who lived in a castle above the town, had managed to save a few head of livestock for himself, and had presented the hungry villagers with an old bull. They took Lehman and me into a barn by the side of the road and showed him to us. He was a big, mean-looking patriarch with all his ribs showing and only one eye, which was bloodshot and rheumy.

"The problem," their spokesman told us, "is how to butcher him. He will not let any of us get close enough to cut his throat."

"How unreasonable of him," said Milton. "And now you want us to shoot him for you? What do you think we are—a couple of killers?"

"Well, *signore*," the man said, "you are soldiers, and you do have a rifle."

"He's right, by God," Lehman said to me. "What will these people think of the brave American army if we're too squeamish to do a simple thing like that for them?"

"O.K., you do it," I said. The truth is that despite my fondness for weapons I have always been faint-hearted about using them on live things. Once in my childhood I actually let a mouse out of a trap. In the process of growing up on a farm, you have to do some bloody chores, such as killing chickens, but I hated it and felt bad afterward. I put a clip into the rifle, got a round into the chamber, put on the safety, and handed it to Milton.

"I have heard," I told him, "that the quick, humane way to shoot a steer is to imagine a cross between his eyes and his horns and hit the middle of the cross."

"Yeah, but this is a bull," Lehman said, reluctantly taking the rifle.

"We're not talking about shooting him in the balls," I said. "Hit the brain and he won't feel anything."

Milton drew a bead. The target was not more than fifteen feet away, but my friend was shaking so badly that I was afraid he would miss entirely, or painfully wound the animal.

"Bull fever," I snorted.

"I can't pull the trigger," Milton said. His face was chalky.

"It would help if you pushed off the safety," I said.

"It's no use," he said. I grabbed the rifle, fearing he would faint and shoot somebody on the way down. The villagers shuffled their feet and shot glances at each other. You could feel them thinking that if all our comrades were like us it was a sure thing that the Germans would be coming back. Clearly, somebody had to save face. I took careful aim at the middle of the X and shot the bull. If I had been nervous before, I was now horrified. The big brute didn't twitch. He stood there with a tiny hole in the middle of his forehead and looked at me with that good eye. I knew he couldn't see me. He had to be dead on his feet. I'm sure he was. But he wouldn't fall. I shot him again, in the spine just behind his head. He dropped in his tracks. Instantly people were all over him with knives. Milton and I got out of there. I wanted to throw up, but wouldn't give my friend the satisfaction. Later, the way Milton told the story around the office, it was a young calf with huge, soft, appealing eyes, and the execution had obviously given me a great deal of pleasure.

"I believe Mauldin has an instinct for that sort of thing," he said. "I don't know why they ever let him out of the infantry."

In the summer of 1944 the old Anzio VI Corps, including the 45th, 36th, and 3rd Infantry divisions, and an airborne task force which contained what was left of the 1st Special Force and several parachute units, invaded southern France. I got permission from Neville to go along, and drew a couple of weeks' cartoons ahead. I figured I knew enough about amphibious invasions by this time to make authentic pictures. They were all right, as it turned out, except that in two or three of them I showed the early waves going ashore in darkness, whereas the actual landings on the Riviera took place in daylight. My jeep was not included in my travel authorization, so with the collaboration of the 45th Division artillery I sneaked it aboard the LST they had converted into a tiny carrier for their spotter aircraft.

The planes were Piper Cubs, about a dozen in all, parked two abreast at the rear of a flight deck which had been rigged from planks and piping and couldn't have been more than a couple of hundred feet long. The first plane to be launched had less than a hundred feet ahead of it. As the pilot ran up his tiny, 65-horsepower engine, two men held his wing struts, two clung to the tail, the LST headed into the breeze and hit flank speed, which must have been all of ten knots. At a nod from the pilot the anchor men turned loose; the airplane darted ahead and simply fell out of sight over the bow. We all gritted our teeth and wondered why the damned fools on the bridge didn't have the decency to reverse the ship's engines. After a while the Cub reappeared, a half mile ahead and ten feet above the water, climbing slowly. The next takeoff was the same; by the time the last four were launched they had so much deck that their wheels were off before reaching the bow. Soon they were all circling around inland, radioing coordinates for the naval guns supporting the invasion.

A few days after the landings, I learned that Corps had dispatched a battalion from the 36th Division in trucks up the Route Napoleon toward

45th Division News

Vol. 5, n° 6 - Grenoble France - August 25, 1944

Roumania Signs Peace Pact With Russia, England, U.S.

The Roumanian radio announced last night that the Government of Roumania had accepted Russian peace terms unconditionally and that they had signed an armistice with Russia, England and the United States.

King Michael announced the capitulation to the people and said the Roumanians would fight alongside the Allies to rid their country of the Nazis.

A democratic government has been formed in Roumania. Premier Antonescu has not been included in the new government.

The Roumanian capitulation came as an aftermath of he Red Army's double drive into the heart of the country.

The advance of General Malinovsky's troops on Jassy ha...

Late News

American troops turned the left flank of the Germans in northern France and crossed the River Seine near Romaine. The Germans are hurrying their forces toward the wooded area of the lower Seine apparently in an effort to thwart any Allied thrust at that area.

The Luftwaffe made its appearance in considerable strenght yesterday in northern France and 50 Nazi fighter planes were shot down. Allied losses were given ... 15.

Paris Freed by F. F. I.

German forces in the Paris area have broken their armistice with the FFI and have resumed fighting for the French capital. The FFI called for Allied assistance.

Fifty-thousand strong, the FFI forces liberated Paris four days before American forces reached the capital city, capturing all the public buildings and the Vichy representatives.

In the meantime, the Americans in northern France were busy cleaning up the remnants of the German Seventh Army.

In the American drive southwest, a junction was made with the FFI forces near Bordeaux.

(No Allied confirmation was made of the new American landir near B...

MATHENY'S NAKED NOGGIN HAS MEANING FOR THE FRENCH

Just in time to catch a crowd coming up the street cheering and hollering, Division Chaplain Robert Matheny, Ludlow, Ky., and Sgt. Stanley Purdy, Oklahoma City, stopped on a corner in the small French town for a ten minute break.

The crow... brandishing scissors, more girls and cut off their hair, ... front th... And ... one again applauded.

THE STARS AND STRIPES

Grenoble - FRANCE ◆ ◆ ◆ August 25, 1944

Roumania Signs Peace Pact With Russia, England, U.S.

The Roumanian radio announced last night that the Government of Roumania had accepted Russian peace terms unconditionally and that they had signed an armistice with Russia, England and the United States.

King Michael announced the capitulation to the people and said the Roumanians would fight alongside the Allies to rid their country of the Nazis.

A democratic government has been formed in Roumania. Premier Antonescu has not been included in the new government.

The Roumanian capitulation came as an aftermath of he Red Army's double drive into the heart of the country.

Late News

American troops turned the left flank of the Germans in northern France and crossed the River Seine near Romaine. The Germans are hurrying their forces toward the wooded area of the lower Seine apparently in an effort to thwart any Allied thrust at that area.

The Luftwaffe made its appearance in considerable strenght ...

Paris Freed by F. F. I.

German forces in the Paris area have broken their armistice with the FFI and have resumed fighting for the French capital. The FFI called for Allied assistance.

Fifty-thousand strong, the FFI forces liberated Paris four days before American forces reached the capital city, capturing all the public buildings and the Vichy representatives.

In the meantime, the Americans in northern France were busy cleaning up the remnants of the German Seventh Army.

In the American drive southwest, a junction was made with the FFI forces near Bordeaux.

(No Allied confirmation was made of the ne...

MATHENY'S NAKED NOGGIN HAS MEANING FOR THE FRENCH

Just in time to catch a crowd coming up the street cheering and hollering, Chaplain Robert Matheny, Ludlow, Ky. and Sgt. Stanley Purdy, Oklahoma City, Okla., stopped on a corner in the small French town ...

PAGE 4 THE STARS AND STRIPES

This edition is the result of combined efforts of personnel from Stars and Stripes and the 45th Division News. It's a makeshift job, and has no relation to the regular Stars and Stripes or its mobile unit which are due to start producing soon in these parts. It was felt that the troops of the combat divisions needed news, hence this sheet.

Because of the conditions under which the paper is produced, many troops will not receive it, and it is not by any means the beginning of a daily. We just saw an opportunity to print a paper and grabbed it.

« This is th' town my pappy told me about. »

The remarkably similar Grenoble editions of the *45th Division News* and the *Stars and Stripes.* Below, how I filled the back page and disqualified myself as an editor.

Grenoble, about 140 miles ahead of us. The French resistance forces had assured us that there would be no Germans along the way. If true, Grenoble would be a nice prize. If untrue, Corps was prudent to send a battalion rather than a regiment up through those canyons. I set out after the convoy with a couple of spare cans of gas and caught up with them four hours later on the outskirts of Grenoble. The resistance had been telling the truth, and I had just enjoyed the most scenic drive of my life. Feeling cocky, I went to *Les Allebroges,* Grenoble's daily paper, with some vague idea about publishing an early edition of *Stars and Stripes* on my own. Inside I found the staff of the *45th Division News.* They had heard of the expedition, too, and had got there first, as usual.

The *News* hurriedly printed a four-page half tabloid, much like our first Sicilian edition, containing general news about the invasion and local anecdotal stuff about the 45th. After Robinson's press run was finished he generously allowed me to take his page forms, replace the *News* logo with the *Stars and Stripes,* and publish my own paper. After shufflling the news around and adding some fresh bulletins from the radio, including an unconfirmed rumor from BBC that Grenoble had fallen, I deleted items of interest only to the 45th, then found I had most of a blank back page to fill. The photoengravers were as helpful as the printers and composers had been: after I had hurriedly drawn a cartoon they blew it up to fill the empty space. (Neville later claimed this proved that cartoonists could never be trusted as editors.) We printed fifty thousand copies of the first post-invasion *Stars and Stripes.* I signed a chit for the printing bill, hoping *Stars and Stripes* would honor it, and started back down the road to deliver the papers to VI Corps for distribution. Halfway back, I ran into an infantry patrol moving up the shoulder of the road, with weapons ready and a five-yard interval between men. I handed each one a *Stars and Stripes* as I went by.

"Some other guys just came by and gave us a *45th Division News,*" one of the doggies said. "What the hell is going on up there?"

Farther along I encountered a weapons carrier hauling the advance staff of the *Stars and Stripes* to Grenoble to publish their first edition. I don't think they were enthusiastic about my publishing venture or the quality of my product (some of the symmetry of Don Robinson's page makeup was lost when I changed the stories around), but they gave me C + for effort and forgave me. They even paid the bill, although this would have been necessary in any case if they wanted to continue printing on the presses of *Les Allebroges.*

In Grenoble, I saw my first execution of the war: an event worth noting because it turned out to be the first legal execution, following a trial and conviction, of World War II collaborationists in France. The proceedings took only a few hours but it was a model of judicial restraint in a country where a lynching mood prevailed and an accusation was usually enough for a man to get shot or a woman to get her head shaved. The culprits were six young local men, in their late teens and early twenties, who had worked as informers for the Gestapo. There was little question about evidence. The city had been taken so suddenly that many Gestapo people had been caught in their local headquarters, even while torturing prisoners in some cases. The condemned young Frenchmen had been helping them. Because of the heavy resistance activity in the region, there had been plenty of torturing and killing by the Germans, and feelings ran high. There must have been five thousand people, two-thirds of them women, watching the executions in the courtyard of the Gestapo building. The boys were tied to stakes erected by the Germans for the same purpose and shot by a platoon of men wearing resistance armbands. While the air was still full of splinters from the posts, each victim then got a pistol shot through the ear. At this point the women went berserk and mobbed the corpses, stamping and tearing at them, before they could be thrown into their pine boxes. One contingent of middle-aged ladies climbed right over my jeep on their way to express themselves. All I could think of was a guillotine scene from the old Ronald Colman version of *A Tale of Two Cities.*

Tooling around the higher mountains in my jeep one day, I got onto a back road which deteriorated into a trail. There I came upon a monk leading a St. Bernard dog, which was pulling a sledge loaded with firewood. Shifting into low-range four-wheel drive and driving at idle to match the dog's pace, I went along with them to their monastery. Although the monk was uncommunicative, he was friendly and clearly fascinated by my machine. He motioned me to wait at the door. Soon an older type came out, with two bottles under his arm. He was followed by a swarm of young monks, who circled the jeep, peering under it and doing everything but kick the tires. All I could think of was schoolboys looking at a new-model convertible. The old man explained that they couldn't ask me in because I was a soldier, but to assure me that it wasn't personal he wanted to give me samples of their product. One bottle was green and one was yellow. Back in Grenoble I showed the stuff to Ed Vebell, one of our staff artists, who was something of a *bon vivant,* and to Stan Swinton, a reporter who often traveled with me.

"My God, that's Chartreuse!" Stan cried. "You get lost in the hills and you stumble over one of the world's fancy booze factories."

Ed explained that they made Chartreuse mostly from flowers. That was exactly what it tasted like. I gave my friends one bottle and kept the other for the trip back to Italy. In Marseille I got my jeep onto an LST headed for Leghorn. It was stormy weather all the way, but sipping the Chartreuse kept my stomach settled. By the time we arrived I had almost grown to like the stuff.

12

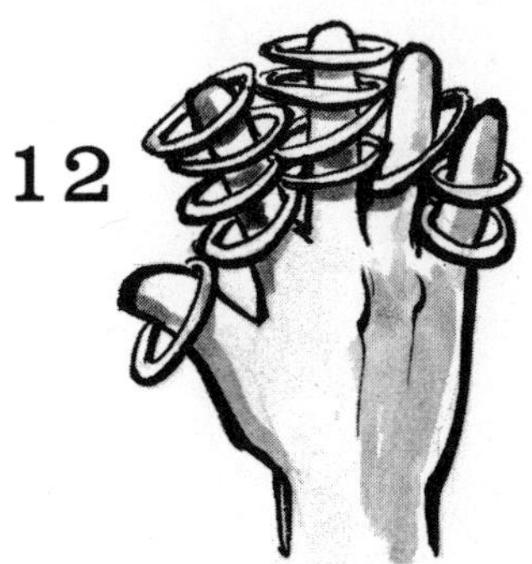

The second winter in Italy was much like the first. The Germans had dug into the mountains between Florence and Bologna and were proving as hard to dislodge as they had been at Cassino. The supply situation had improved for our infantry: large amounts of warm clothing, decent rations, and cigarettes were finally getting past the black marketeers. To offset this, the mountains were a little higher, the snow a little deeper, and the German supply lines a little shorter. They had lost a lot of artillery in the long and bitter retreat from the south, but now they were able to get plenty of ammunition for the guns they still had.

There was no shortage of material for me. The 45th Division had stayed in Alsace, along with the 3rd and 36th, which had also been good sketchbook sources. Still in Italy was the 34th, a grizzled outfit which had been the first American division overseas in World War II. In the end, the 34th logged more combat time than any other division in Europe, yet it never got much publicity because it was seldom involved in glamorous affairs such as taking a major city or disastrous ones such as the Rapido River crossing which decimated the 36th at Cassino. The 34th was a classic footslogger division. Every company had four or five characters who had managed to survive from the beginning.

These were mostly Willie and Joe types. A large part of staying alive was latching onto a good partner. If you had to work with a man who was scared shitless all the time you were in trouble. On the other hand, if he was all gung-ho to kill Germans and win medals he would get you into

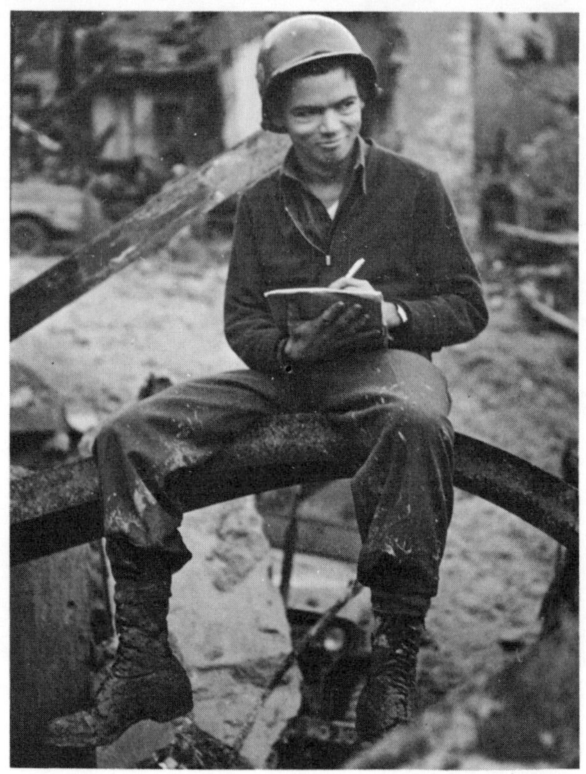

Photo by John Phillips

Business as usual with author back in Italy.

Photo by John Phillips

Photo by John Phillips

Photo by John Phillips

worse trouble. The best life insurance was to find a nice, steady, sane buddy who knew how to stay apprehensive all the time while doing his job without panicking. Some of the best Willie and Joe material I picked up was from listening to infantry partners who were personally incompatible or even hostile to each other, but who worked well as a team on patrols or when taking towns, and so clung together like sick kittens on a hot brick. To hell with personalities—they wanted to get home alive.

Once I happened upon a company in the 34th which was behind the front, in a reserve position, but had taken a hit from an 88 shell and lost one of its old-timers. The body, which was badly mangled, was covered with a blanket, and the dead man's friend, another veteran, was sitting by him. I didn't know either man, and I wondered what sort of partners they had been. Were they friends, sharing a joke in the sleet or a hoarded cigarette butt in a cave? Or was it a professional merger, with the sharp-eyed one, who owned the reflexes, covering the one with the quick feet as they attacked from building to building?

There was no way to tell. The survivor glowered at me until I retreated, embarrassed, then he went back to glaring at the corpse. A sentimentalist in the correspondent corps might have seen a tear coursing down the grizzled cheek of the rough-hewn trooper, but I missed it. Whatever the relationship had been, the survivor's reaction now appeared to be resentment as much as sorrow: "Goddammit, there goes my walking insurance policy. Why didn't he take the long way to the latrine when he knew they were zeroed in on the area? What kind of replacement will they send up? Why doesn't Graves Registration come pick him up and get him the hell out of here?"

Shortly, they did come, in a weapons carrier with THE GREEN TURD painted on the hood and two characters in the front seat who could have played the gravediggers in Hamlet. I had met this pair before, making their rounds like municipal scavengers. In some situations such as this one they were able to retrieve fresh bodies where they had fallen. Usually they got them second hand, often locating a hastily-buried body marked by a stick or slat, or even a broken weapon, with a dogtag hanging from it. They slid this old infantryman into a mattress cover. His partner walked away. The men said hello to me and then loaded the body on top of half a dozen others in the back of the truck. One mattress cover contained a soldier so tall that his feet stuck out to the rear. To my horror I saw that one boot pointed straight up and the other straight down. One of the Graves Registration men took hold of the downturned foot and delicately but firmly rotated it to match its mate. Whatever had happened to the deceased, it was clear that they had put his leg into the bag as a separate item.

I never saw these men handle corpses disrespectfully, although they might have been hasty at times. Little touches of humor, such as the name of their vehicle, were ways of staying sane on the job. As for me, I never put bodies into cartoons. It was not from squeamishness—although I did feel some of that—but a matter of technique. It seemed to me that if my drawings reflected the war accurately a reader would be able to deduce that there were bodies just offstage.

Other old divisions still in Italy were the 1st Armored, which had given me material for dozens of cartoons about infantrymen and tanks, the 85th, and the 88th, which was dug into the hills overlooking Bologna. Somewhat newer were the 92nd, an all-black division staffed with white officers who gave most visitors the impression that they hoped their boys wouldn't do *too* well and upset any theories, and the 10th Mountain Division, a colorful unit full of ski enthusiasts and climbers. For once in the history of the army, a bunch of specialists had been sent to the right place.

Although I kidded the air force regularly in cartoons, especially for such things as claiming that bombs were winning the war and for the comparative youth of their officers, my feelings toward airmen were not generally malicious. In fact, I felt that the air force deserved to be emulated in many ways. Back when the only way a dogface could get out of battle was to be carried out, the fliers had a rotation system. Fifty missions and you went home. It gave a man a goal and kept him from sliding into hopelessness. One day, however, I was visiting an infantry company from the 1st Armored Division, dug in on top of a ridge. The valley in front of them was supposed to contain two or three companies of Germans. The rest of the armored infantry regiment had encircled the valley and was trying to drive the enemy up the slope into the automatic weapons of the entrenched company. It was a swell idea, but a suspicion was growing on the ridge that the Germans had slipped the noose and left the premises. All you could hear was the noise made by the "encircling" troops on the far slopes. My hosts were all out of their foxholes, taking the sun, swapping stories in low voices, and smoking, but staying near their weapons. Suddenly, all hell broke loose. Lead was ricocheting and dirt was flying in every direction. We all thought the entrapped Germans had somehow managed to trap us. Then we heard the airplane engines. A pair of American P-51 Mustang fighters were strafing us. By the time they finished their run and got turned around for another pass at our ridge, we were all cowering in our holes. They made two more passes, presumably using up all their ammunition, and went home, leaving us to look for casualties and vent our opinions of our air force. Somehow, nobody had been hit. I picked up a pocketful of .50-caliber slugs and carried them back that night to the Fifth Army press camp, where I showed the bullets and regaled some reporter friends with the story of the strafing.

"How can they be so blind?" I asked, rhetorically. "We had marker panels out, and those positions have been static for weeks. They must have had them marked on their charts."

One man listening in the background was wearing baggy fatigues like the rest of us, but when he stepped into the light I saw he was also wearing the single star of a buck general. He was the commander of the tactical fighter support for the Fifth Army, and the boss of the two pilots who had thrown the bullets at us.

"Mauldin, I've seen some of those funny cartoons you've done about us," the general said. "How would you like to spend a day flying around with me in a P-51? We've fixed one up with a back seat, and you can see how hard it is to spot ground positions from the air."

It sounded reasonable on the surface. How could anybody turn down such an invitation? Early next morning, I met the general at his tiny liaison airstrip, which had been bulldozed out of the side of a hill near Fifth Army's forward command post. We flew in his personal Cub down to Florence, where his fighters were based, got aboard his two-seater P-51, and roared off into the wild blue yonder.

Many military pilots seem to have a perverted love for the smell of vomit from passengers. My general was no exception. Besides, he was sore at me. I had tried to prepare for the ordeal by skipping breakfast, but it didn't help. Remnants of all my meals for the past week came up to haunt me as we snap-rolled, split-essed, zipped, roared, climbed, spun, and dove our way all over the Po Valley. From time to time the general explained to me over his shoulder that we were trying to tease the Germans into shooting at us and revealing their positions. Any Germans watching us could see we didn't need to be shot down. We were going to fall apart in the air. Finally, as a climax, we strafed the streets of Bologna, although I couldn't see a soul moving down there except a man on a bicycle, whom we missed. Then we flew back over the ridge where the two planes had shot at us the day before. My pilot asked me to point out the U.S. lines and the German lines. Sick and miserable as I was, I did so without hesitation. I don't think he liked that. Up went our nose, and we arrived over Florence at about fifteen thousand feet. Down went our nose—straight down—and we screamed earthward at full throttle. Somebody stuck a butcher knife in each of my ears and twisted. When that plane was built, nobody had heard of pressurization. At the bottom of the dive, the general did a pullup which put my head down between my knees, slowed enough to lower his gear and flaps, and made a nice landing which I was in no condition to appreciate. I had to be helped from the cockpit, bleeding from various orifices in my head and soaked with my own bile. My opinions about the air force remained about the same. My lesson was to be careful who's listening when you tell a story.

Shortly before Christmas in 1944, I was asked by Bob Neville to sketch a congressional junket. The House Military Affairs Committee was taking a fact-finding swing through the European and Mediterranean theaters of operations, and was spending a week in Italy. As far as I can remember, Neville had never given me an assignment before. He had allowed me total freedom, which I appreciated, and now that he wanted me to do something, I was anxious to please.

The congressmen were staying at the Grand Hotel in Rome. I hied myself over there, hoping to see something to satirize, and found that some of the committee members defied caricature. I saw one of them, a portly old gentleman whose name was often in the papers in connection with military affairs, attempting a frontal assault on a chambermaid in a corridor. He was in his undershirt and socks. The girl, squeaking piteously, was trying to duck under and around various folds of fat which he kept throwing in front of her. I remember that his triceps hung down like hogs in hammocks. I don't name him because there is a sort of ethic covering exposure of certain kinds of wartime misbehavior, but it is a strain. I was so disgusted that I just stood there, while he grinned at me and rolled his eyes in a comradely way. I mean, after all, his expression said, war is hell and how can we survive without a little forcible poontang now and then, hey, soldier? There must have been a hundred girls in that hotel who would have leaped into the sack with the old boy at the crackle of a twenty-dollar bill but he had to go at it like a slob. When I made it clear that I was unsympathetic, he lost whatever erection he might have had, and the maid slithered away, whimpering.

"Are you looking for somebody, soldier?" the congressman asked, as haughtily as he could under the circumstances. The Grand was for VIPs and officers of flag rank, not enlisted Lochinvars.

"Why, yessir, I think you're one of the people I'm supposed to see," I said, introducing myself and explaining my mission. The atmosphere warmed right up. He said he had heard of me, and he certainly seemed aware of the fact that the Italian edition of the *Stars and Stripes* had a daily circulation of half a million. He dragged me into his room, broke out a bottle of rare old stuff, and I had almost as hard a time escaping as had the Italian girl.

I spent a day or two in Rome with the committee, then traveled north with them. Not all members were as clownish as the fat one, but several worked at it. Two or three were serious types. One of these was Clare Boothe Luce, then a congresswoman from Connecticut. One day the group set out from the Excelsior Hotel in Florence in a convoy of jeeps to see the war. Whoever arranged the tour did a good job. Not only did the lawmakers get a ten-hour, kidney-busting jeep ride through miles of hub-deep mud and rocky back trails, but they actually got taken near enough to the front so that at one point our own artillery was shooting

"Uncle Willie!"

over them. Several doughty male members of the group were convinced that the explosions were incoming shells, not outgoing, and were outraged that the military would take such gambles with their precious skins. Not Clare Luce. She was bright as a bird through the whole trip, taking notes and talking to soldiers, and that night, when the tour was over and the gentlemen were massaging their sore butts and drinking to their narrow escapes, the lady from Connecticut got hold of a jeep and driver and went back to several of the spots we had visited to complete conversations which had interested her.

Possibly the scruffiest performance of that day's tour was by a Midwestern congressman whom I accompanied through an evacuation hospital, about seven or eight miles back of the front. In World War II, the average combat casualty was carried by litter to his battalion aid station, where he got patched up enough for a ride, by jeep, mule, or ambulance, to a clearing station, usually somewhere near division headquarters. Here, if he was still alive, he got patched up some more and sent to an evacuation hospital. These units, in distance and facilities, were about halfway between the rough first aid at the battalion level and the elaborate and complete general hospitals way to the rear. "Evac" hospitals were equipped for surgery, and did a lot of it, but the basic idea was still merely to keep the man alive for more traveling, often for many miles over rough roads. (This was long before helicopters.) Thus, a casualty in one of these places was often still in a state of shock, still in bloody bandages, and, in the case of amputees, sometimes just beginning to look with comprehension at the flat place in his blanket. He was in a vulnerable condition, physically and mentally.

The congressman entered, escorted by a military aide and members of the medical staff, and followed by a cartoonist.

"Howdy, son. Where you from?" to a torso with a great ball of red-and-white gauze for a head. If the ears heard anything or the mouth said anything, it was muffled by an inch or so of soggy cloth. "I say, where you from, young fellow? Where's he from, nurse?"

"He's from Georgia," said the patient in the next bed.

"Oh," said the congressman. It was not his state. "Where *you* from, fella?" he asked his informant. This one had splints on both legs—the sort of injury that might have come from driving a vehicle over a mine. Might have—but we never found out, hurrying on because this casualty was from the wrong state, too, and so was the next one, who had a tube in his nose, several holes in his belly, and a blue-gray complexion which hinted that he might have endured the last of his ambulance rides. The next man couldn't have been from a wronger state—he was a German infantryman, also full of holes and also blue around the gills. The congressman hovered over this one for a moment, glowering down at him.

"I hope the bastard appreciates what we're doing for him," he said. "I wonder what kind of care the krauts give our boys?"

"Sir, we understand they generally abide by the Geneva rules," the aide said.

"Well, by God, I hope so. And if you get down to your last bottle of plasma, I hope he doesn't get it." With a last glare at his vanquished foe, the congressman continued on his search. Finally, in the next tent, with only minutes left on the timetable, we came to a patient from the right state. He seemed almost as glad to meet his representative as the old man was to see him. They actually embraced, which seemed all right from a medical standpoint because the soldier had no visible wounds. As the aide rushed out to find a photographer (the congressman upbraided him for not having one ready) one of the doctors, whom I knew slightly, leaned over and whispered to me.

"I'm going to tell him the man has the clap."

"Good Lord," I said. "Does he?"

"No, but by the time he untangles his tongue and says it's not true, I'll bet that lard-ass will be two miles down the road."

There wasn't time. The aide burst in with an army photographer even as the sufferer on the cot told how he had been laid low by a recurrence of malaria picked up in North Africa. The pair posed with their arms around each other, and with the doctors, including my friend, smiling in the background. With an admonition to the aide to make sure he got the negative and to try for a hundred eight-by-ten-inch glossy prints, the congressman charged without another word back out past the cots of the long ward tent through which we had just come, because that was the shortest way to the waiting jeeps. Every eye in the place followed him through, except for those behind the ball of gauze and those belonging to a man in traction who was either asleep or unconscious.

Back in the Excelsior, a WAC captain who was serving as aide to Clare Luce found me in the lobby and said the congresswoman wanted to meet me. This was not totally surprising, since *Life* magazine, published by Mrs. Luce's husband, had by now run a lot of my stuff and given me considerable publicity. Still, it was flattering and somewhat awesome. Not only was she politically prominent—she was an all-round celebrity, and *she* wanted to meet *me*. I followed the WAC upstairs and met the personification of Women's Liberation. Mrs. Luce was beautiful and frightening, with the fiercest eyes I had ever confronted.

"What are you going to do with yourself after the war?" she asked.

"Make a living, I hope," I said.

"What are you going to do about your education?"

"I hadn't thought about it."

"Do you realize that you are going to be in a position to reach a lot of people? Don't you think you ought to be educated?"

"Yes, ma'am."

"If you take my advice, you will forget about being successful for a while and get yourself into college. If you need any help, let us know."

I believe she really meant it. In retrospect, I think I probably should have taken her advice. At the moment, however, nothing was farther from my mind than forgetting about being successful.

13

As the Germans were pushed back to their own borders on the western front, they struck back with one last, huge counter-offensive called the Battle of the Bulge. For a while it was successful, and its effects were felt in Italy, where enemy morale went up and they began shouting insults as they continued rolling grenades over the cliffs. The more I heard about the Bulge, the more curious I became. Until then the war I had seen had been a stalemate at worst, usually ending in an advance of some sort. Now we were hearing stories of massive retreats and of regimental clerks picking up weapons and earning their combat infantry badges.

Neville and Herb Lyons, our new managing editor, approved my travel orders. They looked a little unhappy, as did some of my cohorts on the staff, when I said I planned to take my jeep. (From time to time people developed acquisitive ideas about that machine and I had worked out an elaborate security system for locking it. Chaining the steering wheel was not enough: it was a simple matter for thieves to remove the wheel and steer with pliers. I also removed the distributor rotor and coil wire and locked the hood down with a welded hasp. Officially, I did this to frustrate native thieves. It was also to keep Milton Lehman or Jack Foisie from borrowing the jeep for a vacation in Sicily.) After drawing a week's supply of cartoons in advance, I drove to Leghorn, where I learned that the next LST to Marseille wouldn't depart for a week or so. Since the voyage itself took several days, it began to look as if I would have to abandon my jeep (unthinkable) or my plans.

Learning that torpedo boats were making regular dashes up the coast to Nice under the German guns along the Italian and French Rivieras, carrying high-priority cargo, messages, mail, and whatnot, I approached the skipper of one of these and asked permission to tie my jeep on his deck. He seemed intrigued by the idea, but told me I needed authorization from Fifth Army headquarters. Time was running out. I tore up the road to the mountains above Florence and parked in front of the tent of Lieutenant General Lucian K. Truscott, the new Fifth Army commander.

Truscott was one of the really tough generals. He had swallowed carbolic acid as a child, corroding his vocal cords and giving his natural drill-sergeant's bark a gravelly quality which made other strong men quail. He could have eaten a ham like Patton for breakfast any morning and picked his teeth with the man's pearl-handled pistols. Patton never went near the front without biographers and photographers in tow. Truscott spent half his time at the front—the real front—with nobody in attendance but a nervous jeep driver and a worried aide. Back when I was in trouble with the Peninsular Base Section in Naples, Truscott, who then commanded the crack 3rd Division, which won more Congressional Medals of Honor than any other army or marine division in World War II, was one of the field officers who spoke for me, and for the right of *Stars and Stripes* to express soldiers' gripes. Later, when he took over the VI Corps and was in charge of the Anzio breakout, I met him for the first time and thanked him for his support. He told me that when I stopped pissing off martinets I wouldn't be doing my job right.

I was on friendly terms with one of his aides, Major Jim Wilson, who had once arranged for me to spend a day riding around in the back seat of Truscott's jeep as he toured the front. As far as I know, it was the only time a newspaperman had this opportunity with Truscott, and I had no wish to repeat the experience. I spent the trip cowering in the back seat, with my helmet jammed over my ears, as we drove time and again past a divisional headquarters, where army commanders usually stop, then past regimental, beyond which they never go, then past battalion, where everybody did double-takes at the jeep with the three stars, and right into company positions, where they were receiving small-arms fire.

"Come here, captain," Truscott would rasp at some bearded unfortunate peering from his dugout. "Tell me your situation." He would pull a map from under his seat, unfold it on the jeep hood, and discuss things. It was from this experience that I got such cartoon ideas as one of some soldiers asking a general not to draw fire while he was inspiring them.

"Actually, he is careful not to drive into situations where he will draw fire on the people there," Wilson told me later. "He's not a showboater. But he feels that it's important for senior generals to deliberately go where

"He's right, Joe. When we ain't fightin' we should act like sojers."

Breakfast in bed.

"Fresh, spirited American troops, flushed with victory, are bringing in thousands of hungry, ragged, battle-weary prisoners." (News item).

Willie and Joe weren't bums. They just looked like bums. This cartoon eventually won the Pulitzer Prize.

"Yer lucky. Yer learnin' a trade."

"We calls 'em garritroopers. They're too far forward t'wear ties an' too far back t'git shot."

"Papa, I think we have been liberated."

fire already exists. Too few American officers of any rank let themselves get shot at. He feels that it's good for morale and forces subordinate commanders to follow suit. He and Patton agree in this matter: Patton often says, 'We didn't get enough of our officers killed last week.' "

Well, if the PT boat captain needed Fifth Army authorization to carry my jeep, I figured it wouldn't hurt to start at the top. Going through channels could take days. My friend Wilson was in. After congratulating him on his longevity and continuing good health, I explained my problem.

"You're crazy to go by PT boat," he said. "At the speed that thing travels it's plowing under waves half the time. Even if you don't lose your jeep it'll get all rusted out. Besides, the Germans take pot shots at those boats. What if they hit you? You'd have a hell of a time getting another new jeep. Things have tightened up. Why don't you go by plane?"

"But I need the jeep," I said. "I've got it rigged with blackout curtains so I can work in it at night, and it's got all my notebooks and working materials stored in the back. Besides, it's the only way I can cover a lot of territory and still make my deadlines."

"And, besides all that, it's spoiled hell out of you." Wilson grinned. "Anyway, I meant you ought to fly the jeep over, too. Troop Carrier Command in Pisa has got a bunch of C-47s with cargo doors that can take it."

He gave me the name of a squadron commander in Pisa. By the time I arrived at the airstrip a C-47 was waiting with a ramp for the jeep in place. Loading was simple. I drove up the ramp, four crewmen grabbed the jeep and slid it sideways, and we were in. They lashed it down and suggested I stay in my driver's seat for the trip, since it looked a lot more comfortable than the aluminum bucket seats lining the cabin.

When we landed in Lyon, I read in *Stars and Stripes* that the Battle of the Bulge was all over, so when I drove out of the airport I headed for Paris. This was a violation of my travel orders, which authorized me only to visit the Seventh, First, and Ninth armies in Alsace, Belgium, and Holland, and made me technically AWOL, but when you are driving your own jeep with a pocketful of trip tickets, Paris is within reach, and your original mission is blown, what can you do?

I was in trouble from the moment I entered Paris. The MPs were skeptical about my trip tickets and outraged by my clothing. Thinking I was going straight to the war, I had worn my usual Italian getup: a Russian-style rabbit-fur cap from the 10th Mountain Division, an armored-force tanker's jacket with knit collar and sleeves, and fatigue trousers with patch pockets for carrying pencils and papers. In Paris this did not add up to a legitimate uniform. They seemed to be operating a more formal war up that way. I was taken into custody almost immediately, but when I insisted that I belonged to *Stars and Stripes*, I was escorted to the paper in the building of the Paris edition of the New York *Herald Tribune* instead of to jail, and delivered into the hands of Lieutenant Bob Moora, the editor. I had never met Moora before. All the different editions of *Stars and Stripes* operated independently of each other. Moora was so cordial to me, in spite of my uniform, that I smelled brimstone almost immediately.

"Mauldin, you have a great sense of timing," Bob said. "You know we print your stuff here."

"Yes, sir."

"Well, the day you pick to arrive in Paris is the same day we get a message from General George Patton about you. He was already sore at us for running pictures of some unshaven soldiers, but now you're the target."

"Forget it," I said, grinning. "This sort of thing happens all the time."

"Forget it?" he cried. "He threatened to ban the paper from the whole Third Army."

I was taken to Major Arthur Goodfriend, one of the officers in charge. He told me I had done much to liven his job since they had started printing my stuff. A staff officer from De Gaulle's headquarters had practically challenged Goodfriend to a duel because I had insulted the competence of French military-truck drivers in a cartoon. General John Lee's headquarters (Lee was the European equivalent of the Italian base section commander) had threatened to cut off the *Stars and Stripes'* newsprint because of another cartoon of mine, according to Goodfriend. He mentioned a few other complaints, but said nothing about Patton, which puzzled me. Also, like Moora, he was cordial to a degree that made me suspicious, considering the trouble I seemed to have caused for him.

"Have a good time in Paris," Goodfriend said as I left. "By the way, General Solbert, who runs Information and Education, would like to see you today if you have a chance."

"Yes, sir." The general would like to see me *if* I had a chance. Have a good time in Paris. They *knew* I was AWOL.

Downstairs I ran into Sergeant Bill Estoff, a portly ex-bookie from Syracuse, New York, who used to run the *Stars and Stripes* circulation department in Naples and was now doing the same job in Paris. Bill was really too old and fat for the army and shouldn't have been drafted, but we were all glad it had happened. He had been assigned to *Stars and Stripes* because during his classification a young clerk had asked his civilian profession. Bill had said he was a bookmaker. The clerk had put down "publishing." Estoff was a wise duck who acted as father confessor to everybody on the paper with enough sense to listen to him. He reminded me of the late Medicine Man.

"The problem is that Patton got pissed and made a threat about you

The costume that fascinated the MPs in Paris.

This hitherto-unpublished photo from Italy by John Phillips shows that unlike my characters I tried to set a good example by patronizing barbers regularly.

and it's all over town," Bill said. "He keeps sticking his foot in his mouth about politics and now it's freedom of the press that's involved. They're trying to figure a way to cool it off before it becomes another episode, like him slapping that soldier in Sicily."

"I'm not looking for trouble with Patton," I said.

"That's not the point," Bill said. "The issue is a lot bigger than you are. Where the hell does he get off telling newspapers what to print?"

"Listen," I said, "I just sneaked into town for fun. This thing is getting over my head."

"Boy, that's the understatement of the week. You go see that general. Don't let him snow you. Meet me back here tomorrow and we'll figure something out."

Solbert was a disarming man who went right to work putting me at ease.

"Enjoying Paris, son?" If he knew I was there illegally he didn't let on.

"Yes, sir. Very nice."

"Well!" Fingertips together briskly. "I hear you're having a little trouble with George."

How do you like that? *I* was having a little trouble with *George*. The room reeked of good fellowship.

"That wasn't very smart of him," the general said. "The press is a pretty delicate institution to fool with. Even the soldier press. Especially for a man in George's shoes. Er, I'm speaking of General Patton, of course."

"Yes, sir."

"I'll be frank with you, son. A lot of us around here are worried about the way he keeps getting himself into peculiar situations, publicity-wise. And this is just the sort of thing that might make a story. A lot of correspondents are laying for Patton these days, anyway. General Ike thinks highly of George's talents and wants to keep him in there pitching, not getting into trouble. Patton lives in a little world of his own, sort of a medieval world, where officers are knights and soldiers are dumb peasants. Only two kinds of people in his little world: heroes and ciphers. All civilians are ciphers, of course. Heroes are soldiers who act happy doing what George wants. Sometimes I wonder if he didn't get into the wrong army."

Solbert must have seen my distress, because now he got around to making his pitch.

"I want you to know that *I* think George is all wrong about those cartoons," he said, smiling. "*I* happen to like your stuff. You'd be surprised how many of us think your drawings say things that need saying." I had a mental image of SHAEF's staff huddled over the morning paper, chuckling.

"There is just one little item," he said. "I'm not going to say you ought to do this. Just that you ought to think about it. Can't you clean up those characters of yours a little? They're pretty scruffy."

"Well, sir, that first winter in Italy . . ."

"I know, son. I know. It was a terrible time. For a while I'm sure the infantry did look like that. And I'm sure you regard it as a sort of trademark for what the infantry goes through. The trouble is that you've made it stick. Some of these kids fresh from the States as infantry replacements think they've got to roll in a muddy ditch and grow whiskers before they're socially acceptable."

"Do you mean my cartoons are making them behave that way?"

"I can assure you that George Patton thinks so. That's how he is. Me? I don't think so. It's ridiculous to think that if a cartoonist reformed his ways the army would become all spit and polish. Why, if you had that kind of power, I guess we'd have to figure a way to put you out of business, wouldn't we?" He laughed. I grinned weakly.

"All I'm suggesting," he concluded, "is that you think a little more about the journalistic aspects of this thing. The accuracy of it. Sure, maybe draw a scruffy-looking fellow once in a while. There are scruffy soldiers. But not the majority. Why, do you realize that less than ten percent of the army ever sees the front lines?"

"That's the ten percent I draw pictures of."

"Well, maybe you ought to broaden your scope, then. All I'm trying to say is that if you'll clean things up a little and get George off everybody's necks, we can get on with the war back here. I tell you, that fellow has got a fixation about this thing. We'd like to get him back to thinking about the Germans."

On the street outside, I decided that if I was to see Paris I had better hurry before the Patton plot got any thicker. I made my way to a café on the Champs Elysées to look for a French photographer named Alex, who had worked for us as an interpreter in Grenoble. Alex was in his early forties, was witty and charming, had a way with the ladies, had promised to show me Paris if I ever got there, and had told me to go to this particular café any afternoon. Sure enough, he was there, looking jaunty in a homburg and pin-striped suit, trying to make a young girl at the next table. I stood at his elbow for several minutes, unnoticed, until an American corporal came along and picked up the girl.

"Allo, Bill," Alex said. "This is terrible. All these women sleeping with Americans. There is no pride left in France."

He had a way of awakening my latent chauvinism.

"What the hell is wrong with sleeping with Americans?" I demanded.

"I don't know. I never tried," he said, sweetly.

"Maybe you'd like the Germans back."

"Well, do you call this liberation? Is it liberation when a French patriot, a man who carried food to the Maquis *at the risk of his life,* comes all the way from Grenoble to Paris and can't find a woman of his own country to keep his back warm? Tonight I will find an American nurse or a WAC and I will have my revenge. I will give her such a time she will scream, first with shock and then with joy. What do you think of *that?*"

"Good show," I cheered him on.

"You laugh? It wouldn't bother you? You have no more regard for your women than respect for ours."

Alex looked at me appraisingly. "Have you ever been to the Sphinx Club?" he asked. ". . . No, of course not. Have you ever heard of the Sphinx? No? My God, before I met you I thought I knew what provincial meant. Why do I waste time on you?"

"Because I have a jeep and can write my own trip tickets, and you still hope to figure out a way to make a fast buck out of me."

"The Sphinx Club might interest you. It's the sort of place American tourists brag about going to, and you are a tourist if I ever saw one. The waitresses at the Sphinx are all beautiful and they are all naked."

"No kidding!"

"Have you any money"

"Some." I had already checked my roll: about 2,200 francs, worth about $44 at the flexible exchange rate.

"Cigarettes?"

"Couple of cartons."

"Ah, you sly cowboy!" Alex cried, delightedly. "I *knew* you carried something besides virtue in that jeep."

"Listen, I bought 'em to smoke."

"Isn't it painful to smoke something worth a dollar a pack in Paris?"

"It might hurt you but it doesn't hurt me."

"Those waitresses have many talents besides serving tables."

I bought Alex a Dubonnet. He had the good sense to sit in silence while I searched my soul. What kind of war veteran would I be without a Paris story for my sons when it was time to tell them the facts of life? I didn't expect my wife to give up society in my absence; could I help it if social life was one thing in Abilene and something else in Paris? Surely she wouldn't begrudge me this. All I had had out of this misbegotten trip so far was an arrest and a snow job in a general's office.

"Listen, Alex, are those waitresses really *naked?*"

"Nude would be a less uncouth word," he said. He knew he had it made now. "They are too splendid to be naked. They are works of art. You can take your sketchbook if your conscience bothers you. You have been to an art class? Americans do allow themselves to study nudes in art classes, do they not?"

"In some of the more daring schools, maybe," I said. "By the way—

isn't a place like the Sphinx likely to be off limits?"

"But of *course* it's off limits. Everything nice is off limits to your nice army. Your hat," he said. "That will get you in."

"In where? The stockade?"

"Leave it to me. Where is your sense of adventure? Trust your friend Alex. Have I ever let you down?"

I reported to the *Stars and Stripes* office, and told Goodfriend I had seen the general and had been given a great deal to think about. He seemed pleased that the matter was out of his hands.

We arrived at the Sphinx shortly after dark. It was plastered with off-limits signs and guarded by two MPs with the demeanor of the Watch and Ward Society and the physiques of San Francisco waterfront bouncers. These worthies looked at me in a pained, puzzled way as Alex began explaining that I was a Russian soldier who had been shot in the throat, captured by the Germans at Stalingrad, recently recaptured by our side, and was being treated by U.S. army doctors who hoped to restore my voice while I awaited repatriation. It was not only an incredibly stupid story, but I thought it was badly told, and I stood out of reach and ready to bolt. It was a tribute to the Big Lie. The MPs not only went for it; Alex had them almost in tears.

"Have fun," one of them said, shaking my hand. "God knows you haven't had much so far. Translate that to him, willya, monsoor?"

" 'Comrade,' " Alex corrected him.

" 'Scuse me, comrade."

"I am glad to see not all your MPs are anti-Communist," Alex said as we went in. The place was jammed with French civilians, all smoking Camels with abandon and eating slabs of pâté like cornbread. Every black marketeer in town must have been there. Alex was greeted at several tables as we passed, the occupants staring curiously at me. A head-waiter bustled up with a no-vacancy look; Alex repeated the Russian bit; we not only got our table but became the center of attention. The waitresses were stunning. They wore lace caps and high-heeled shoes, with absolutely nothing between, except that two or three of them had saucy little aprons about two inches square, possibly to cover unsightly appendicitis scars. And every one of these girls found reasons to pass our table, pause, and stare admiringly at me. I reciprocated with such intensity that Alex had to remind me to take up the slack in my jaw and look the part of a tragic Stalingrad victim, not a gaping Yankee. He had not lied about those girls. I thought they were the prettiest things I'd ever seen. Of course, I had been in the mountains for quite a while. The girl who served us took special pains to brush against me every time she brought something. The dinner must have been good—the check took eighteen hundred francs and all my cigarettes—but I don't remember much about it. It is hard to taste food with a pink nipple dangling in your ear.

After coffee the headwaiter said the girls upstairs wanted to do a special show in my honor. We were directed to a small room, where we arranged ourselves on cushions with a bottle of cognac between us. This took my last four hundred francs, but as it turned out I don't know what I'd have done without that bottle for support during the next half hour. Two bare chicks announced they were going to take us on a world tour of connubial customs. One of them strapped on a dildo and they both went to work.

"This is their funniest routine," Alex whispered.

They showed us how Americans screw: the "husband" kept looking at his wristwatch. In England the wife asked: "Feel better now, dear?" In Germany the couple counted cadence. In Russia they both kept looking over their shoulders. After a few more countries the girls fell into our arms, exhausted by their artistic efforts.

"I'll take the husband," Alex said, gallantly helping the girl unstrap her equipment. "It's a favor to you, since you've already seen what the wife can do, whereas this one is of an unknown quality."

"Listen, old buddy, you're perfectly free to take him or her or whatever it is wherever you want," I told him. "The question is, what are you going to use for money?"

Alex had worked himself around behind the girl and taken a breast in each hand. Now, like a child about to be deprived, he clutched those precious baubles so tightly and gave such an anguished howl past her ear that she winced.

"Do you mean you brought me here with no more money?"

"I *said* I didn't have much," I howled back. "And *you* brought *me* here, you bastard."

"Shh! Your throat," he remembered. The girls had caught the word "money," divined our trouble, and now it didn't matter whether one of us was a wounded Russian or not. They were beginning to suspect they wouldn't even get a tip. I never saw two pretty faces change so fast.

"We'd better get out of here before the word gets around that I'm a phony," I said.

"We'd better get out before we get killed," Alex corrected. The girls were chattering to the headwaiter, who had come in a side door. I smiled ingratiatingly at him and raised the almost-empty bottle with great gusto in what I hoped was a Russian-style salute. He did not smile back. I held on to the bottle as we backed out.

Happily, the news of my miraculous recovery hadn't reached the MPs out front; they shook our hands warmly in farewell. They seemed to have taken quite a fancy to us.

"Hey, is that show upstairs as rough as they say?" one of them asked.

"One of the few bits of old Paris left," Alex assured him. "I must get this man back to the hospital."

"You guys sure didn't stay very long."

"He is very weak."

"Boy, he must be. Imagine a young guy like that, tore up so bad he can't even handle a little poontang."

14

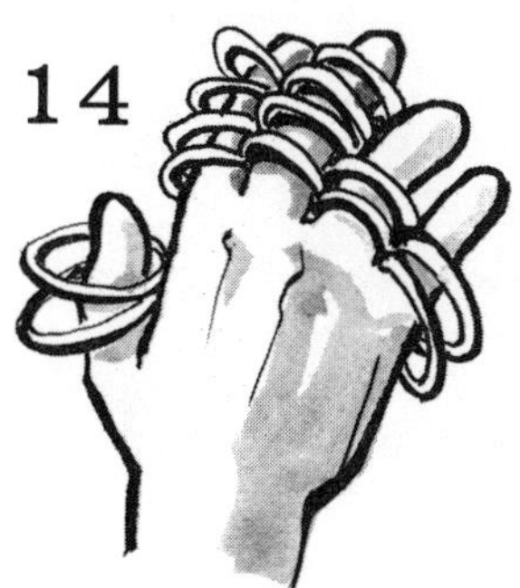

"It's just like the trouble you had back in Naples, only more so," Bill Estoff said when we met next day. We sat in his favorite bar, a gloomy little dive around the corner from the office. This was like Estoff. In a city full of beautiful sidewalk cafés, his bookie instinct led him to a hole in the wall. With his tie loosened and his sleeves pushed up, all he needed was his cigar box and form sheet. "That chicken little ribbon clerk in Italy only had two stars," Bill said, "but Old Gutsy-Blood's got stars all over his hat. You're in the big league now."

"I'm not playing against anybody, least of all Patton," I said.

"You're in it, whether you like it or not," Estoff assured me. "You've got the army in a bind. If they make you change your stuff, everybody will ask how come your dogfaces got creases in their pants all of a sudden. If they leave you alone, they've still got old Georgie chewing the rug and trying to push the paper around."

"I suppose they could arrange to get me run over by a tank," I said.

"Too late for foul play now," Bill said, grinning. "If they were gonna get you, they should have thought of it in Naples."

We were joined by Will Lang, the *Time-Life* correspondent whom I hadn't seen since Italy. Seeing Lang and Estoff in the same morning made Paris a far less hungover place for me.

"I've been trying to convince Mauldin we're going to help him out," Estoff said.

"Affirmative," replied Lang, ordering an eggnog.

"What I don't get," I said, "is why somebody doesn't just tell General Patton not to write any more letters to the editor."

"The good general," said Lang, "has all kinds of talent for getting publicity but very little knowledge of public relations.

"Enough chatter," said Estoff, polishing off his drink. "Let's swing into action."

"The only action I can think of is for you guys to get me on a fast bomber for Rome," I said.

"Will and me got better ideas," Estoff said.

They escorted me to the Paris office of Captain Harry Butcher, Eisenhower's naval aide. I had never dreamed Estoff and Lang knew people like Butcher. He greeted my two friends warmly, asked them to wait outside, and put a proposition to me bluntly and briefly: "We've all decided the best solution is for you to go have a talk with the general himself."

"You want *me* to go see Patton?"

"Certainly. Why not? Meet your chief critic face to face. Talk it out. Tell him why you draw those things. He'll tell you what he doesn't like about them. Maybe he'll change some of your ideas. Maybe—" Butcher chuckled slightly at the thought—"maybe you'll change his. Something bothering you? Speak up; don't be afraid."

Since he had invited frankness, I said I thought it was a long way to drive just to get my tail chewed out.

"Nonsense, Mauldin. He's not half as bad as he sounds. Pretty nice guy in some ways when you get to know him. Tell you what: I'll call him right now, and if he won't agree to see you and talk this thing over privately, man-to-man, no rank, then I won't ask you to go. How's that? Think it over and you'll agree with Lang and Estoff and me that it's the only sensible way out of all this. You do want to help us out, don't you?"

"Yes, sir." I was scared. I remember thinking that I had come a long way in a few years but that I had finally overplayed my hand.

"Don't think Patton won't see the logic and humor in this, too," Butcher said, placing the call to Third Army headquarters in Luxembourg. "That man can be pretty surprising at times. Did you know he writes poetry? . . . Hello, hello. Thank you. Morning, general. Fine; yourself, sir? How's Willie?"

He was referring to Patton's pet bull terrier. Obviously the conversation was going well. The aide pointed to an extension phone, so I could hear for myself how easy this was going to be.

"General, I won't take much of your time," Butcher said. "You'll remember you had a few criticisms about the Paris *Stars and Stripes* which goes out to Third Army . . . yes, yes, sir . . ." (There were squeaking noises which at first I ascribed to the French telephone system.) "General, it was the cartoons I was calling about, and the fellow who draws them. What's that, sir? Oh, no. No, we haven't done anything like that—in fact, I've got him right here in my office. Just been talking with him, and, general, it seems to me that a great deal of good would come of it if he heard your viewpoints on . . . yes, sir, I'm sure he's already heard them, but I meant in person . . . came and talked to you . . ."

Now the shrill voice at the other end took form: "If that little son of a bitch sets foot in Third Army I'll throw his ass in jail."

Now I was on familiar ground, and it was the captain's turn to look distraught. He recovered fast, though, and it was my privilege to watch a real pro at work. His tone was still jovial and personal, but whereas he'd said "I" before, the perpendicular pronoun now gave way to "we," and there was little doubt about who Ike's aide meant by "we."

"General," he said, "we feel around here that it might be a good thing to do. We're convinced Mauldin means well; he's as interested in getting the war over as the rest of us. He has told me he'd be happy to talk with you. Fine, sir, fine. Oh, yes, by the way, general, we've promised him that the conversation will be private, just the two of you, no rank. . . . Sir? Well, I'm afraid we've already assured him of it that way. Goodbye, sir, thanks again, and we're sure this will be most constructive all around. . . . Goodbye, sir."

We cradled our phones and he looked at his for a moment, grinning, before turning to me. I found myself liking Butcher, even if he was sending me on a suicide mission.

"I believe I already mentioned that Patton can be a surprising man," he said. "At least you know this deal wasn't rigged with him in advance."

"Does General Eisenhower really know about this?" I couldn't help asking.

"He thinks it's a great idea. Now, Mauldin, Bill Estoff tells me you have a pretty fancy jeep. I have a few suggestions for your trip to Luxembourg. Unfancy it. Make sure your vehicle is regulation, windshield folded and covered and so on, and for crying out loud get yourself regulation, too, from head to foot. You have a helmet? Necktie? Sidearm?"

I assured him that I had been in Patton's army in Sicily and could still recite all the fines, right down to untied shoelaces.

"Of course. I forgot," he said, smiling. "You're always drawing pictures about it. Well, good luck. Report to Major Quirk in Third Army public relations. We've done all we can at this end."

A thick, cold rain was falling as I neared Luxembourg. Up to the borders of Third Army I allowed myself the comfort of a windshield. Then I lowered the glass, slipped on its canvas hood, donned helmet and pistol, and checked myself over carefully. Within a mile I was stopped at an MP roadblock.

"Kee-rist, Mac, why don'tcha at least turn up your collar if you got to drive in this rain?"

"I thought it was against regulations. No fines for turned-up collars this year?"

He laughed and asked for my trip ticket. The good humor drained from his face.

"Cute," he grunted.

"That's what everybody says when they see one of those," I told him. "But it's legit."

"Balls. Where you headed and what's your business?"

"I've got an appointment with General Patton."

"I'm getting to where I don't like you at all. It's a long, muddy road to the provost marshal's office."

"Then we'd better get started," I told him, "because this is going to sound worse and worse to you."

The provost riffled my papers, noting that I was temporarily detached from the Mediterranean Theater of Operations and attached to the Seventh Army in Alsace.

"So we find you driving a stolen jeep from Paris to Luxembourg. And the corporal here tells me you didn't act a bit worried when he picked you up. Where'd you get the jeep?"

"It isn't stolen," I said. "It was issued to me by Fifth Army."

"Vehicles are not issued to enlisted men as individuals. Did you know that?"

"Yes, sir."

"But this one was issued to you?"

"Yes, sir."

"You say Fifth Army. That's Italy. Suppose you tell me how you got that jeep up here."

"Flew it."

"He flew it, corporal."

"Yes, sir. I heard."

"I mean the troop-carrier boys in Pisa did it for me. They put it in a C-47 and flew it from Pisa to Lyon."

"A buck sergeant has a personal jeep and the army flies it around in C-47s for him," the provost said to the MP.

"He says he has an appointment with General Patton, sir."

"It figures. Corporal, you didn't handle this man roughly—speak loudly or profanely, or anything like that?"

"I have never been stopped by a nicer MP," I put in.

"Good. Whatever happens, I don't want it said that we handled a delicate case roughly. Smoke?"

"Thank you, sir."

"The thing that gets me about you," the provost said, holding a match for me, "is that you're so goddamn *reasonable*. So rational."

"Seemed that way to me, too, when I picked him up, sir," the corporal said.

"If you'll make a couple of calls we can get all this straightened out," I offered.

"No doubt. The question is, who do we call?"

"Well, you could try General Patton's headquarters—there's a Major Quirk there—or maybe you could try Captain Harry Butcher at SHAEF."

"Butcher?"

"He's General Eisenhower's aide."

"Now we got Eisenhower in the act, with a lousy captain for an aide. If you're going to try to bullshit your way out of this, you ought to at least study the tables of organization."

"Sir, he's a captain in the navy. That's the same as a colonel in the army."

"So Eisenhower, who runs the army in Europe, has a ship's captain for his aide. . . . Listen, I'll make a deal with you, you loony bastard. I'll call this Major Quirk. I don't guarantee I'll get him, mind you, but I'll speak to his office. You got this thing on your mind about calling somebody's office, maybe it'll relieve you or something. Actually, by rules we're supposed to check all stories later anyway for a report, but as a favor I'll do it right now. Meanwhile, we're going to keep that jeep. You won't need it any more.

"It's a deal," I said. "If I don't have an appointment with Patton you keep the jeep."

"*General* Patton, sergeant!"

He made the call. He didn't get Quirk, but somebody in the office straightened him out. The provost was a sport. He even laughed a little.

"We'd better get this man on his way, corporal. We've made him late."

"Oh, that's all right," I said, airily, "the appointment was pretty well open, depending on when I got there."

Patton had taken over Luxembourg's royal palace. I was scrutinized and passed by a small task force of vitamin-packed MPs with mirror-toed shoes and simonized headgear, then directed to Quirk's office in a downstairs wing of the magnificent building. The major turned out to be a nice man—so far I was having remarkably good luck with Patton's subordinates—and although he too inspected me carefully from head to toe, I could see that he was doing it for my own good. He led me through the story-book palace, full of huge, ornate, high-ceilinged rooms. Patton's office must have been the throne room, the grandest of them all. It had great double doors. One was ajar; standing slightly behind the major as he discreetly rapped, I could see the general's desk at the far end of the room, across an acre of carpet.

There he sat, big as life even at that distance. His hair was silver, his face was pink, his collar and shoulders glittered with more stars than I could count, his fingers sparkled with rings, and an incredible mass of ribbons started around desktop level and spread upward in a flood over his chest to the very top of his shoulder, as if preparing to march down his back, too. His face was rugged, with an odd, strangely shapeless outline; his eyes were pale, almost colorless, with a choleric bulge. His small, compressed mouth was sharply downturned at the corners, with a lower lip which suggested a pouting child as much as a no-nonsense martinet. It was a welcome, rather human touch. Beside him, lying in a big chair, was Willie, the bull terrier. If ever dog was suited to master this one was. Willie had his beloved boss's expression and lacked only the ribbons and stars. I stood in that door staring into the four meanest eyes I'd ever seen.

"Come in, major," Patton said. Somehow, it broke the spell. There was that shrill voice again. Like the lower lip it brought him down to human proportions. We made the long trek across the room and came to a parade-ground halt before the desk, where I snapped out the kind of salute I used to make in high-school ROTC. Whatever of the parade-ground soldier was still left in me, Patton brought it out.

"Hello, sergeant." The general smiled—an impressive muscular feat, considering the distance the corners of his mouth had to travel—and came around the desk to offer his hand. I don't know who was more astonished, Willie or me. The dog, rising with his master, literally fell out of the chair. As we shook hands, I stole a glance at the general's famous gun belt. He was wearing only one of his pearl-handled six-shooters. Undergunned, shaking hands, smiling—all were hopeful signs. Patton told me to sit. I appropriated Willie's chair. The dog not only looked shocked now but offended. To hell with Willie. Butcher had been right. This was going to be O.K.

"Well, sir, I'll be going," the major said.

"Going where?" Patton snapped. "Stick around. I want you to hear this."

The major hesitated for the barest instant, glanced at me—he was aware of the agreement for privacy—and took the adjacent chair. The old chill started back up my spine.

"Now then, sergeant, about those pictures you draw of those god-awful things you call soldiers. Where did you ever see soldiers like that? You know goddamn well you're not drawing an accurate representation of the American soldier. You make them look like goddamn bums. No respect for the army, their officers, or themselves. You know as well as I do that you can't have an army without respect for officers. What are you trying to do, incite a goddamn mutiny? You listen to me, sergeant, the Russians

"*My, sir—what an enthusiastic welcome!*"

"*Beautiful view! Is there one for the enlisted men?*"

tried running an army without rank once. Shot all their leaders, all their brains, all their generals. The Bolsheviks made their officers dress like soldiers, eat with soldiers, no saluting, everybody calling everybody Comrade—and where did it get 'em? While they ran an army like that they couldn't fight their way out of a piss-soaked paper bag. Now they've learned their lesson. They put uniforms back on their officers. Some men are born to lead and don't need those little metal dinguses on their shoulders. Hell, I could command troops in a G-string. But in wartime you're bound to get some officers who don't know how to act without being dressed for it. The Russians learned you have to have rank and if some comrade looks cross-eyed at a superior today he gets his teeth kicked in. When somebody says 'frog' he jumps. And now he fights. How long do you think you'd last drawing those pictures in the Russian army?"

The question turned out to be rhetorical. I opened my mouth to say that I realized the necessity of discipline and had never thought officers should be called Comrade, chosen by popular elections among their troops, or deprived of the dinguses on their shoulders. But I quickly shut it again, and kept it shut for the next twenty minutes or so as the general reeled off examples of the necessity for rank through four thousand years of military history.

For a while it was fascinating. Patton was a real master of his subject. I have an affinity for enthusiasts, anyway, in any field of endeavor; as I sat there listening to the general talk war, I felt truly privileged, as if I were hearing Michelangelo on painting. I had been too long enchanted by the army myself—as a child listening to my father's stories, as a high-school boy dreaming of West Point—to be anything but impressed by this magnificent old performer's monologue. Just as when I had first saluted him, I felt whatever martial spirit was left in me being lifted out and fanned into flame.

At one point, somewhere around the Hellenic wars, when once again the value of stern leadership was being extolled, I absently reached out to see if Willie's ear needed scratching. I was stopped by a dog owner's reflex which reminded me never to handle another man's pet uninvited. A glance at Willie confirmed this. Had I touched his ear it would have been with my left, or working hand, and I think he would have put me out of business, accomplishing in one snap what his master was trying to do the hard way.

When Patton had worked his way back through the Russian revolution to the present again, he got around to my cartoons.

"Sergeant," he said, "I don't know what *you* think you're trying to do, but the krauts ought to pin a medal on you for helping them mess up discipline for us. I'm going to show you what I consider some prime goddamn examples of what I mean by creating disrespect."

He opened a drawer and came up with a small batch of cutouts from *Stars and Stripes*. On top was a street scene I had drawn of a French town being liberated. A convoy of motorized infantry was being deluged by flowers, fruit, and wine, handed up from the street and dropped out of windows by hysterically happy citizens. Some of the soldiers were taking advantage of the general confusion and pelting the convoy commander, in an open command car in front, with riper samples of the fruit.

"My, sir," says a junior officer, "what an enthusiastic welcome."

The general held the next one up by the tips of his thumb and forefinger as if it were contaminated. It was a night scene of a war-battered opera house with a USO show advertised on the marquee: "GIRLS, GIRLS, GIRLS. Fresh from the States!" Queued up in the snow at the front door was a long line of weary-looking soldiers of various nationalities, mostly British and American, with their coat collars turned up against the raw weather and their sad faces filled with anticipation of the charms within. It was one of my better drawings: loaded with poignancy, I thought. Queued up at the stage door were the officers, of course, all spruced up and waiting to take the girls out. Some even had bouquets.

"Now this," shrilled the general, "is the kind of goddamn . . . where are the words under this one? Somebody cut off the goddamn words!"

"Sir, there wasn't any caption under that one." Willie, the major, and I all jumped at the sound of my voice.

"No words!"

"No, sir. I didn't think it needed any."

"All right. You've got a bunch of messy goddamn soldiers in one line and a bunch of officers in another. What's it mean?"

He was going to let me speak again. It was really too much for Willie, who got up and stiffly walked to his master's side, ready for anything.

"Sir, it means the soldiers want to look at the girls and the officers want to take them out."

"Well, what the hell's wrong with that?"

"Nothing, sir," I weaseled. "I didn't imply anything was wrong. I just thought it was a humorous situation." No ordeal is worse than that of a cartoonist who has to explain his creation to a reader.

"You think the soldiers ought to get laid instead of the officers, don't you?" Patton growled.

In spite of himself he couldn't help grinning slightly at this; in spite of myself I couldn't help liking him a little for it.

"Sir, it has been my experience that when USO or Red Cross girls are to be had the officers usually get them."

"And what business is that of yours, sergeant?"

"None, sir. I just thought it was an amusing situation and I drew it as I saw it."

"It doesn't amuse me."

"To tell you the truth, sir, it doesn't seem very funny to me, either, any more," I said, honestly.

"Well, by God, now we're getting somewhere. Now, why did you draw this picture if it wasn't to create disrespect for officers?"

He sat back in his chair, put his fingertips together in a listening attitude, and I got my chance at my only speech of the day.

"General," I said, "suppose a soldier's been overseas for a couple of years and in the line for a couple of months without a break, then he gets a few days in a rest area and goes to a USO show. He knows there's not much chance of getting next to one of the girls, but it would mean a lot to him if she'd circulate among the boys for a while after the show and at least give them the pleasure of talking to a girl from the States. Usually, there's not a chance. She arrives in a colonel's jeep two seconds before showtime and leaves in a gen . . . some other colonel's staff car before the curtain's down."

Patton's eye glittered menacingly, but he did not interrupt.

"All right, sir, the soldier goes back to his foxhole," I said, "and he's thinking about it. He doesn't blame the girl—after all, he figures, she's a free agent, she did her bit by entertaining him, and it's her own business how she entertains herself. Nobody in her right mind would go out with soldiers when officers have better whiskey and facilities. The soldier knows all this. And he doesn't blame the officer for going after the girl, either. That's only human. . . ."

"Jesus Christ, major, does this make sense to you?" the general growled. "Well, I told Butcher I'd let this man speak his piece."

"I'm almost finished, sir. My point is, the soldier is back in his foxhole stewing about officers and thinking he's got the short end of the stick in everything, even women. Whether it makes sense or not, the fact is that he feels there's been an injustice, and if he stews long enough about this, or about any of the other hundreds of things soldiers stew about, he's not going to be thinking about his job. All right, sir, he picks up his paper and he reads a letter or sees a cartoon by some other soldier who feels the same way, and he says, 'Hell, somebody else said it for me,' and he goes back to his job."

"All I've got to say to you, sergeant," Patton said, "is that if this soldier you're talking about is stewing it's because he hasn't got enough to do. He wasn't put in that hole to stew, or to think, or to have somebody else do his thinking for him in a goddamn newspaper.

"I don't know where you got those stripes on your arm, but you'd put 'em to a lot better use getting out and teaching respect to soldiers instead of encouraging them to bitch and beef and gripe and run around with beards on their faces and holes in their elbows. Now I've just got one last thing to say to you." He looked at his watch. Forty-five minutes had gone by. "You can't run an army like a mob."

"Sir," I protested, "I never thought you could."

"Think over what I've said. All right, sergeant, I guess we understand each other now."

"Yes, sir."

We did not shake goodbye. My parting salute was at least as good as the first one, but I don't think anyone noticed. The major and I started the long hike across the carpet and I heard Willie's chair creak as he climbed back on his perch.

Will Lang was waiting outside. As one of the instigators of the meeting he felt entitled to first crack at the story. I said Patton had received me courteously, had expressed his feelings about my work, and had given me the opportunity to say a few words myself. I didn't think I had convinced him of anything, and I didn't think he had changed my mind much, either.

Years later I read Butcher's account of reading Lang's *Time* story to Patton over the phone. When he quoted me as saying I hadn't changed Patton's mind, there was a chuckle. When he came to the part about the general not changing my mind, either, there was a high-pitched explosion and more talk about throwing me in jail if I ever showed up again in Third Army. *Time* didn't print the part about the general violating the agreement by keeping the major in the office during the interview. If I'd been quoted on that I'm convinced he'd have set Willie after me.

15

I finally headed for the Seventh Army, where I should have been all along, spending some time with the First and Ninth armies on the way, but carefully skirting the Third at all times. Driving through part of the Huertgen Forest, I passed miles of burnt-out tanks from the Battle of the Bulge and had half a dozen flats in as many hours from shell fragments littering the roads. It had been a huge fight. Everything about the European theater of operations was gargantuan compared to the Italian campaign, which began to seem like a small family war, bitter and intense as it was.

In the German hamlet of Aldenhoven, where the Ninth Army's 29th Division was getting ready to cross the Roer River for the drive on Cologne, I saw my first jet airplane. Two American P-47s jumped a small, twin-engine German bomber directly overhead and set one of its engines afire. The bomber spiraled down, apparently out of control, with the fighters following and pumping more bullets into it. It began to dawn upon me that the victim was going to crash on or near me. I looked for cover, then my attention was drawn upward again by an unearthly howl as the German pilot hit the throttle on his good engine, flattened out at roof-top level, and streaked for the enemy side of the river a couple of miles away, leaving his pursuers with egg on their faces. Even as I asked myself how all this was possible with no propellers, the German jettisoned his single remaining bomb and just happened to lay it onto one of our forward ammunition dumps, which went up like a volcano. Through the smoke I could see that the bomber made it home across the river.

"What do you know!" said a soldier a few feet away. "I was actually rooting for the bastard."

That night engineers from the 29th swam the freezing river and laid slack cables under the surface. At three in the morning I was awakened in a battalion headquarters by ceiling plaster in my face as one of the great artillery barrages of the war was laid down and the town of Jülich, across the river, fell into dust. The cables were tightened, pontoon foot bridges were run across, and Bob Capa, the *Life* photographer, whom I hadn't seen since Anzio, invited me to go over the Roer with him. I pointed out the advantage of cartooning: you don't always have to be right there to draw certain scenes. Besides, I had borrowed a good pair of binoculars.

Soon Capa returned with a bloody leg. Crossing with a couple of riflemen, he had encountered a German soldier, apparently dazed by the shelling, in an attitude of surrender. As soon as the trio was close, the German had lifted his hands a little higher and released a U.S. grenade from his armpit, killing one American and wounding Capa and himself. The surviving American had shot the culprit, tossed Bob his first-aid kit, and gone on. Meanwhile, the photographer had gotten the whole episode on film. He hadn't even bothered to open the kit, although he was bleeding badly. He wanted to get his film to London. He caught a ride west, made it to London, and was at the front again within a day or two.

Back in Italy, the breakout from the mountains above Bologna and the last big push across the Po Valley soon started. Near Verona on a bright spring morning I had breakfast with some tankers from the 1st Armored Division, who told me they were on their way to Milan, which had been encircled. After hastily taking some cartoons to the Leghorn office of *Stars and Stripes* for delivery to Rome, I set out for Milan in my jeep, which by now had almost thirty thousand miles on the odometer. On the way I ran into more people who assured me that Milan had fallen. I drove into the city at high speed, wondering where all the welcoming crowds were. It turned out that a lot of them had exhausted their festive spirits in the square by the cathedral, spitting on what was left of Mussolini and his girl friend, who had been hanging by their heels in an Esso station. The remainder of the populace stayed home, behind shutters, out of simple discretion. Our armor had bypassed the city for the moment and proceeded northward. Technically, Milan was not yet ours.

Turning a corner downtown, I almost ran over a German paratrooper in camouflage clothes, with a Schmeisser burp gun in the crook of his arm and a couple of potato-masher grenades in his belt. I discovered that when properly motivated a good jeep driver can go into reverse from high gear at thirty miles an hour. In a nearby bar, which was miraculously open, I found a man named Donald Downes, who worked for the Office of Strategic Services, forerunner of the Central Intelligence Agency, and had just arrived by parachute. We had several drinks as I told Downes of my near collision with the hostile soldier.

"The odd thing was that he didn't really look so hostile," I recalled. "He could have shot my ass off if he'd wanted to."

An Italian partisan, who wore a red armband and Mauser rifle, and was helping us lap up grappa, explained that a battalion of SS troopers had holed up in the Regina Hotel, their old headquarters, and had dug pillboxes and posted sentries around it. Reinforced by remnants of a paratrooper battalion, they had shown an understandable reluctance to surrender to partisan "irregulars," whose numbers they had been depleting by torture and execution for a long time. The partisans, on the other hand, saw no point in forcing the issue and losing more men at this stage of the war. Obviously, the Germans were going noplace, having been cut off to the north. Both sides had tacitly agreed to wait for the Americans to arrive.

"If you hadn't been in such a hurry, that trooper would probably have offered you an ersatz cigarette," Downes said.

"He's still there, if you want to ask him for one yourself," I reported, after a quick peek around the corner. This time, besides the soldier, I had glimpsed the ugly muzzle of an MG-34 in the slit of a pillbox at the hotel's corner.

"Let's both go," Downes said. The partisan cheered us on, saying the Germans would probably roll out a carpet for us, since we would be added security for them.

He was right. The paratrooper called out a sergeant, who summoned a lieutenant as we approached. The lieutenant, wearing his natty little death's-head cap, greeted us in passable English, pulled back a barbed-wire barricade, and urged us to come in and set a spell. Full of fermented courage, we accepted. Upstairs, we found two more Americans: an OSS colonel who had jumped into the city with Downes and was arranging the surrender, and an Army Pictorial Service photographer who had come along to record the scene. The higher-ranking Germans were upset because they had been told they couldn't keep several elegant cars, including a couple of big Mercedes roadsters, or their wardrobes, or their sidearms. Distressed by this harrowing scene, Downes and I wandered into the lobby, where we were approached by a pink-cheeked young SS corporal who spoke beautiful English.

"I want you to know I'm not German," he said right away. "I'm a Dutch citizen."

"That's what you claim," Downes retorted. "It will be interesting to hear what your fellow Dutchmen say."

"Them rats! Them dirty, cold-blooded, soreheaded, stinkin' Huns. Them atrocity commitin' skunks . . ."

The Germans retreated, but to the e
they hardly ever ran.

"Able Fox Five to Able Fox. I got a target, but ya gotta be patient."

"What could I do? We were occupied."

"Now don't tell me they drafted you into the SS," Downes said. "They're elite. I'm surprised they even let you join. Every red-blooded German boy would kiss ass to wear that black uniform. What did *you* have to do? Turn in your family?"

"Please, I am only asking for information. As a Dutch citizen, will it be necessary for me to go to prison camp with these Germans? Can't the matter be straightened out?"

"Let's straighten it out right now," Downes suggested. He found the SS lieutenant who had let us in, pointed out the Dutchman, and reported the entire conversation. The lieutenant's eyes narrowed and the corporal's cheeks lost their healthy flush.

"I don't think you'll have to worry about spending much time in jail now," Downes told the young man. "Your pals are going to pull off your legs and beat you to death with them, you fink."

Upstairs, the parley ended with permission for the SS battalion commander to address his men. As they assembled in the lobby, under a huge swastika flag flanked by portraits of Hitler and Himmler, Downes and I had another encounter, this time with a captain who had a French blonde on his arm and a magnificent white Alsatian bitch on a leash. He introduced the girl as Yvette and the dog as Anna. Downes and I were still drunk enough to respond graciously.

"I realize the girl must go with me to prison camp and I must leave the dog," the officer lamented, "but I wish it were the other way around." He had probably murdered six dozen people but he had tears in his eyes about Anna. "She's a trained bodyguard but not vicious," her owner said to Downes. "In fact, she's affectionate. Will you try to find a home for her? The partisans will shoot her if she is turned loose. I would rather shoot her myself."

Downes, no fool, had already noticed that I had eyes for Anna. If it hadn't been for her associations, it would probably have been love at first sight for me. She had let me rub her head and had already made it clear that she could be rehabilitated. Downes took the leash from the captain, allowed the man a quick hug with his pet, then brought the dog straight to me and struck his deal.

"I want that big swastika flag on the wall," he said.

The SS colonel had begun his speech.

"We are surrendering," he said, "to save ourselves for a newer and greater Reich. If some good blood is preserved, the fatherland shall rise again." And so on. Finally, there was a roar of "Heil Hitler!"

"Hey!" the American colonel cried. "I didn't tell 'em they could say *that!*"

Even as the *heils* were still bouncing among the rafters I pushed past a group of officers who were piling their Walthers and Lugers on a large table in the middle of the lobby. I tore down the flag, rolled it into a ball, and delivered it to Downes. The thing must have weighed twenty pounds.

"Only a drunk would have done that while they were still pulling off those holsters," Downes said, giving me Anna's leash.

"Who's drunk? I've got the bodyguard dog and you're holding the flag," I said.

At this point the festivities were interrupted by the roar of tank exhausts outside. It was the very group from First Armored that had given me the information outside Verona that Milan was in the bag. The tanks' cannon were leveled at the Regina and three or four men stood on each vehicle with M-1 rifles and submachine guns aimed at the lobby entrance. Several weapons wavered and several eyes bulged when I strolled out among the prisoners, with Anna heeling nicely.

"Shit, man, I thought you were on our side," one of the tankers hollered at me.

While Anna might have had some reservations about me at first, she was crazy about my jeep. She liked the windshield down; since the weather had turned balmy I didn't mind. For the next few weeks we traveled all over northern Italy with her rump in the right-hand seat, her forepaws on the hood, and her ears twitching in the wind. Fortunately, C-rations appealed to her, too. In the end, I won her heart myself. I knew it had happened when I woke up with a suffocating feeling one morning (I slept on the locker in the jeep's rear) and found Anna sitting on my chest and washing my ear.

16

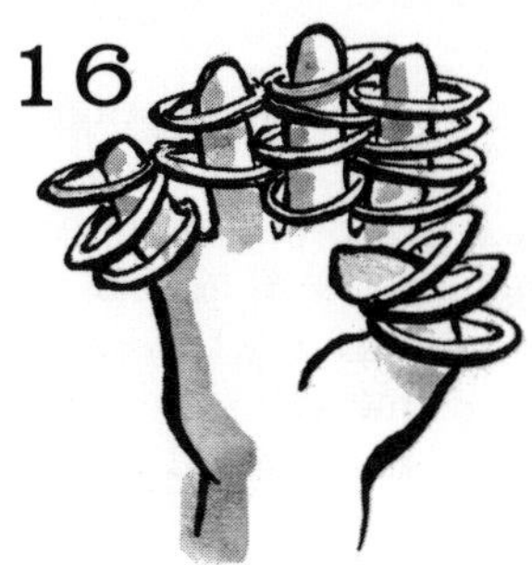

When I was growing up in New Mexico I used to see a lot of Morton's salt ads, printed on blue tin and hung from barbed-wire fences: "WHEN IT RAINS IT POURS." It sure does. Early in May, 1945, as I was watching the end of the war in northern Italy, I read in *Stars and Stripes* that I had won a Pulitzer Prize. I wasn't even sure exactly what a Pulitzer Prize was, except that it had something to do with journalism and literature and was prestigious. You would see the name of a writer, photographer, playwright, or cartoonist preceded by it: "Pulitzer Prize winner Sam Bronstadter was in town briefly today en route to his summer residence on Hammerhead Lake." Like most people, I pronounced it "Pewlitzer," when it should be "Pullitzer."

There was a check for five hundred dollars, too, but that wasn't all that came with the prize. I got a message from Neville that *Time* Magazine was doing a cover story on me and wanted me to do a full-color portrait of my character Willie. Since my painting set was in Rome, I headed there with Anna. There was some static about a dog sharing my bedroom-office, but Pulitzer Prize winners can get away with things like that. As I was working on the *Time* cover, Neville called me on the phone.

"Mauldin, have you got any medals?"

"Well, there's that Purple Heart, and a Good Conduct Medal for staying out of jail, and a ribbon for being in before Pearl Harbor, and one for being in this theater of operations. . . ."

"That's what I thought. General McNarney, who is the head man now in the Mediterranean, called me up about your Pulitzer. He wanted to know if the army had ever decorated you and I said no. He wanted to know what they should give you and I said they would have to work that out for themselves, since it was their idea."

"Thanks."

"There was more to the conversation. He suggested the Legion of Merit. That's a pretty fancy medal."

"It sure is. The last guy I heard of winning one of those was a master sergeant in the Cooks' and Bakers' School in San Antonio. He invented a pie-crust formula that saved the army thousands of tons of flour."

"Now I'm really convinced that's the one for you. The general gave me the job of writing the citation. How would you like to write it yourself?"

"I wouldn't want to deprive you."

"Well, what'll I say?"

"It's the general's idea and your problem, sir."

As Neville struggled with my medal, Memorial Day came. I drove to Anzio to hear a speech by General Lucian Truscott, who still commanded the Fifth Army. Normally, I am allergic to Veterans Days and Armistice Days and the like, but Truscott was somebody special. Besides, I was curious to hear that gravelly voice over a PA system. The Anzio-Nettuno cemetery was a collecting point and there were about twenty thousand American graves. Families hadn't started digging up the bodies and bringing them home. The speakers' platform, covered with bunting, was arranged with its back to the endless rows of white-painted temporary wooden markers. Before the stand were spectator benches, with a number of camp chairs down front for VIPs, including several members of the Senate Armed Services Committee.

When Truscott spoke, he turned away from the visitors and addressed himself to the corpses he had commanded here. It was the most moving gesture I ever saw. It came from a hard-boiled old man who was incapable of planned dramatics. The general's remarks were brief and extemporaneous. He apologized to the dead men for their presence here. He said everybody tells leaders it is not their fault that men get killed in war, but that every leader knows in his heart this is not altogether true. He said he hoped anybody here through any mistake of his would forgive him, but he realized that was asking a hell of a lot under the circumstances. One of the Senators' cigars went out; he bent over to relight it, then thought better of it. Truscott said he would not speak about the glorious dead because he didn't see much glory in getting killed in your late teens or early twenties. He promised that if in the future he ran into anybody, especially old men, who thought death in battle was glorious, he would straighten them out. He said he thought that was the least he could do.

Back in Rome I finished the *Time* cover, aware of the fact that the real

Willie was in one of those Anzio graves or not far north or south of it. I told Neville of a plot I had hatched some weeks before. I had thought of arranging for Willie and Joe to be killed on the day the war ended.

"Having it happen at the last minute is what every infantryman dreads the most," I said, "and the idea isn't unrealistic. If these guys were real they would have been dead long ago."

"An atrocity like that would never get printed in any paper of mine," Neville said.

"Besides, it would relieve me of the temptation to exploit those characters in civilian life," I pointed out.

"That'll have to be your problem, not mine. Speaking of my problems, your citation is ready, hero."

He read to me about how I braved shot and shell to gather authentic material for my morale-building work. The next time I heard it was in McNarney's office in Caserta. A whole bevy of his staff generals were summoned to witness the ceremony. The lowest-ranking man in the room aside from me was an eagle colonel who quoted the citation. After McNarney had hung the medal on me and trooped out with his major generals and brigadiers, the colonel drew me aside.

"It's almost lunchtime and you must be hungry after driving from Rome," he said. "The sergeant at the reception desk will show you to the enlisted men's mess."

There were two more fulfillments for me in those last days before I went home. I had sent a rough of a cartoon idea to Harold Ross at *The New Yorker*. Now it came back O.K.'d and initialed personally by him as well as by the cartoon editor. Later in the year, I met him in the flesh and he asked why I had never sent the finished drawing. I told him about all the midnight oil I had burned in Chicago thinking up ideas and how I had always sent them to *The New Yorker* first—thousands of them. I explained that in the midst of all my current success I had needed to be sure I had *really* made it.

"As for the finished drawing," I said, "I just didn't have time to do it then. Do you still want it?"

"Nah," he said. "It was a soldier cartoon and the war's over."

In the same mail with the O.K.'d rough from Ross was a manila envelope from Phoenix Union High School containing my diploma and a letter from Superintendent Montgomery, who was still running the place. He told me they had discovered I had not received full credit for the artwork I had done in my senior year, including the design for the 1939 yearbook cover. The board felt this more than made up for my scholastic deficiency of a quarter credit, so I was officially graduated with the class of 1945, only six years late. When it rains it pours.

The time came to give up the jeep and Anna. Neville accepted the former and promised to handle whatever paperwork was necessary to prevent the army from asking me ten years later what I had done with it. As his driver took it from me and headed for the *Stars and Stripes* motor pool, the exhaust header blew off the manifold with a roar and you could see from the clouds of blue smoke that poured from under the hood that a ring-and-valve job was long overdue. Anna went to Caserta to live with a female U.S. State Department employee who already had one German Shepherd and promised to ship my dog to me as soon as possible. It was the last I ever heard from the lady or Anna.

Late in June, 1945, exactly ten years from the beginning of this book, my agent got through to me by phone at the barracks in Fort Dix, New Jersey, where I was being processed back into civilian life, and told me I had over two hundred newspapers signed up for my future output, a hard-cover collection of my cartoons with a running text I had written was number one on the best-seller list and a Book of the Month Club selection, *Ladies' Home Journal* had paid ten thousand dollars for excerpt rights, the *Time* cover story was beautiful, the movies wanted to pay a hundred thousand plus ten percent of the gross, and General Patton, home for triumphal parades, had said I was the Bruce Bairnsfather of World War II and that he hadn't liked Bairnsfather, either. It just wouldn't stop pouring.

Editor John Willig in back of my now-worn-out jeep, author in front with Anna, near *Stars and Stripes* office in Rome.

The medical lieutenant who gave me my final physical was a downy-cheeked fugitive from a junior internship.

"Have you regained full use of your arm and hand?" He studied my papers as I stood before him naked as a jaybird.

"Sir?"

"It says here, 'Gunshot wound, right shoulder.' "

"Oh. No, I never lost use of my arm and hand."

"How long were you hospitalized?"

"I didn't go to the hospital."

"Show me the scar."

"There is no scar."

"And they gave you a Purple Heart for that?"

The man waiting behind me, who had at some point in the past been stitched across the belly and lower chest with half a dozen machine-gun bullets, lost his temper.

"Christ, lieutenant, he didn't make the rules! We take what we're given and do what we're told."

"Thanks, buddy," I said.

Uncle Billy, Willie, and Pop. A family portrait.

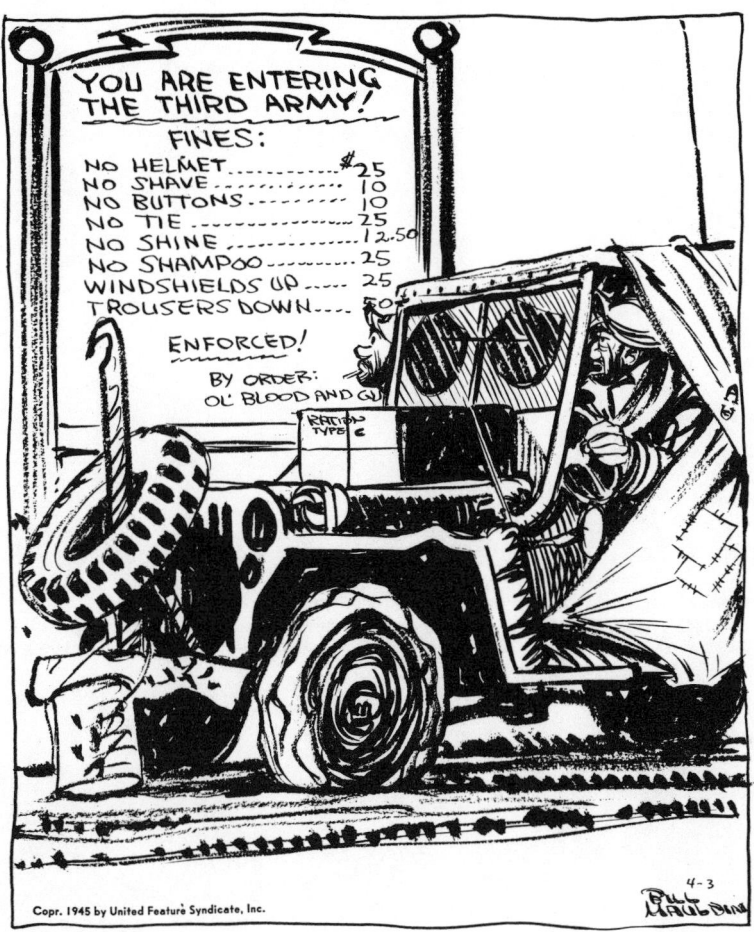

"Radio th' ol' man we'll be late on account of a thousand-mile detour."